Libya. A Love Lived, a Life Betrayed

To Nate

So many thanks for
you helps.

Best Wishes

Susan H. Sandove

Octobe 2018

City Solicitor, London - 'A beautiful love story of two people from two very different worlds who managed, successfully and against all odds, to build a very strong and powerful combined world'

The Jordan Times – 'Susan Sandover is able to narrate events from their 1980 meeting until his 2015 cancer-related death with compelling impressions and vivid details…. a resilient, upbeat tone in most of the book. Yet one comes away with a deep sadness for the Libyan people as the problems in the book are ongoing'

Jersey Evening Post – 'Libya and Love as the wife of a Libyan ambassador when Susan Sandover met a dashing diplomat while on holiday in Africa her life took a turn that would bring her under the often, terrifying influence of the Gaddafi regime.'

Brand South Africa – 'Susan has beautifully captured their Libyan love story in her book displaying vast insider knowledge on Libya's political, social and cultural history together with details on the final year of the Gaddafi regime.

EL Gazette – Sandover's advice is given on the 'drill' when you are faced with being evacuated home at a moment's notice, possible ways to mitigate family law in other legal systems and how to land on your feet and pick up your career again on arriving back in the country you left long ago'

London Book Fair 2017 'Write Stuff' – shortlisted author

Libya, A Love Lived, a Life Betrayed

9/36

Susan M. Sandover

Matador
9 Priory Business Park,
Wistow Road, Kibworth Beauchamp,
Leicestershire. LE8 0RX
Tel: 0116 279 2299
Email: books@troubador.co.uk
Web: www.troubador.co.uk/matador
Twitter: @matadorbooks

ISBN 978 1785899 393

British Library Cataloguing in Publication Data.
A catalogue record for this book is available from the British Library.

Printed and bound in the UK by TJ International, Padstow, Cornwall
Typeset in 11pt Aldine401 BT by Troubador Publishing Ltd, Leicester, UK

Matador is an imprint of Troubador Publishing Ltd

For Bashir
'The Bringer of Good News'

الى بشير
حامل الاخبار السعيدة

Contents

One

9/36 is the end of the tale but the beginning starts with so many previous events that have had to be sealed in my memory box for safety. Many times I have wished that I could have kept a diary of the past 35 years, but the fear of my writings being found and incriminating the man I loved has always stopped my ever beginning. Even today when I have nothing to lose, all of those past years still haunt me.

When I was asked recently in an interview what qualifications I believed that I had for working abroad, I felt a certain amount of frustration at the woman who had quite clearly not read my CV and was obviously just reading the next question on her formulaic list. In a probably rather inappropriate answer I responded that I had been bombed by the Americans, lived through two attempted coups, a major earthquake and two typhoons, lived under a dictatorship, through a revolution and a NATO bombing. A silence ensued for a few moments; I could see what was going through her mind, wondering if I was some kind of Walter Mitty character, and if what I had just said could be true? It was. What she had failed to notice in my eyes and tone of voice was that I am a survivor despite even 9/36 being hurled at me.

At the tender age of four I went around the world with my parents, out via the Suez Canal and back through the Panama Canal. Although I can remember little if nothing of the journey it might have ignited my Christopher Columbus spirit since travelling from then onwards was in my bones; any chance, anywhere, I was game. But this story begins in 1980 when I was 32 and weaves between my flat in Frognal, North London and Freetown, Sierra Leone on the West Coast of Africa. The country was preparing to host an Organisation of African Union Summit (OAU) new hotels had been built and it was swarming with security experts and intelligence agents from Western, African and Arab countries.

For my travelling companion Kathy and me it was a cheap winter holiday destination and if I were to believe in fate then certainly my destiny was decided when we set foot on the tarmac and on to the ferry taking us to Freetown that night.

The capital was bubbling with frantic businessmen eager to capitalize on the many construction projects necessitated by the hosting of an international summit. We were two not unattractive young women out for some fun in the sun with little or no competition. Africa was a complete revelation to us with its noises, colours and heat being so very different from the suburban London where we had both grown up. The ubiquitous music, clubs, casinos and stunningly beautiful beaches were all so exciting, as was the charming male company. With numerous bottles of champagne arriving at our dinner table, we enjoyed the attention as we danced the night away before returning to our shared hotel room to compare stories and laugh about them. Our days were spent enjoying the sun and the glorious unspoilt tropical, palm fringed sandy beaches. The backdrop to our carefree fortnight throbbed with rich Africans, Lebanese and Indian brokers and traders all vying for a share of the lucrative contracts on offer, while the poor Sierra Leoneans were left with little or nothing to look forward to.

It is difficult to remember every detail of that time where Kathy and I met so many extraordinary people but we were thrust into a novel, different world. The president's son, the infamous Nigerian millionaire playboy Jimmy Ahmed, the head of intelligence at the Libyan embassy Mohammed Marouf, Anwar Sadat's Egyptian presidential head of security and amongst others a former SAS man called Ian, whose reason for being there we never quite discovered. A motley crew in a tropical climate all wanting to make money and have fun. Without a doubt we were two single females in the right place at the right time with enough worldly experience to know how to say no when it was necessary.

So vividly I remember when we first met Bashir wearing a yellow shirt and beige trousers. Why I remember this detail until today I have no idea but for some reason he caught my attention with an ever – mischievous smile that I came to adore. At that time he was sporting his glorious long black locks and a Mexican moustache. I am sure there was also the interest factor of being the first Libyan I had ever met. Of course we all knew of Gaddafi and a little of how this revolutionary colonel had turned the oil markets upside down and was now trying to impose his own form of socialism on his oil rich country. This however, was far away from our thoughts as Bashir came to say hello to our table of new friends. There was an instant magnetic connection as we shook hands, before he disappeared off to the casino. For the rest of the holiday we were to pass each other at different times generally stopping to chat about music. His passion for it became apparent on hearing him play the classical oud some days later. He always sang in Arabic, seemingly channelling a faraway, beautiful place.

Such was the fun we had in Sierra Leone that I returned for a second time a month later. A lucky chance meeting at a London party had secured a photo journalism assignment to write on Sierra Leone. I met Bashir frequently. He was Charge d'Affaires (Head of Mission) at the embassy while the ambassador was out of the country. During this period I encountered many more interesting and intriguing people from the world of international diplomacy. As the commencement of the African Union summit drew closer the inevitable behind the scenes politicking increased. Between Bashir and myself there was a strong mutual attraction in that unknown atmosphere of frenetic international diplomacy; that *unknown* then would play quite a large part in our future lives.

Arriving back in London at the end of my second visit I commenced writing up my commissioned articles and it is here that our story truly begins. Shortly after my return I received a call from Bashir in Switzerland. He was undergoing medical treatment and suggested I join him in Geneva. Kathy joked (and still does) it was not 'a platonic invitation'. I flew to Geneva in the summer of 1980 believing that he was genuinely ill, and that maybe I could cheer him up, he had sounded depressed. Needless to say a week in Geneva, beside that scenic lake, is always a divine prospect and no other thoughts were in my mind. Bashir was waiting at the airport looking thin and weary, yet still sparkling. The rest is history as they say, and Bashir admitted later that he was determined to have an intimate relationship with me. However, the reason for his being in Geneva, I was only to learn several years later were founded on a plot to assassinate the Egyptian President, Anwar Sadat, who was due to attend the summit in Freetown. This was with the almost certain knowledge of the Libyan Foreign Minister Dr. Ali Treki who was also going to be in Sierra Leone and presumably authorised by Colonel Gaddafi himself because nothing of this nature happened without the hand of the Colonel. Bashir knew if

3

he remained in Freetown that he too would be implicated and he strongly opposed any talk of assassinating a head of state or come to that, anyone. The only solution was to plead an illness needing specialist treatment in order to escape to Geneva where he would be far removed from the plot.

It was in truth a half excuse: in reality, he was sick, worried and nervous to a point where he could hardly keep down any food. I do believe that the pressure and stress of being a career Libyan diplomat under Gaddafi was to a large extent the cause of poor health throughout his life. Much of our time was spent consulting specialists in and around Geneva. Nonetheless, he seduced me and we fell in love; he was the most amazing lover. By the time it came for him to return to Sierra Leone the OAU had finished. The Egyptian president eventually never attended the summit and life resumed there as normal. Bashir was back to being a diplomat and not a political assassin. However, undercover arms were being smuggled into the country by Mohamed, the Intelligence Officer with the connivance of Ali, the embassy's Financial Attaché. Gaddafi was starting his pan – African interference and power building even as early as 1980.

Before leaving Geneva we had decided that I would return to Freetown for an extended visit at Christmas. I was pretty foot loose and fancy free at this stage in my life since working for agencies on an assignment basis allowed me to pick up and leave as and when I wanted, provided that I had the money. I headed out to Freetown and moved in with Bashir who was sharing a house with Ali, the Financial Attaché a surly character who spoke no English. It was quite apparent that he neither respected nor liked western women, probably thinking us debauched.

Later I discovered that Ali had been the instigator of the plot to assassinate Sadat. The man was an opportunist believing that such endeavours would gain him favour with the revolutionary committees of which he was a new member. Words to describe him such as completely unscrupulous, corrupt and utterly contemptible are probably inadequate. Further into the future he would become pivotal in more dark activities at the embassy, shattering its already dubious reputation. It was he who remained in the country and negotiated and dealt with Charles Taylor, later to become the President of Liberia. Ali remained in West Africa for many years, rising in power within the Revolutionary Committees. His place today should be in The Hague for war crimes but I have no idea where he is or whether he is alive or dead since the revolution. Sierra Leone made him a multi – millionaire through appallingly blatant corruption and the snuffing out of so many West African lives.

Christmas in Freetown was buzzing with tourists as it was starting to become a winter holiday destination. Miles, a London friend joined us and we befriended an interesting group of people over that Christmas break. I awoke on brilliant mornings to go water – skiing, fishing and take spectacular boat trips whilst descending on the city for huge nights out. Poor Bashir was working of course, though I was to discover in the years to come he was a man who could function on a little sleep, party until the small hours yet still work effectively in the morning and complete a full day's work.

By 1980 Gaddafi had realised that his dream of Arab unity was just a dream where he would not be at the helm so instead he turned to Africa as being the place where he could build his empire. When one has unlimited wealth, one can buy and sell people and this he was able to do with relative ease in Sierra Leone. Gaddafi was a master strategist in *dividing and conquering* as he lifted people up and then knocked them down. By 1986 he had declared his intention to become the Emperor of Africa. Through using Libya's vast oil wealth it allowed him to create instability well beyond Libya's borders. The recruitment by Gaddafi of Foday Sankoh, who was the leader and founder of the Sierra Leone rebel group Revolutionary United Front and Charles Taylor, later to become Liberia's President was to be the birth. They received much of their training from Libyan forces and endless funding from Gaddafi's Libya. The civil wars in these countries in 1991, which lasted for eleven years, saw an estimated 50,000 people killed with over 500,000 displaced in neighbouring countries. It was the start of this instability in the 1980s that began to worry the United States about Gaddafi's activities in Africa.

Life in Sierra Leone in this period was pretty laid back for diplomats. It was considered a hardship posting and once the OAU Summit was over, little if anything happened in Freetown. Despite the intensely hot, humid, mosquito infested climate there were the glorious sandy beaches, long, lazy langoustines and shrimp lunches to savour in tasty dishes and romantic beach club locations. The Italian Ambassador who used to arrive at the beach everyday particularly amused me, putting up his chair, table and shade and relaxing. Fifteen minutes or so later one of his attachés would arrive with the mail for the day. The attaché would return at twelve

5

presumably to collect the papers for the appropriate actions to be taken. The ambassador would then have a swim surrounded by Italian female tourists. He was not a young man and quite obviously enjoyed female company. By twelve thirty he left the beach and the next time we saw him would be in one of the casinos, again surrounded by beautiful women. Not a bad life for a widower close to retirement. He was a delightfully, charming man who was excellent company, even if only for a brief chat. He had one of the necessary qualifications for a diplomat.

By contrast for those in the Libyan diplomatic corps, life under Gaddafi was becoming complicated. He wanted all embassies to be controlled by political appointees (his cronies) but was realistic enough to know that he still needed the backbone of career diplomats and their expertise. From 1980 onwards no new career diplomats would be appointed until the beginning of 2000. Poor Bashir's timing in joining the foreign ministry in 1976 could not have been worse. He had graduated from the Diplomatic Institute and subsequently worked in the Department for International Co – operation. He was fortunate having a boss who was a highly skilled diplomat with years of experience and who encouraged young attachés. Bashir accompanied him on missions to Singapore, Malaysia and southern European countries. By shadowing this man he began to learn his trade. Sadly background and tribal allegiance were important requisites for positioning in the Foreign Ministry in 1980. Unfortunately Bashir's family background was a hindrance to his career prospects. His father had been born in Gargaresh, a suburb of Tripoli, but became an orphan at seven. He was adopted by an uncle who raised him, albeit somewhat minimally. Sharia inheritance law should have meant that in adulthood Mohamed Shkuka would inherit his father's considerable wealth but it was sadly sequestered by the uncle. Thus Mohamed became a lowly janitor in a school. He was however, highly respected in the Gargaresh community, being thought of as a man of high morals and deeply held Muslim beliefs. He was to become known as '*Hacouma*' – *Governor* in Gargaresh. Bashir was to inherit his father's goodness. At times I heard him too being called 'Hacouma' in the Gargaresh area.

At the end of 1979, it was Bashir's time to go on a posting. Despite having passed out of the Diplomatic Institute with high scores, he was given Sierra Leone as his first posting, a country considered a backwater. He was furious not to have been assigned to one of the key embassies such as London, Paris or Washington, especially given his good language skills and placing in the Foreign Office exams. However, it was his departmental boss who gave him the best advice. 'In a small embassy you will have responsibility but in London you will probably not even go to the Foreign Ministry'. This reasoning proved to be very prophetic. Within one week of being in Freetown, Bashir was meeting the President, something that would not have happened as a lowly Third Secretary in the Paris embassy. In Sierra Leone Bashir was able to glean experience that he never could have imagined, experience that would serve him well in the years to come. He always remained a career diplomat, carefully avoiding those who were in the service only to join the gravy train of revolutionary appointed diplomats, a requirement for any of those ever wishing to become an Ambassador.

After the New Year Miles returned to London and I stayed on with an open agenda. I was thrilled with my Africa adventure. Dream worlds never last long and hardly more than a week later Bashir returned from work announcing we were moving temporarily to share with the embassy Administrator since he was living in a large, spacious house, his wife and family being in Libya. Although slightly puzzled, I accepted the explanation given then that an additional Third Secretary was joining the embassy and Ali preferred to share with another male rather than with the two of us, which seemed quite understandable.

The truth was quite different. When Gaddafi wrote his Green Book his main theme was that all Libyans are equal and that there should be no owners but only 'partners not wage workers'. Gaddafi realized that there were elements in the foreign ministry who came from the old, rich, elite families and these people he wished to crush. He set about renaming the embassies as *People's Bureau*. Every embassy was to be managed by a committee and these appointees could come from all walks of life, educated or uneducated and mostly quite unsuited to interacting with other nationalities. There would no longer be ambassadors instead the name to be used was *Secretary of The People's Bureau*. Pivotal to their appointments was the necessity to sign up to both the Revolutionary and their local area committees. The latter would put forward elected candidates to join an embassy for a period of four years with secondments from their current jobs to these new positions. The embassy in London had already been taken over by the revolutionary committees and what had happened there was about to happen in Freetown. This would mark the end of my Sierra Leone adventure; the end of stage one and the start of many more such upsets, which we had to weather and accommodate, during our 33 – year love affair.

Bashir seemed to feel reassured when he learned that one of the members of the new People's Bureau to be established in Sierra Leone was Anwar a career diplomat who had joined the ministry the same year as Bashir. This man had however, decided to sign up with the revolutionary committees, as a way of being fast tracked in the Foreign Ministry. Bashir knew instantly that he did not fit in with this group who were forever brandishing and quoting from the Green Book and talking about how they would bring revolution to western dominated countries. His living with an English woman was quite obviously exceedingly inappropriate in their eyes, particularly a 'western prostitute' as they were fond of branding me. Both of us realising that I could no longer remain in Sierra Leone a flight back to London was booked. In some respects it was well timed since my brother was about to get married and I wanted to be at the wedding. I did not however, want our relationship to end in Freetown in this way. Neither did Bashir.

The Sierra Leone chapter for me was over and I was en – route back to London and my Frognal flat. I am always overwhelmed by sadness when I see or hear any talk of Sierra Leone. I think of how things could have evolved had it not been for the cruel and mindless civil war using child soldiers to fight against each other. First there were the most abject, inhumane mutilations of innocent people followed some years later by the horrific Ebola outbreak when the country was barely even beginning to recover. The country has quite astonishing mineral wealth, but it is embezzled and hoarded by only a few. Sierra Leone was and is the country of black diamonds.

On a final personal memory, I feel I must include my being made aware of the horror and inhumane treatment of some of Sierra Leone's young girls. Like most people at the time I knew nothing of female genital mutilation (FGM) before travelling to Africa. On the first night of my third visit I was to hear, see and learn of this inhumanity. Bashir lived in a tiny hamlet away from the centre of Freetown. A balcony at the back of the house overlooked a pathway covered in dense vegetation leading to a group of about five small ramshackle homes. Darkness used to arrive at 6 pm and in this half – light I heard the sound of drums ceaselessly pounding out a rhythm. A short while later in the half light of dusk I saw the strangest sight, women and girls with grey painted faces and white lines streaked on top of the grey. I remember questioning Bashir as to what on earth was going on, not then realizing that it was just one example of a practice that causes untold emotional trauma to millions of females worldwide while enforcing an inherent gender inequality. The drums would continue pounding and pounding out their sombre rhythm night after night until their agonising wounds had healed.

One final memory has to be of Sami, our house help. Prior to leaving our duplex he had begged that both of us should go to London where he would work for me. I could see in his eyes a total disbelief when I told him that I lived in a tiny one bedroom flat and had no room for him let alone need of any help. I wonder whether he is alive or dead as I wonder about so many of the people whom I met during that year. It is incomprehensible even for me today to understand how the political greed and power of so few can destroy the lives of so many. How do these people not only get into power but also manage to stay in power, in some cases, for decades?

I was forced to leave Sierra Leone without the Committee knowing where I was or what I was doing. In the final days before leaving they had put guards on the house wanting to know where I was living and so my ignominious departure from Sierra Leone was under a blanket in the back seat of a car. As Bashir and I sat on the ferry taking us out to Lungi airport, the city's lights fading in the background, we held each other tightly with tears streaming down our faces. That feeling of love being taken away, the ache and pain are desperate emotions but now I realise it is a rare and wonderful blessing to have such strength of feeling for someone else. As the British Caledonian plane took off neither Bashir nor I realized quite how quickly we would be back in each other's arms; we were deeply in love and determined not to be separated.

Two
٢

Our love calls between Sierra Leone and London were made long before the existence of the internet and Skype. There were times when it would take days and endless waits to make contact due to the poor communication infrastructure in Freetown. Imagine my joy when after no more than a month of separation I heard Bashir's voice giving me the news that he was leaving Sierra Leone and flying to London before heading to Libya.

At the same time alarm bells began to ring in my head but on asking him why I received the reply I was to come to know so well in the future, that he would explain on arrival. Once again I was to have our next meeting in an airport, but this time I was in Gatwick, London Arrivals and Bashir was wearily pushing his two suitcases looking stressed, sleep – deprived and pale. I had been hoping to whisk him straight up to my flat. Of course he as ever the consummate professional, told me his first London destination was to the Libyan embassy to meet, as he was now called, 'The Secretary of the Peoples Bureau.' It was no longer *His Excellency the Libyan Ambassador to London*. The country had also been renamed and the flag replaced by an all green one. A protocol nightmare had begun to always ensure that in case Gaddafi should visit the new flag was to be hoisted, the new anthem was to be played and all officials would call the country by its new name *The Socialist Peoples Libyan Arab Jamahiriya* at all times. A number of diplomats had been sent home with their careers in tatters due to mistakenly forgetting to apply these changes in front of Gaddafi, who never had any mercy. Pre – 1969 days returned in 2011, when again for diplomats the old flag, anthem and the country name were resurrected.

We took the train into central London together from Gatwick caressing each other between passionate kisses I am sure to the embarrassment of other travellers in the carriage. Victoria station saw Bashir into a taxi and

I into a further taxi complete with his two suitcases back to my flat in Frognal. What seemed a long, endless wait was only in fact four hours before my buzzer rang and Bashir was with me alone in the flat. I am an impatient person in stressful situations and having had to leave Sierra Leone for Bashir's safety I was anxious to know that I had not jeopardised his position. Before he even had time to sit down I was begging him to tell me what had happened. This however, was not the way Bashir worked. Always taking his time and after his habitual glass of whisky and a large steak and salad I was to learn of the demise of the Libyan embassy in Sierra Leone.

My observation over the years has brought me to an understanding that African nations were much more tolerant of Gaddafi's antics and power plays than the West. Obviously this was at the very least in part due to the generous sweeteners being given to the appropriate people in power together with phenomenally expensive jewellery being handed over to their wives. By 1981 this had worked well up to a point in Sierra Leone, but in all likelihood it was one step too far when five revolutionary, Green Book brandishing Libyans arrived in Sierra Leone without diplomatic passports (these had now been banned by Gaddafi and diplomats were to be considered ordinary people travelling on ordinary passports). Bashir continued that these men had established links with officials without going through official protocol and were also distributing the Green Book and the propaganda surrounding Gaddafi's Third Universal Theory. Naturally Sierra Leone officials became edgy and were probably also receiving prompts and warnings from USA officials. The ambassador, Abdallah, was out of the country so Bashir as Charge d'Affaires was called to the foreign ministry. He was told to advise the Libyan government that Sierra Leone did not recognize the structure of this new type of embassy. The people newly arrived from Libya were not considered conducive to the well – being of the country and thus were no longer recognised by the state and were persona non gratia. The embassy had 48 hours to close and all Libyans working in the embassy were to leave the country. Bashir, not considered part of this new order, was not asked to leave and in fact was the Sierra Leone government's preferred candidate to stay on as head of a Special Interests Section under the umbrella of another Embassy. To find another country willing to take on this mantle within the timescale and with the approval from Tripoli was totally impractical so the closing operation was taken. Besides which Bashir was unwilling to remain in an increasingly difficult environment without diplomatic protection of a negotiated third country.

To close an embassy down under the best of situations would take time, but 48 hours to exit staff and families onto planes back to Libya, close down a building, and shred reams of documents were among the many necessary tasks going through Bashir's mind at that time. Plus of course losing all the armaments stored beneath the embassy which had been smuggled in as diplomatic cargo, was probably the most paramount. As Bashir sat face – to – face with the Ministry staff he felt overwhelmed by the task at hand. They finally reached agreement that one diplomat could stay, and Ali the Financial Attaché, was nominated. This seemed like an obvious choice in terms of the logistics, but in the future this decision would in small part lead to the rise of Taylor and Sankoh.

As he recounted those last days Bashir told me of the dumping of the armaments. Looking back on this event in years to come we laughed at the absurdity of the situation but at the time it must have been terrifying. Mohamed, the Head of Intelligence, was a colonel and pretty level headed when not drinking and gambling; he rose to the task. Bashir spoke of how they waited until one in the morning, sitting in one of the casinos drinking and playing blackjack. Perhaps it was an unorthodox way to calm one's nerves. By the time they were to start the exercise they were not exactly sober and had fortunately won a bit of money. Both of these two factors were to prove to be their saviours later in the arms dumping exercise. They took two of the embassy cars and loaded them up with rocket launchers, RPGs, guns, revolvers, bullets and almost every description of weapons all in the back of the two cars covered by blankets. A desolate part of beach with a rocky shoreline, which they knew had deep water had been chosen as the best location to heave the weapons into the sea. Having dumped the first two loads of this dangerous cargo there were still two more remaining at the embassy waiting to be thrown into the waves. On returning to the embassy they loaded up the second pile and headed back towards the secluded spot but this time they didn't have such a clear run. A two – car police patrol stopped them on the return trip back to the dumping ground wanting to know why they were driving in that remote area late at night and what was under the blankets. Although the cars had diplomatic immunity to start arguing on the rights and wrongs of drunkenly driving them at 2am with aggressive, late – night policemen did not seem like a good idea. However, money did talk. Bashir and Mohamed pretended to be considerably drunker than they were, telling the police that they had prostitutes hidden under the blankets who could not be seen in public with them. Thanks to the dollars won earlier in the casino that night they were able to persuade the officers to let them on their merry way. Two happy police cars left with the casino winnings and my darling, intrepid Bashir and his colleague continued on theirs down toward the sea again to resume the dumping operation. The relief at having outwitted the police made them truly elated as they flung the next load of weapons into the sea whilst joyfully singing Abba's 'Money, Money, Money' at the tops of their voices. Thank goodness they were in a remote spot. What a bizarre, hilarious sight; I smile as I picture it today. I do wonder if anyone ever found this arms haul and if they ever questioned where or whom it had come from. I am sure Bashir's Sierra Leone experience has not been replicated by many diplomats if any, and I rather suspect there aren't many who would wish to be in such a situation. These were the building blocks for surviving as a Libyan Diplomat during the Gaddafi years that his former boss said he would never find in the big prestigious embassies, which proved incredibly pertinent in the years to come.

Bashir now had to stay in London, waiting to be told which course of action he should take and where he should go. From Sierra Leone they had had few if any instructions from Libya as to the steps that should be taken. This was 1981, no computer, poor telephone lines, no fax in Sierra Leone; there was still only telex communication. The secret codes had been brought by Bashir to London and were deposited at the embassy. He had left with just two suitcases leaving behind furniture unsold, deposits on the house and other administrative and financial loose ends. The Foreign Ministry was still directly in Gaddafi's firing line, thus for Bashir as a career diplomat there was no precedent or a requirement to pay him any compensation for what he had left behind or lost. Of course the members of the revolutionary committee were more than well compensated. You either beat them or joined them, and the latter never was or would be an option for Bashir and the former would not happen until 2011.

Nonetheless for now we were in my beautiful, Frognal garret very much in love and thrilled at being reunited so quickly. It was the middle of February and a typically bleak, English winter. Bashir was dressed in a safari suit with no coat, no warm clothing and only short – sleeved shirts. As was to become common for future shopping exercises, he wrote a list of what he needed against the damp, cold, London weather. I knew where clothes could be found and bought cheaply so quickly returned with everything to protect him from the winter elements. We were then in business and mentally blocked out what was to come. How long would he be in London? After this how long would he be in Tripoli? Where to if anywhere, next? Our relationship hinged on answers to these questions as at that time there would be no chance of my being able to join him in Libya.

By this time Bashir was known to Kathy and Miles but was yet to meet my brothers and other friends. To anyone observing it must have seemed pretty unusual, the number of diplomats in my extended family congregating for dinners together; we could have held our own General Assembly. Within a week Bashir received his orders to return to Tripoli. He hated visiting the embassy and said the atmosphere was depressing with those against the new arrangement, namely his colleagues and friends from the foreign ministry and university, and the 'invaders' as he called them from the new set up. This arrangement was to explode in 1983 and cause our lives to be completely upended.

All too quickly those unwelcome instructions to return to Libya and leave London saw us on yet another train ride to Gatwick Airport, but this time in Departures. Airport farewells were becoming a regular feature of our lives and this one was no less tearful on my part, as we had no idea when we would be reunited. My only consolation was the proximity of Libya to London, or to the southern Mediterranean countries where we could possibly have an opportunity to meet in the future. However, at this time exit and re – entry visas for Libyans were strictly controlled by the Gaddafi regime as it was starting to go into lock down given the opponents he was beginning to garner.

We had expected that it would be a long separation but in less than two months Gaddafi decided that there should be a Peoples' Bureau in Liberia and that a People's Committee should be sent to Monrovia, the capital, to set up the new embassy under its new Libyan title. Bashir was nominated to go as the only career diplomat along with financial and administrative attaches. It must have irked Gaddafi that by this point in time, despite all of his bullish manoeuvres he still had to rely on diplomats to run his missions abroad.

Thankfully as there were no direct flights from Libya to Liberia, Bashir had to fly via London and we managed to steal a few more days and nights before his onward flight to his second West African adventure. Life was always fun despite the hardships and underhand political events that were affecting us at any given time. The two of us loved people, loved to socialise and debate, all the while enjoying good food and wine. Bashir was an absolute charmer and always attracted interesting people. All too quickly however, we were back at Gatwick Airport for yet another farewell. We clung onto each other right to the final minute, a few last kisses and Bashir disappeared into the tunnel with neither of us knowing when we would next be together.

When Bashir flew into Liberia along with the committee, apparently the government had not been informed they were arriving, nor did they have any idea that a Libyan Peoples Bureau was about to be established in the country. This was typical Gaddafi, the presumption that everyone would accommodate his every whim; he seemed to think that his authority over the people and institutions of Libya could be replicated wherever he turned his attention. Of course these agreements were always greased with dollars. This was something that was instilled in his children and cronies, and was to cause endless diplomatic crises in the future.

The Committee had dollars pouring out of their suitcases and set themselves up in the best and probably the only five Star Hotel. Bashir found the country, unlike Sierra Leone, dangerous and the people unfriendly. After just a few days when walking back to the hotel from a Portuguese restaurant he was held up by a gang, and had his expensive Rado watch and money stolen. This was a fast lesson, and from then on he would go out with no more than $50 in his sock and would make every effort not to look wealthy, walk quickly and have a car and driver wherever possible. He felt that Liberia was the Wild West, having come from relatively safe territories.

Of course Liberia is considered by many to be a United States outpost and by this time the international community was well aware that Libya's policies were in direct conflict with the West. The arrival therefore of Libyan revolutionaries in Liberia with cash to spend on people attracted to the Green Book doctrine was not something that either the Liberian government or the US embassy welcomed. I was absolutely delighted to receive a call from Bashir just a short while later to say that they had once again been told to leave the country within 48 hours. For Bashir this was by now almost becoming a routine. Thankfully on this enforced departure there was little to pack up, and nothing to leave behind. There was no holding him he rushed onto the London plane, in fact happy to be leaving the country he had barely had time to get to know. I was to meet him yet again in Gatwick Arrivals.

By now it was a well – rehearsed routine from the airport back to the embassy in London to report what had happened and to await further instructions. This was becoming a well – trodden path for Bashir. Being the only diplomat and the only one well versed enough in the procedures and protocols that had to be followed, he was the one to negotiate and relay the information. Gaddafi, furious that this African country was not going to accept his answer to the evil colonial capitalist West's domination as he saw it, now set in motion his cultivation of Taylor and Sankoh. This was to prove the undoing of both countries. Libya still had their man Ali in Freetown who was eager to do his great leader's wishes and able to do so with unlimited Libyan funds. Thus the unhappy saga of West Africa began to unfold, in part bankrolled by Gaddafi.

It is an uncommon experience for a diplomat to have to leave a country once due to a breakdown in diplomatic relations, but for it to happen twice within a period of three months was quite extraordinary. Being a Third Secretary in a backwater was proving to be far more interesting than Bashir ever could have imagined and he was up to the task, utilising all of his diplomatic skills, most of which had not been taught at the diplomatic institute. This was new ground for a Libyan diplomat. He now had no regrets about not having been posted to Paris or London.

Bashir had by this time developed a feel for African diplomacy and could see that this would be an area of great interest for a Libyan diplomat, requiring demanding skills. When Diplomats talk and discuss where they have been and where they would like to be posted, their criteria sometimes does seem to be measured to talk on the quality of the social life and living conditions. While Bashir certainly enjoyed life's comforts, he was also motivated by the interest and importance of the work to be done and he had earmarked Kenya as being somewhere he would like to be posted from the point of view of African interest. Also he wished to be in the vicinity of two Nairobi based United Nations' headquarters one being the United Nations Environment Programme (UNEP) and the other United NationsHuman Settlements Programme (HABITAT). By choosing an African country there would not be much competition from his colleagues who viewed any posting to Africa as being a failure. Furthermore, he wanted to work with a UN agency as a way of working for the Libyan good within Libya rather than as an opponent abroad. Therefore when he returned to Libya he lobbied everyone he knew to be posted to Nairobi.

As luck would have it there was a vacancy in the embassy and so almost immediately he received his posting papers for Kenya; he was moving from West to East Africa. He had been in Liberia on an ordinary passport but now needed to be reissued with a diplomatic passport, as Kenya had not been asked to recognize a Peoples' Bureau and the Libyan Embassy was still an embassy with an ambassador. I seemed to be spending more and more time waiting in Arrivals and Departure halls for Bashir. Once more I made my way down to Gatwick to be reunited before his departure for Kenya. We were to have a little precious time together, or so I hoped, before he left for Nairobi.

London, September 1981; it was Bashir's 31st birthday and we went to the Palm Beach nightclub in the Berkley Hotel to celebrate. It was a great evening as we both loved dancing. I could never match Bashir's wonderful moves but had a great time nonetheless. He was never one to hold back or be embarrassed, always wanting everyone to join in whether they were able or otherwise. For him it was the most blissful release from all the pressure that work was beginning to lay at his door.

It was around this time that I received the first copies of the books that I had contributed chapters and photographs to on Sierra Leone. It was a truly exciting new career that I was deeply motivated by. Bashir was enthusiastic about the contents of the books as there were detailed sections on Kenya. Thinking that I would just buy further copies, I gave him mine and that was the last that I ever saw of them.

Protocol can be an exceedingly good way of delaying something one country does not want to happen without causing a diplomatic incident. So it was when Bashir arrived in Nairobi airport that the Kenyan Foreign Ministry's Protocol Department very politely advised him that they had received no information on his appointment to the Libyan embassy and therefore they would be unable to approve his appointment. Whether this was due to their having got wind of Gaddafi sending revolutionaries to all the African embassies or a genuine error in communications was unclear. Bashir was refused entry into the country despite having a visa issued in London. Tarah, the Libyan ambassador was a career diplomat with whom Bashir had worked in the International Cooperation department. He was keen for Bashir to join the embassy and suggested waiting in nearby Seychelles rather than returning to Libya. The problem would be quickly solved and in the meantime the Seychelles embassy would take care of his needs. Those were the days when certain embassies were flush with money and one of those, for some reason, was the Seychelles. Bashir flew to the Seychelles capital, Mahe where he was about to enter Paradise. He believed he was flying with two suitcases, one of which contained my two books.

On arrival at the small airport in Mahe, Bashir was greeted with the traditional highly fragrant jasmine necklace delivered by one of their stunning female airport staff. A welcome indeed, but where were the suitcases? Eventually one was tracked down. It had never left Nairobi, but the other with my books was never recovered. Until today I feel sorry that I did not go out and buy my own copies but they were expensive and I had limited funds.

Not only had my books been lost forever, but Bashir now had only the shoes he was wearing, the others being in the lost suitcase. In those days, 1981 Seychelles was still a relatively unknown tourist destination apart from the holidaying super rich who had no need to buy clothes or shoes when they came to the islands. It was a beautifully relaxed, casual place with a tropical climate so flip – flops were the standard footwear. There were no shoes to be found in Bashir's size in the country, so the pair he was wearing would be all that he was to have for his stay. He was a stylish man but throughout his life he hated shopping, and now another shopping expedition was needed with no simple way to get anything into the country. I hinted that perhaps a London shopping trip and a visit to Seychelles bringing shoes could be a solution? I think the idea began to be considered as the beauty of the Seychelles became all too apparent.

Notwithstanding the shoe problem, for Bashir, who loved the sea having grown up in a house on the shores of the Mediterranean, it was a home from home. His entire childhood had been spent swimming and enjoying Gargaresh beach, so the Seychelles was the last word in a perfect, tropical Eden. Even better the Secretary of the Peoples Bureau, Habib was a career diplomat who had worked with Bashir in the International Cooperation Department. Habib had a massive budget and looked after Bashir royally, putting him into one of the very few five star hotels on the island at that time.

Obviously, Bashir's intention was to be issued with his Kenyan visa and return to Nairobi quickly. An African – wide mistrust of Libya was beginning to ferment. Daniel Arap Moi, the Kenyan President was also the current President of the OAU and wary of Gaddafi and the Libyans he was stationing across Africa. Hence by the end of two weeks there was no update on the visa situation. Bashir was besotted with the Seychelles and called to say that I had to drop everything and come to Mahe to see this country, which was like no other he had ever visited; the marine life was beyond belief. It was impossible to resist the call and of course I brought the shoes. For once, it was a change Bashir meeting me at the airport looking totally relaxed from Seychelles life. I promptly discovered that the perfume of the frangipani, the lush landscape and the brilliant blue of the sea were exactly as he had described. In fact it was cheaper for me to be in the Seychelles than to part with the money we had been spending on those long, longing phone calls.

It could not have been more wonderful. The next weeks were utterly free of all cares. We swam snorkelled and saw every imaginable type of sea life. The Seychelles in 1981 was blissfully empty, tranquil and peaceful during the day. At night there were countless evenings in the hotel bar and the Segar dance competition which Bashir had predictably won the previous two weeks. On my arrival he had been banned from re – entering to give others a chance. Not many people could afford to stay in such a hotel for an extended period and Bashir's stay was to last for 45 days until his visa finally came through.

One highlight of our stay was a flight on a six – seater plane which took us to Praslin Island; our heaven. We were the only people staying in a small complex of wooden huts on the beach. I can visualize that beach to this day with the two of us walking, swimming, lying, kissing and laughing in that remote idyllic place. Perhaps one of the best gifts Bashir gave me is the unique and wonderfully happy memories and his spirit of carpe diem. He was insistent not to leave anything until tomorrow, always do it today.

We had so much of what we built together taken away in later years, but nobody could ever tarnish my vivid reminiscence of those magical tender loving days.

The Secretary of the People's Bureau, Habib and his wife offered us the hand of friendship by inviting us to their glorious residence and introducing me to my first taste of the spices and flavours of Libyan cuisine. We were to meet again in Manila as colleagues. By contrast there was Abdu, the youngest member of the committee who seemed to be chiefly concerned with drinking and womanising, much to Habib's annoyance. Abdu was from Sirte, the birthplace of Gaddafi, hence his luck at being sent to the Seychelles to earn a handsome salary and have fun. I think he looked at me as being Bashir's European catch and was not interested in much more about us.

It was the other member of the committee, whose name I fail to remember, who was obviously put out by Bashir having an English girlfriend. Probably it is selective memory loss. Year after year I was to encounter his type, every night hanging out in bars drinking alcohol, picking up different women and then returning home to their unsuspecting wives. It was the hypocrisy of these men that was so repugnant, rather than their activities. Bashir warned me to steer clear of this man as he had labelled me a prostitute and a non – Muslim and therefore believed I would lead Bashir into evil ways.

At this time the People's Bureaus were newly formed and included the new elite revolutionaries as members of the committees. No one knew quite what power they had, but it was obvious that they were Gaddafi men and he was building his power base in the foreign ministry and in all parts of Libya. Bashir was concerned at the influence that these people seemed to have given his experience in Sierra Leone and Liberia. This might be a good place to look back to pre – 1969 Libya under King Idris and at what was to come as well as where Bashir stood at the beginning of the revolution. This history would impact and colour his life in the future and our lives together.

Three

Bashir was born in 1950 when Libya was a desert backwater having suffered from the ravages of occupation by the Italians, Germans and the Allies during World War II. He remembered vividly United Nations food parcels arriving at the house and of there being vitamin tablets which were forced down his throat by his mother saying *'they will do you good'*. Food was scarce and there were no mains electricity or water. Life was tough for the majority.

The country became independent in 1951 with King Idris being crowned the country's monarch. The new King was from the large and powerful infamous eastern tribe of Senussi which had been politically active during World War ll giving vital support to the British 8th army in North Africa against the Italians and Germans. As head of the tribe and grandson of the Grand Senussi, Sayyid Mohamed Ibn Ali Senussi, King Idris was a popular choice both with the allies and the Libyan elite from eastern Libya. *'Elite'* accurately describes the situation in Libya by 1969. Oil wealth was flowing into the country and the profits left over after foreign oil companies had taken their large slice were then generously distributed to members of the old clans and the King's family.

Libya was divided into three fiercely autonomous regional areas. Gaddafi by overthrowing the monarchy and later declaring *the Jamahiriya (a republic of the masses in which political power is passed to the people)* made Libya into a one nation state. This fragile unity was maintained with an iron fist during his 42 years in power a fact frequently overlooked when assessing the pros and cons of NATO intervention and post – revolutionary Libya.

Events can impact our lives dramatically and for Bashir growing up during this period they were to heavily colour his view. Although I am not trying to write a history of Libya since the Second World War it is important to be aware that there are dramatically differing points of view on the reign of King Idris, both positive and negative. Also, at the start of the 1969 revolution, Bashir was nineteen and of a generation that is steadily disappearing, being the last to be able to accurately describe how the landscape was at that time. Gaddafi ensured that nothing positive could really be written about Libya under King Idris. The history was to be lost, buried, and forgotten. By September 1969 there were two groups: the old elite and tribal elders and the marginalized. Members of the latter group were initially to become Gaddafi supporters on the night of the 31st August and the following morning, as the news of the coup trickled through.

Bashir would be the first to say that under the Kingdom he received a first rate primary and secondary education given that Libya was a developing country coming out from the ravages of World War ll. Teachers were qualified, many coming from Iraq, Egypt and Sudan and the professors in the universities were from the USA and UK. Up to date textbooks were supplied to every child free, and there was a desk for each one of them in clean, airy classrooms. Bashir started to learn English at his state secondary school an institution in stark contrast to the fee – paying elite Tripoli College where only English was used as the language of instruction. When he reached university his best friend was the late Bashir Bishti (the son of a former foreign minister and to whom from now on I shall refer simply as Bishti) who had attended Tripoli College and whose, Arabic as a result was poor. The joke was that Bishti helped with the English assignments while Bashir did the Arabic. Bishti had little or no idea of how to write literate Arabic but had a wonderful grasp of English and the two of them made good companions.

On the medical side the hospitals were well maintained and staffed by qualified expatriate doctors and nurses with all treatment being free. There was also a private hospital, and those patients needing treatment unavailable in Libya would be sent for private treatment in London, paid for by the government. When Bashir's cousin needed a kidney transplant (which sadly was unsuccessful) he was sent to Hammersmith Hospital in London.

There was little if any crime; gold shops packed with expensive wedding jewellery would be closed at prayer time with two broomsticks across the door. A population of approximately three million lived more or less harmoniously. However, the distribution of the oil wealth, property and the allocation of the choicest jobs were not based on merit but rather through nepotism, cronyism and tribal influence, overseen by the royal family. The most coveted jobs were in oil and the military as for both there were opportunities for training abroad, huge salaries and the chance to skim large helpings of cream from multiple deals. Where there is inequality, there is fertile ground for dissent and uprising.

I have talked to numerous expatriates who were in Libya before and after the revolution and without exception they will all say that living and working in Libya was pleasurable before 1969. Huge salaries, luxurious housing, wonderful beach clubs just for expatriates and a few elite Libyans, casinos, restaurants, excellent shopping coupled with a very pleasant Mediterranean climate made for an extremely easy lifestyle and an opportunity to build quite a nest egg.

Throughout Libya's post world war history the expatriates have been beneficiaries whereas the majority of Libyans have been the losers. For the Shkuka family Bashir's brother Ismael had recently spent six months in prison for joining a rally expressing dissatisfaction at the inequalities within the society. The majority of Libyans, certainly outside of Tripoli and Benghazi, tolerated appalling infrastructure and lacked any of the benefits such as mains water and electricity that I in London had taken for granted as a child growing up at the same time. Even in 1969 it is hard to imagine studying by candlelight and a kerosene lamp and getting news through a makeshift radio, yet this was how Bashir studied as a child and in his first year at university. For a society with new found oil wealth it was becoming apparent that despite improved aspects in the area of health and education there were a few who lived lavishly with the majority eking out a living.

On the evening of the 31st August 1969 Bashir and his brother – in – law to be, Shaban, were enjoying the twilight on Gargaresh beach. They could see the sports cars being driven into the New Florida and Polyranna casinos. The floodlights were shining on Underwater and Rimmal, the two exclusive sports and social clubs for expatriates and a few select Libyans, occupying the best positions on Gargaresh beach. Of course these two young Gargaresh lads could in no way ever dream of joining these famously exclusive playgrounds. They sat on the beach discussing their lack of opportunities and marginalization within the society. Late in the evening as frantic sports cars began screeching out of the clubs, Bashir and Shaban had their first inkling of the peaceful coup that had taken place in Benghazi. Gargaresh beach and Libya would never be the same again.

Initially there was euphoria on the Libyan streets and it was rumoured that in the Libyan embassy in London some were seen jumping on the tables to celebrate the overthrow of the monarch. King Idris was in Turkey at the time: he never returned to Libya but instead went into exile in Egypt. The monarchy was abolished and a new state formed with the ideals of 'freedom, socialism and unity'. The charismatic and exceedingly handsome Gaddafi had taken power along with his compatriots and formed the new governing revolutionary council. Bashir recounted how it took him along with others, less than a year to realise that they had replaced inequality with a monster.

Alas, as I try to review the historical facts I continually find differences in the sequence of events and how they are recounted. Gaddafi rewrote his history and his sycophantic followers assisted him in recording their own versions of the pre and post 42 years of Gaddafi rule. I do so wish that Bashir had lived to write this story rather than myself, his wife. He always promised that either when he retired and was living in England or when Gaddafi was gone that he would write his memoirs. I have had to keep all my memories in my head. However, whenever Bashir spoke of the political events which occurred prior to our meeting, he always described them as being as clear in his mind as they were when they occurred.

My recollections are those of a foreigner living in my adopted country of Libya but also through the eyes of my Libyan husband. Right up to the beginning of the revolution in 2011 nobody talked about Libya before Gaddafi apart from perhaps in very tight family groups. It is suspected, and I believe it to be well grounded, that Gaddafi recruited one third of the country's adults into the intelligence service in various capacities to act as 'antenna' or listeners/reporters as Bashir liked to call them. In this way Gaddafi was able to write history through his own eyes. Fairly accurate smuggled stories were occasionally reported in the western press, but more often news of life under the Gaddafi regime was based on hearsay and assumptions. People lived in very real fear of being caught speaking against the leader or his family, so silence was the rule for all but the bravest.

Gaddafi was a disciple of President Jamal Abdul Nasser who had led the

Egyptian revolution against the monarchy in 1952. Nasser introduced far – reaching land reforms and cracked down on the Muslim Brotherhood. He was to become an iconic figure in the Arab world due to his anti – imperialist stance especially in his successful nationalization of the Suez Canal out of the grips of the French and British. He was equally admired and lauded for his efforts for Arab unity and his moves towards social justice for Egypt.

Emulating his role model Gaddafi immediately promoted himself to the same military rank of Colonel. He then set about tackling the unfair legacy of foreign domination of the Libyan oil industry. He demanded the renegotiation of oil contracts and threatened to shut off oil production if the oil companies refused. He memorably told oil executives 'people who have lived without oil for 5000 years can live without it for a few years in order to attain their legitimate rights'. The gamble paid off and Libya became the first developing country to secure a majority share of the revenues of its own oil production. Production levels, matched those of the Gulf States with Libya having one of the smallest populations in Africa of (less than 3 million at that time). It was at this early point, that Gaddafi enjoyed the support of most, including Bashir. There should have been more than enough for one and all.

However, it was perhaps the in – flow of wealth that became Libya's 'curse' as Bashir called this black gold. It is easy to say 'what if' but I do wonder whether a Gaddafi, without billions of dollars to hand might have been a very different Gaddafi. Perhaps the Libyan people might have enjoyed a different kind of prosperity and freedom? Gaddafi may have secured vast wealth for Libya but shortly after renegotiating all the contracts the ten members of the revolutionary council awarded themselves 10 million dollars each for leading the revolution, with no such largesse for the rest of the population. In later years Gaddafi was to claim the oil wealth was for himself and his family, the rest of what little remained being for the Libyans. This greed has never been admitted or even acknowledged by any of the Gaddafi clan.

There were two individuals who received very different treatment at this time. The first was Ali Mdorid, a high ranking military officer and the second was Ahmed Bishti, a former Libyan foreign minister and father of Bashir's university friend, Bashir Bishti. The purge between 1971/72 saw seven former prime ministers, numerous government officials, as well as King Idris in absentia, brought to trial on charges of treason and corruption in the Libyan People's Court. A good number of these men were subsequently acquitted which was also the fate for both Ali Mdorid and Ahmed Bishti but in different ways. Ali had taught Gaddafi at the military college and had gone with the young Gaddafi to England for training at Sandhurst. For some reason or other the Colonel (as Gaddafi began to become known by Libyans) never forgot how Ali had taught him so on learning that he had been arrested, ordered his immediate release. It was at this point that Ali resigned his commission and joined the Foreign Ministry. Ahmed Bishti on the other hand was imprisoned but later acquitted. When these former senior officials and ministers were arrested the majority of people were terrified at what was occuring and wanted more than anything that this new legal authority would see no connection with themselves and those arrested or their families for fear of being found guilty by association. Nonetheless, Bashir and Bishti went to the prison to discover the circumstances of Ahmed's incarceration. They were horrified to find the old man sitting on a concrete floor with no bedding and a bucket in the corner that had not been emptied and stank of excrement. He was restricted to a daily ration of a loaf of bread and a cup of milk or water. Perhaps the only piece of good luck was that he had a cell to himself. Despite these circumstances Ahmed Bishti was dignified and stoical; he was a deeply religious man who still somehow believed that justice would result in him being released. The two young men visited him daily for a period of around three weeks. His family and relatives stayed away as did his so – called friends. This shunning of those in political trouble seems to be a characteristic of many Libyans and was certainly the case when it came to Bashir being on the Gaddafi blacklist for eight years. No one was willing to help, even his own family. The experience of Ahmed Bishti's imprisonment was one of the events that had a profound effect on Bashir in turning him from being a Gaddafi supporter to becoming one of the many silent opponents.

Bashir had had no contact with the pre – revolutionary elite and his view of them was that they lived an opulent lifestyle with no regard for the majority of Libyans. Ahmed Bishti though, he saw as a devout man wishing to promote Libyan interests. Bashir, like the majority of Libyans, had genuinely believed that summary arrests, torture and disappearances were to be a thing of the past but seeing Ahmed Bishti in prison was a clear illustration that things had not changed and were in fact changing for the worse. When Ahmed Bishti was released he retired to his farm in Zawiya where he lived quietly until his death. His wife was still alive in 2002, aged 91 when we left Libya for Manila. I wish I could have interviewed her but Gaddafi was still very much at the helm and no one spoke or asked, ever.

By 1973 Gaddafi had handed over the day – to – day running of the country to Major Jaloud while he started writing his infamous Green book. The model that was created was an ultra – hierarchical pyramid with the Gaddafi family and close allies at the top wielding power unchecked, protected by a brutal security apparatus. Tales abounded of torture and lengthy jail terms without trial, executions and disappearances. This saw the beginning of many of Libya's educated and qualified citizens choosing exile rather than paying lip service to Gaddafi and his Green Book supporters. The majority of those able to go into exile were the wealthy elite who had the financial means to enable them to escape. Gaddafi also began his reward system for allegiance at this time with scholarships to study abroad. Many who took advantage of this benefit would never return to Libya, choosing to settle primarily in the UK, USA and Italy as the Gaddafi regime became ever more robust and fearsome. Bashir wished to do a MA abroad but was only offered a Canadian scholarship to study Library Science, a subject in which he had no interest, so chose not to take up the offer.

There was one more episode of friendship and another of terror that confirmed Bashir's belief that Gaddafi was a colossal error. He had been at school with Milad Awassa who of the two was slightly older. Milad was not a particularly spectacular student, and was held back several times. His family was from a wealthy clan in Aziziyah, twenty kilometres out of Tripoli. Their income derived from farming and owning extensive property in Hay Andulus an upmarket Tripoli suburb, which was primarily rented out to expatriate oil workers for high rents. Bashir and Milad become inseparable friends and on one occasion he remembered going with Milad and his father to collect the rent money. To a young and impressionable poor Gargaresh lad this must have seemed like wealth beyond belief. Nevertheless it did not impact on their friendship. Happy times were spent together down on the beach and Bashir grew to know and like the whole family. Based on Milad's family background it was therefore in many ways strange that he became one of Gaddafi's *last bullets* (a Libyan/Arabic expression for a close confident and the final protector). He joined the Libyan forces fighting in the Yom Kippur war against Israel and through this came to the notice of Gaddafi on his return to Libya. There was no harm to their friendship at this stage but while Milad had been away, Bashir had made new friends at the university with different ideologies to those of Gaddafi's. He had completely lost faith in Gaddafi as a leader, and was about to devastatingly lose faith in his friend Milad.

The events leading to this chasm began to become apparent in 1973 when Gaddafi gave a speech in Zawarah, a city 102 kilometres west of Tripoli in which he initiated a five – point plan that included the removal of all opponents of the revolution and all traces of bureaucracy and the bourgeoisie; to 'expunge Libya of all foreign influences'. Storm clouds were appearing on the horizon. In 1974 a legal reliance on sharia law was introduced with adultery and homosexual activity to be punishable by flogging (although I have to say that I heard no account of flogging ever being used as a punishment). Alcohol at the beginning of the revolution immediately became illegal and this led to some enterprising expatriates, unscrupulous foreign diplomats and the Gargaresh mafia setting up illicit stills and becoming millionaires through the sale of illegal alcohol.

Also it was around this time that conscription for all 18 year olds was enforced. No longer could the sons of the elite be exempt, and those at university would be targets for over enthusiastic revolutionary officers. It was a truly miserable time for those undergoing training. There were many stories of young men having to crawl on bare knees across the yard for two hours and then having to stand for hours in the hot Libyan sun without hats or water; Bashir was one of these young men. This was revenge for the newly appointed revolutionary army officers and it was payback time for those who had marginalized them. It must have been incredibly hard for ordinary Libyans to know where to position themselves.

These radical reforms combined with the abolition of a parliament being replaced by The People's Committees led to widespread discontent, especially when it became known that the Revolutionary Council Committee (RCC) had decided to spend money on foreign causes. By 1975 as well, members of the original RCC were beginning to recognize that Gaddafi was moving the revolution in the wrong direction. Bashir Saghir al Hawaasi and Omar Mfeheshi then launched a failed coup leaving just five members of the original ten – member council.

The red line had been crossed with this seeming blanket imposition of new laws. Bashir remembered going to the University in April 1975 and joining his friends to demonstrate against these laws and enactments brought in at the maniacal whim of Gaddafi and his followers. They were also joined by conservative Muslim brotherhood followers who had been outlawed as being anti – revolutionary. What they failed to know was that the police and the newly formed and very well armed revolutionary brigade had been called in to put down the demonstration. Bashir recounted there were pools of blood spilling everywhere, students and demonstrators screaming, shouting and yelling all desperately trying to escape the bullets and the brutality of the police clubbing, hitting and kicking them. Imagine his horror when along with Major Jalloud he saw his best friend of old Milad brandishing a Kalashnikov as he stood on a roof top mowing down the students. Bashir swore never to have any personal contact with Milad again; the friendship of so many years was cut, over, irreconcilable. At one point much later when we were homeless, people suggested that Bashir should ask Milad for help as he was powerful and could undoubtedly have found a solution. Bashir never went back on his word. Their lives had gone in dramatically different directions. Milad became one of Gaddafi's last bullets; his reward was complete control of meat importation to the entire fiefdom, a highly lucrative contract. He committed suicide during the revolution when his Gargaresh house was surrounded by the revolutionaries. It was after long drawn out fierce fighting that he jumped from the roof in a hail of bullets. He and Bashir had made their choices long ago. When Bashir heard this news despite everything I saw a tinge of sadness in his eyes, he made no comment and I did not ask.

Bashir and his friends were lucky on that day and escaped to their homes unhurt but were aware that there had been countless injuries and deaths. Could it be possible that Libyans had harmed each other in such a brutal fashion? They were having difficulty believing what they had witnessed, the sheer carnage of what they had just seen and experienced. Gaddafi did not want it known that there was any dissent; nothing was reported in the press. It is believed at least thirty students were killed on that terrible day.

Bashir and Bishti, *the two Bashirs*, were to discover in the evening, that one of their friends, whom they called Sheikh because of his deeply held religious beliefs, had been arrested. Once again it was down to the two of them to locate their friend and to see how they could help. As was beginning to be the pattern, other so called friends faded into the woodwork. Thankfully Sheikh was released after two days and allowed to return to a small flat where he was living, not wishing to bring attention and danger to his own family. He had begun writing against the regime and this in all probability was the reason for his imprisonment. Bashir recalled it was a desperately sad meeting as Sheikh begged the two not to return and visit him again as he knew that he was going to be rearrested and that they should not put themselves and their families in danger, this being especially true for Bishti. These events left such a deep impression on Bashir and cemented his belief that Gaddafi had to go, but the question was *how*? The terrifying reign of terror was to continue through to 2011 when the bubble burst. Bashir lost so many of his friends; Bishti went into exile in the USA and died there, Sheikh was arrested and rearrested, spending long periods in prison, and Milad was a dead name. The friendships of Bashir's youth were shattered. Gaddafi had fractured the foundation of Libyan society and in so doing was able to control it. Fast – forward to the present and perhaps it can be better understood why the revolution has failed. These people had been cooped – up in this desolate desert setting and pitched against itself for decades, Gaddafi's handiwork is still endemic in every level of Libyan life today.

Four
ع

Sierra Leone had been our introduction, Seychelles a brief but beautiful, romantic interlude, and now Kenya would be the backdrop for the next stage of our logistically difficult romance. It would be my learning curve of how to live with a Libyan diplomat with amazing highs and ultimately a life making decision.

The Committees had not contaminated the embassy in Kenya and Bashir could barely wait to start working as the Libyan focal point for the United Nations Human Settlements (HABITAT) and for the United Nations Environment Programme (UNEP). The latter would hold an increasing importance for him as an organization where it might be possible to help in improving Libya from within. Nairobi proved to be way beyond all of his expectations. One of the things I found interesting being with Bashir in both West and East Africa was a question that he was continually asked by the locals '*where are you from?*' to which he replied '*like you, I am African.*' A look of incredulity was always followed by a repeat of the initial question, '*No really, where are you from?*' This split of Arab North and Sub Saharan Africa would be an increasingly sore point for the Libyans as they saw their wealth being given to a sub – continent of which they felt little or no part. Gaddafi felt otherwise.

From Seychelles I had flown back to London. Meanwhile Bashir in Nairobi had found a place to live opposite the Ethiopian embassy on a hill close to the residence of the President. Being on the 8th floor it had the most fabulous, panoramic views of Nairobi, especially at night from the picture windows in the living room. For both of us renting flats was still a new experience. We were to learn from living in Kenya never in future to rent a property near the President's Palace, nor near a TV or radio station, a military barracks or the airport. If there is ever a coup these are the first places to be hit. At this time nothing could have been further from

Bashir's thoughts when searching for a flat, although it would become a major factor in where we chose to live in the future. Untypically, Libyan diplomatic personnel were not helped with accommodation; they were thrown out into the city and expected to sink or swim.

A Libyan Second Secretary's salary in Nairobi at that time was US$1000 a month and included in this was a housing stipend that was increased over the years with one's grade. The majority of Libyan diplomats chose to live in tiny flats in order to save money rather than present a good face of their country. Very rarely did the Libyan diplomats mix socially, perhaps due to a lack of language coupled with their refusal to be accompanied by their wives. They did not make particularly inspiring, dinner party guests. It could also have been that under Gaddafi they believed the diplomatic rules had changed. They knew the diehard intelligence officers and *'antenna'* in the embassy were watching and eager to report back to Tripoli on what they considered to be any misdeeds. Later, whenever Bashir was under investigation he was to discover report after report on which had been written such statements as *'he was seen drinking in a bar with a blonde western woman who could have been CIA, MI6, or Mossad?'* This comment highlights how ineffective they were and how their main thrust of work was primarily on checking their career diplomats. When out we would jokingly ask if we were being watched as these officers seemed ridiculous to us, but later their observations were to land us in serious trouble.

Nairobi was still relatively safe at the end of 1981. I arrived just in time for Christmas and the New Year armed with a couple of bottles of exceptionally good red wine and meticulously planned gifts. Kenya was to be the only place where we felt comfortable celebrating Christmas. Although I have never held deep religious beliefs the 25th December has always been a joyous day when people celebrate together, decorate their houses and give presents. Being married to Bashir and to be seen celebrating Christmas was tantamount to heresy as I was to learn when living in Libya. Bashir was extremely private about his religion; despite drinking alcohol, not going to the mosque and not fasting during Ramadan he was always the first to be overly generous in helping the under privileged financially in his Sadiqkah (The Arabic word for giving to charity). At times I would hear him praying quietly at night before sleeping and increasingly so with age right up to the end. He hated those who committed heinous crimes, who stole and embezzled and then went weekly to the mosque on Fridays and made their Haj to Mecca to be given absolution, only to return to their fiendish ways. We both believed in the simple mantra of *doing as you would be done by*, though we clashed on one spiritual point. He believed in fate whereas I in luck and chance. Today I am no longer convinced either way although I have to say there has been a great amount of fate, luck and chance in my life.

Nairobi's climate is a temperate 25C all year round, just perfect. We made new friends and life was good. Horse racing has long been one of my passions and so on finding that there was Sunday racing I encouraged Bashir to have a day at the races. My enjoyment is not for the betting, but rather being on the rails and watching and hearing the horse flesh race past. For Bashir it was a new experience and one that he too would grow to enjoy. Imagine my surprise when on placing a bet I heard a voice saying '*bloody hell Susie what on earth are you doing here?*' It was one of my friend's from when I had lived and worked in Cambridge in the 1970s and she had taken a job at the Banda School by the National Park. Mandy and her husband Dave became firm friends and we often visited the school at weekends to enjoy the tennis courts, swimming pool and the fine company of the two of them and their friends. I still smile when I remember a Cambridge GCE exam at the school being interrupted by an escaped lion from a nearby nature reserve being found in the playground. The comment written on the Disruptions paper stated that '*a lion entered the school compound during the maths exam which was postponed for two hours until the animal was captured and returned to the reserve*'. I have no doubt that this was the first time and quite possibly the last that anyone had found cause or used this particular reason.

Our ability to enjoy mixing socially wherever we went was a feature of our lives that enabled Bashir to be such a successful diplomat. He had contacts and friends everywhere we went and always maintained those friendships. He was a good mover and both of us brought friends from our different circles which made for a fascinating social life. We loved entertaining and being entertained and there were plenty of receptions, parties, and social get – togethers in Nairobi with its 120 or so missions. Added to which of course there were all our new contacts and friends working for the UN organisations.

I was anxious to find work and it was through Soleiman a Libyan exile working for UNEP that I was to have my first experience of working for the United Nations as an English Editor within the United Nations Human Settlements Organisation (HABITAT). This was still in the days of electric typewriters and no spell or grammar checks and for those of us in the English section we were tasked to produce documents ready for translation into the five other UN languages. Through the editing work I was to learn of the aid projects and assistance being administered by this organisation; it gave an insight into the immense value of UN work.

It was from Soleiman that we came to learn of the plight of his brother – in – law Jaballa Hamad Matar. He was born in Ajdabuya a town some 150 kilometres south of Benghazi to an old and respected Libyan family. He joined the Libyan Diplomatic service and initially at the start of the revolution he, like Bashir, had been euphoric about the overthrow of King Idris. However, later he found Gaddafi's new socialist ideology repugnant and by 1972 felt unable to continue working as a diplomat and resigned his post. Subsequently he became a businessman and was one of the most prominent Libyan opposition figures. His organization had a training camp south of the Libyan border in Chad. This perhaps accounts for one of the reasons why Gaddafi commenced the Chadian war. By 1979 Jaballa had been arrested and imprisoned for six months and on his release was warned that Gaddafi was going to re – arrest and imprison him again as being a powerful enemy of the state. Gaddafi never had any mercy for those who opposed him. Realizing that it was untenable for him and his family to remain in Libya, he escaped to Cairo in the same year.

The family frequently visited Nairobi and likewise Soleiman went to Cairo to see his sister, nephew and Jaballa. I never recall having met any members of the family but we often heard from Soleiman of harassment, intimidation and assassination attempts on Jaballa's life. Gaddafi was resolute in not letting people just leave Libya and go into exile; they were constantly followed. Eventually, in March 1990 Jaballa was kidnapped from his Cairo apartment by the Gaddafi secret police and taken to the most dreaded of prisons, Abu Salim in Tripoli. This was where he spent the remainder of his life for the most part in solitary confinement in appalling, miserable conditions. For his wife the three letters that were smuggled out are pitiful in the extreme. She must have found them soul destroying. It is not known when and how he was murdered but all Libya knew of his plight and lived in fear of what could happen to them if they too questioned or spoke against the regime either at home or abroad. It was becoming clear that anybody thinking of challenging or leaving did so at their peril.

I mention Jaballa's story as a Gaddafi opponent to illustrate that we knew first – hand rather than through hearsay of what happened to those who were brave enough to organize any resistance. This was to have an impact on the decision Bashir took in 1983 and later when living in temporary exile of being unable to return to Libya, his home. Soleiman's poems on the loss of his country and an inability to return to Libya for fear of imprisonment or death are hauntingly beautiful. Jaballa will remain in Libyan history as one of the major but also one of the *many* victims of Gaddafi's intolerance to opposition.

Bashir and I argued for years after whether it was fate or good luck that made us move from the flat with the view on the Nairobi hill. After Christmas 1981 we both felt that living on the 8th floor was too high, especially as the lift was continuously out of order so we relocated to a small flat in a compound in Hurlingham. This was a magical home with a huge balcony overlooking a garden. Our nights of always going out were replaced by balcony nights. I look back on this period as being when we really began to know each through much intense talk, discussing, laughing and loving each other. Both of us were busy with routine work and conferences, the latter with the inevitable long deadline negotiation nights. Work was intermingled with the inevitable national day receptions. Nairobi receptions were always splendidly set in embassy and hotel gardens and we had the pleasure of knowing many people at these social events.

As time goes on in a diplomatic career receptions become increasingly hard work and a chore but at this time they were still a novelty. In the future our rule would be talk to two people in depth, five quickly and then try and leave. This may sound flippant but sometimes we had two or three to attend in one night and often every night for week after week. It was exhausting, plus in smaller countries we would frequently be meeting the same people. A standout reception for over the top opulence was that held by the Philippines embassy when Mrs Marcos came to the HABITAT conference. No expense had been spared with champagne and chocolate fountains, with the gorgeous perfume of colourful Kenyan flowers in abundance, Mrs Marcos always demanded beauty with not a thought for the millions of Filipinos living in abject poverty. Like Gaddafi, the Philippines' money was her money to spend as she pleased. This was especially ironic on this occasion since she was in Nairobi specifically for an organization that was established to provide help to the poor and homeless.

One of my fondest memories of Kenya is of leaving the city at midday on a Saturday and throwing sleeping bags into the back of the Range Rover and driving to the Mara to watch the animals. It was such an amazing experience and what a privilege to be living in Nairobi and to be able to do this weekend after weekend. On our first safari we were accompanied by a Masai guide who later became a firm friend. During the day we had seen elephants, giraffes, zebra and rhino but no lions. We had our binoculars but his eyes were sharper and better than any manmade device and it was he as the sun was setting who spotted the tiny movement of grass and the tip of a tail. We drove to within fifteen feet and then out emerged a lioness with her two cubs. It was more than we had ever imagined although one tinged with fear on my part but not so Bashir whose comment was 'we have been driving round and around all day looking for lions now here they are and you want to drive off'.

Life seemed perfect until on the night of the 1st August 1982 the peace was broken and the events served to remind us of the instability of African living. We had been out with friends and on arriving home sat on our balcony having one last drink before turning in. Suddenly we heard and saw low level jets screeching across the night sky. This was unheard of, especially as it was midnight, and we wondered what was happening and why? Bashir had heard no rumours and as we were completely in the dark it was more than alarming. Thankfully he was able to understand Swahili and therefore the later radio broadcasts. We learned that soldiers from the Kenyan Air force had taken over the radio station and announced they had overthrown the government. Their plan had been to force a group of air force pilots to bomb State House. The pilots pretended to follow orders on the ground but once air borne ignored the coup leaders and instead dropped the bombs over Mount Kenya's forests. Had we still been living in our old flat we would have been in the very thick of very heavy fighting. Lessons were well learnt for the future: always think doubly carefully about what buildings are in the neighbourhood before finally choosing where to live (although as we shall see later, failure to do so when we chose a house in Tripoli led to some interesting consequences).

Fate had been on our side, as Bashir muttered at the time. This was 1982, so there were no mobile phones and we had no house phone apart from a public telephone in the courtyard of the compound. Fortunately living in a compound we felt relatively safe but gunfire and the noise of jets flying overhead continued throughout the night. Coming from London I had never heard guns being fired in anger and it was extremely frightening. I have to say that whatever bad situation we were in Bashir always managed to keep calm and clear – headed or at least he pretended for my benefit.

Listening to the news early the next morning we learned that in the wealthier areas, especially those inhabited by the Indian community, mob justice had taken over. There was widespread looting and burning of shops downtown and houses were robbed and women raped. By midday it was announced that the coup attempt had failed and relative peace had been restored with a night curfew. The Indian community especially was shell – shocked, having been hardest hit by vindictive attacks.

I marvel to this day at Bashir's belief that as a diplomat he would be respected whatever the situation. He was determined to drive to the embassy to ensure that it was safe and report on the coup attempt to Tripoli. Although Amar as Charge d'Affaires should have been the first to give orders, he refused to go, as did the intelligence officer. Both of them showed their character that day, or rather a lack of it. Bashir had managed to contact Gilban, another career diplomat and Iyat the administrator. These three diplomats set out for the embassy. They were gone a couple of hours which was nerve racking as there was no way of knowing what was happening and whether or not they were safe. Later Bashir stated he was fuelled by a good measure of bravado but in fact he was petrified, not wanting to show either me or the other two the reality. Although they were stopped by innumerable checkpoints, fortunately there had been respect for their diplomatic car throughout the drive. They saw men running through the streets brandishing pangas and looting. An African mob is fearsome and on reflection they were pretty foolhardy to have ventured out that day, but they had done their duty nonetheless and could not be accused of shirking their responsibilities.

The next day people bought up everything in the shops and we were reduced to eating corned beef that neither of us could stand. We learned from colleagues at the UN, who were old hands at these sorts of situations that we should always be prepared for any upheaval, either natural or human. Bottled water, tinned food, candles, batteries, a good FM radio, a container of petrol and always fill up the bath with water at the first hint of trouble. We were about to become *prepared for anything* diplomats. Life in Nairobi was no longer uneventful. Later we were to experience a minor earthquake and this time we were ready and knew exactly what to do Nairobi, Liberia and Sierra Leone had been our training grounds.

I have always been a firm believer that birthdays should be celebrated as the means of recalling where and when one was at a particular point in time. We had made many friends by September 1982 and all were invited to Bashir's 32nd birthday party. The ambassador, Taher, suggested using the Libyan residence. This large, beautiful house with gorgeous garden and swimming pool was used for entertaining and for weekend activities for the embassy children. I think that Taher had an ulterior motive as the International Telecommunications Conference was taking place at the same time and the Libyan Telecommunications Minister was attending. He was a known playboy and partygoer and was nicknamed 'the dancer' and Taher presumably believed our party would give him a good time. Neither Bashir nor I were in favour but were not in a position to dissuade Taher and so it was set. On the morning of the party close friends and I cooked a wide array of international dishes and Taher generously provided drinks – alcoholic of course.

Everyone arrived including the minister and all seemed to be going well until some friends arrived bringing with them two Cuban exiles. My approach up to this point had always been to have an open house. Bashir though, was uncomfortable with their presence and his sixth sense warned him to keep an eye on them. As ever he was proved correct as midway through the evening one of them left the main party and disappeared upstairs. Bashir followed the man to discover him taking photographs of the celebration from the upstairs balcony. Alcohol is banned in Libya and it was very dangerous for its diplomats to be seen drinking publically. Furthermore it was a mixed gender dancing party attended by the Minister, so it would have been frowned upon in certain quarters and was of course not something we wanted on film. On asking the Cuban for the film, explaining that photos were not allowed in a private party he refused, saying it was his personal camera and there was no harm. Thankfully, the German who had brought them to the party intervened and exposed the film, resolving the situation, but with the Cubans leaving in an acrimonious huff. It could have been perfectly innocent but I rather think it was not.

This was yet a further education in terms of dos and don'ts when living with a Libyan diplomat. As the Libyan profile became less and less acceptable internationally, we became more and more watched. It wasn't just the USA with a keen eye on us either, later we would become aware of the UK Government and of course, always, the Libyans. At this time the Iraqis too were our watchers but as the political picture changed they too became the watched.

The final death knell to the party hit when the Minister asked me to come to his hotel room. It was a tricky situation to extricate myself from. It needed an explanation of my relationship with Bashir which to any normal person would have been obvious. His response to that was to remind me of his status and to find one of my friends' to entertain him. This exemplifies yet again many Libyan men's attitude towards women; for this man and his kind the only reason an adult female could possibly be out of the house must be that she was loose, easy and would respond positively to *any* sexual advance.

Taher the ambassador had told me some time earlier that Libyan wives had the best life in the world. For him this meant women staying at home, producing children, cooking, cleaning and socializing solely with other females for which they were provided gold and clothes. Taher's was in fact a love match; he was from Tripoli and his wife from the mountains. They had met at the university and her family had been very resistant to the marriage due to the Libyan tribal system. She was a well – educated lady but like so many of that generation marriage meant retirement to the home. I suppose for the majority that may have been enough but certainly stepping out of this norm would have brought shame on your family at that time. For the few women who did work, the only socially acceptable jobs were teaching and medicine. The life of a housebound wife certainly wasn't for me. This was my first real taste of Libyan gender inequality. Bashir's mother and sister were illiterate and his brother – in – law refused to allow his first daughter to go to school despite Bashir's intervention on her behalf. Even by 2013 when things had changed dramatically within the society, with the exception of his youngest brother's second wife who taught in a primary school, all the Shkuka women remained at home. They had husbands who did not need 'the other tap' (meaning another source of income) although economics were to change the position of many women regarding work by the turn of the century in Libya.

Fast – forward to May 2015 and the scandal surrounding the Libyan soldiers who were on a training course in Bassingbourne, Cambridge. Two of these soldiers were given sentences of 12 years imprisonment for rape. They were caught on closed circuit television moving around Cambridge city harassing men and women and finally gruesomely raping a man. The judge perhaps rather inappropriately described them as 'hunting dogs'. The Gaddafi family and their cronies set the standards of behaviour for many Libyans. They had no morals when it came to sexual activity and their way of life trickled down into society.

A further illustration is of a Welsh friend, her Libyan husband and their exceptionally eye – catching daughter, who were on Regatta beach during the 2000s where the Gaddafi Boys had built their Tripoli beach palaces. Saif, Gaddafi's son was driving along the beach and saw their daughter and came down to talk to her and her parents. Imagine their horror when he invited her, which of course meant *ordered* her to come to a party he was hosting at his Regatta house that evening. Everyone in Libya knew what such an invitation meant. My friends drove straight home, packed up their house and drove across the border that night, deciding to live in the UK; the alternative was just too appalling for their beautiful daughter. Others were not so lucky and tales of rape and sexual exploitation were extremely prevalent. For ordinary people living in Libya this was an everyday fear; thugs, however loosely, connected to Gaddafi's all – powerful apparatus raping women and young men at complete liberty, with no fear of prosecution. Now looking at Libya today I cannot help but feel that the Libyan diaspora returning to Libya in 2012 had not fully realized the extent to which the Gaddafi regime's violence, lack of morals and propaganda had so corrupted the society. They came to the New Libya with their western way of life perhaps with a rather high handed set of values and ideas. Yes the beast had been removed, but he had sown his demonic seeds far too well during his 42 years of tyranny.

As I have said birthdays were and are markers in my life and this party coincided with my mother's death. That week I had received what was to be her final letter saying how much she and my father enjoyed learning of my weekly African adventures. Sadly that letter is with my possessions in Tripoli which in all probability I will never see again; items such as this are the valuables in my life. Time and again poor communications were to play a part in the period before the Internet and mobile phones. Not having a home phone my contact number was either Bashir's office extension or that of my office. On that Sunday evening a friend passed by our flat saying that they had heard a message on the BBC World Service asking Susan Sandover to call home. Without an international phone line at the flat we drove to a friend's house and called my parents' number but there was no answer. The only solution was to call my dearest childhood friends Penny and Steve. I could tell immediately when Steve said *'I am so sorry Susie, about Barbara'*. My mother had been suffering from ill health but her death was unexpected. She had spent a day out in the countryside with my father and on arriving home said she felt a little tired and wanted an early night. She died beside my father in bed silently in the night. My father found her when he woke in the morning.

When talking about a parent it is always difficult to use the correct adjectives, especially for my mother, as they would all seem inadequate. She was deeply religious, although without ever forcing this on anyone else, kind to all and always willing to help everyone who asked. Perhaps the greatest tribute was that in nearly all the hundreds of condolence letters we received from all over the world they all mentioned how Barbara was their best friend. Her example has been a guiding light for how I have tried to live my own life. Today the changes of how one communicates with family and friends when living abroad is easy using internet, mobile or skype. The World Service Call Radio Service has been discontinued as no longer necessary, but at that time it was invaluable.

I flew to London immediately in order to support my father who quite obviously was in an extremely shocked state. My mother had always been a wonderful stay at home mother and was the one who organized their social life and the entire running of the house; my father didn't have a clue. In fact she was not too dissimilar to a Libyan wife. Sometimes I think one forgets how women's rights are still something relatively new in our British society and culture.

The church had standing room only for the funeral, a clear reflection of how much she was loved by so many. It was typical that she had long ago asked that the very un – funereal 'Lord of the Dance' with its fabulous words should be sung at that time and place.

Being the eldest, only female and single sibling it was assumed that

I would return to London to look after my father. My father's sister explained this was my expected duty probably relating it to her own life as she had looked after and lived with her father after the death of her mother. For her, perhaps times had not moved on but for me I was 33 and however much I loved my father, I certainly never could have imagined moving in and living with him. In fact I rather doubt whether he would have liked that living arrangement, perhaps apart from the cooking. Again there is a similarity to Libyan society in the expectation for an unmarried female to look after a widowed father. I decided that I would remain with him until just before Christmas and then return to Nairobi, as my brother would then take over for a month coming from Vienna. Unfortunately on talking to my boss at UN HABITAT I was to learn that they were unable to hold my job open for an extended period and so I was forced to resign. This was a bitter disappointment.

I had loved my HABITAT job, working alongside people who had so much to give in the field of helping the homeless. It was fascinating to work with such an international workforce. Additionally my colleagues Marguerita from Chile the Spanish translator, George the French translator and Mercedes from Brazil and our boss Charlotte, known for her famous panama hat, we made a jolly team. Weekends were spent together regularly in Marguerita's gorgeous garden. George and Marguerita playing guitars, Bashir on oud and the rest of us on spoons and drums, we could be heard playing music from all over the world. It was in her garden that we planted our Christmas tree when we left the country. From my mother I had learnt to always buy a Christmas tree with a root. Not having a garden in Nairobi and only a balcony we had to find a home for our tree. I do so hope that it has grown into a massive fir as our legacy in that scenic country that gave us so many happy memories.

When I returned to Nairobi, Soleiman once more helped me find interesting work this time as a conference room officer within the organisation where he worked UNEP. I equally loved this work as I felt absolutely in the thick of things, especially when it came to the Drafting Committee; I also really began to understand the difficulties of accommodating every comma, full stop and nuance.

The casino in Nairobi was to be another eye – opener as a window into the hypocrisy of corrupt officials from different territories supported by the Gaddafi oil wealth. Perhaps one group that shocked us the most was that of ministers and diplomats representing the Polisario Front (the separatist movement seeking independence for the Western Sahara region in the South of Morocco) who were so often seen in the casino. In 1981 Gaddafi was an ardent sponsor of their cause and substantial funds would arrive in suitcases from Libyan coffers to support their fight. We both loathed seeing these men in the casino drinking, picking up women and losing Libya's easy – come money on the blackjack and roulette tables. Likewise whenever certain Libyan ministers came to Nairobi, the casino was always their first port of call and more Libyan dollars were frittered away like Monopoly money. The Libyan ambassador even had to pimp for Abdul Arti, the Libyan Foreign Minister when he came to Nairobi as he had a favourite Somali prostitute. There was also Ali, an army Colonel who came with his South American girl friend. She was a total embarrassment. On one occasion we had to sit through her parading like a fashion model wearing her latest French designer dresses and new pieces of jewellery bought by Ali presumably from official Libyan government funds; it was nauseating. Ali would recount on numerous occasions that he had everything to thank Gaddafi for, as without him he would have owned nothing. He carried huge bags to Nairobi stuffed with dollars for the various causes that Gaddafi was supporting which were based in Nairobi.

Ali, ever generous with the Libyan money had wanted to give Bashir financial help so he could buy a house. Bashir refused. When we were in Manila years later we discovered that Amar Hanesh, one of the members of the committee in the embassy had taken a substantial amount from Ali. This discovery was absolutely incredible to us, as at the time we had no idea as to who were the chancers or thieves in the embassy.

So who was Amar? His family name was Hanesh, which translates from the Arabic to little snake. He was in reality a really very big snake. Kenya had stated that they would not accept a change from an embassy to a People's Bureau. Gaddafi was desperate to become the next Chairman of the OAU so he was prepared to back down on the People's Bureau issue in order to accommodate President Moi, the then OAU Chairman. There would be an unofficial committee within the embassy consisting of three members: Taher as the Secretary with Amar a businessman, and Abdallah from the Libyan intelligence office as the other two. These two new members of the embassy were to become Bashir's new bosses despite

43

speaking poor or little English and having no knowledge of international politics or diplomacy. All seemed to be well initially but obviously Bashir was especially wary of Abdallah.

At that time we had met the Philippine Ambassador Mendoza and his wife and three children. Their daughter Peachy was our age and we started inviting her to our home where on one occasion she met Amar. Coming from Zwarah, Amar was already involved in an arranged marriage that was due to take place in the autumn of 1983. Possibly initially Amar thought of Peachy as a last fling but it was to develop into something much more intense. He was like a moth to the light. It was fascinating in 2002 when by fate or possibly chance we reconnected with the Mendoza family at a Manila ball and learned how Amar and Peachy's love affair had ended.

It all seems such a long time ago and my memory as to the sequence of events is fuzzy. Taher relied on Bashir as being a capable but junior diplomat to go and meet envoys, political opponents and diplomats that he could not be seen to have consultations with either publically or privately. Bashir was in effect the go – between. From 1972 to 1979 Gaddafi had sent Libyan troops to bolster the brutal regime of Idi Amin in Uganda. He also called for a Jihad by the Congolese Muslims against the western backed Mobutu Sese Siko. Finally, as I mentioned previously, Libyan opponents had set up a training camp in Chad and in 1980 Gaddafi began his horrendous military intervention in the country, which was to cause great loss of both Chadian and Libyan lives. Gaddafi used the pretext of a border dispute in that part of the country but it was the uranium deposits that were of most interest.

Gaddafi had seen his Arab dream fade and he now swapped his pan Arab robes for Pan African garments. President Daniel Arap Moi was the current Chairman of the OAU at the time and Gaddafi was desperate to succeed him. However as a result of his African meddling, many African heads of states had become suspicious of Gaddafi and were not in favour of seeing him take up such an influential position. In the hope of gaining support, Gaddafi began courting Yowen Muserveni, one of the Ugandian opposition leaders in exile. One of Bashir's roles in Nairobi was to be the intermediary at secret meetings and negotiations with Muserveni in the hope of ousting the then Ugandian President Obete. Bashir had great admiration at that point in time for Museveni wishing that Libya could have such a potential leader. President Moi managed to coerce a few other

African heads of state to attend the Tripoli summit. No doubt offers of suitcases full of dollars were promised for attendance but the majority boycotted the summit. Taher flew on ahead to brief Tripoli and Bashir was chosen to fly with President Moi to Libya, much to the irritation of Amar. I was still in London looking after my father since my mother's funeral.

Bashir had never flown on a presidential plane and that in itself was a unique experience. He sat with the press corps at the back of the plane but was asked to go forward to brief President Moi. His description of flying up over Sudan as dawn was breaking and viewing the amazing landscape of the Sahara as they crossed into Libya, he said was unforgettable. Suddenly two Libyan MIG jets flew up along either side of the Kenyan plane and accompanied them all the way to Tripoli diving and turning like birds in the sky. Every time I too have flown over the desert I marvel at the grandeur and beauty of this isolated place.

Alcohol had been banned in Libya and yet a great many Libyans wanted a drink, its scarcity massively boosting its demand. If I had known what Bashir was up to on that Presidential flight I would have died a thousand deaths knowing what the consequences could have been if exposed. Curiously as it was on a presidential flight no questions were asked about what went onto the plane and what went off at the other end; times have changed. With the connivance of a member of the Kenyan Protocol, two cases of Johnny Walker Black Label whisky were put on the plane and taken off at the Tripoli end by Bashir's cousin who was in the CID. I tell this here to show what I came to learn about Libya in how to survive; that everything was possible and nothing was impossible providing one was patient and knew the way and had the right contacts. Everyone had contacts in Libya.

Apparently four happy nights were spent at the conference after hours with Bashir being the folk hero of the event. To my way of thinking he was foolhardy and rash but he was young and carefree. The summit was intense with of course Tripoli being unable to cope with organizing the event efficiently, not surprisingly. Rightly Gaddafi felt shamed that so many African leaders had shunned him, resulting in a tit for tat series of events for those who hadn't attended. President Moi flew back to Nairobi and Bashir flew to London for twenty – four hours en route back to Nairobi. Yet another hello and goodbye; this was our lifestyle.

Bashir and I at this time began to realize that what was happening in

Libya had made it impossible for us to get married. A new law had been passed that Libyans were forbidden to have foreign wives. Added to which, it was 1982 and Bashir had only one more year before the end of the four year posting. It was drawing close to decision time but what decision to reach was incredibly difficult as it would be momentous. Bashir had a passion for his work and both of us loved being in Nairobi. The people, the wildlife, the climate and our new friends all brought us so much happiness. We discussed with Soleiman the possibility of Bashir applying for a job with either of the two UN Kenya based organisations. All UN senior jobs are subject to quotas based on the size of each member state's population. Due to the Libyan population being small, their allocation of senior posts was likewise tiny and the few jobs there were went solely to Gaddafi cronies, of which Bashir was not one. If we were to stay together then the only option was for Bashir to abscond from the service and come to London and for us to be married there.

In the meantime the two new members of the committee began to exert their authority and crunch time came when the ambassador was away. Amar, being the age senior member of the committee was made Charge d'Affaires, under the old style embassy it would have been Gilban a career diplomat at the grade of Minister. Gilban was highly educated, open – minded, spoke excellent English and was fascinating to talk to about the Libyan antiquities as his degree was in archaeology. As I write of him it is with sadness, as during his time in Nairobi he must have contracted AIDS, as he was to die from the disease some three years later. Bashir went and visited him in hospital in Tripoli but at that time little was known of AIDS and it was covered up as being shameful for the family. He was a remarkable man and one of the diplomats of whom Libya should have been very proud.

Amar's new role went completely to his head and he began instigating new rules in the embassy, taking all the embassy cars from the career diplomats Gilban, Iyat and Bashir and imposing late shift after late shift on the three of them while coming into the embassy around midday, himself having spent the night with Peachy in night clubs and the casino. Petty gripes in a small team build up and the sacking of Anna, the embassy secretary, because she had not acknowledged Peachy one day when she came to the embassy, I think was the icing on the cake. Amar was in charge despite having had no diplomatic training and limited English. By the time Taher returned, the atmosphere had completely soured. He wisely did not want to rock the boat with Amar but at the same time tried to smooth ruffled feathers with the foreign ministry staff. He had lost his trusted secretary but was one to always see where his best interests lay. The three diplomats realised that things were deteriorating, especially as Taher's term was nearing completion resulting in his return to Libya. Gilban, Iyat and Bashir all requested to be posted home early, but Bashir had a different agenda.

By the time of my return to Nairobi for my second Christmas, Bashir and I had decided to get married and London was going to be where we would start our new life together. The big question however, was how this could be accomplished. The Financial Attaché in the embassy was Ahmed Arajoul who came from Sebha in the south of Libya. Ahmed also worked in Libya's embassy in Rwanda and when he was out of Nairobi Bashir took over as Financial Attache. Ahmed liked Bashir and sympathized with our situation and so we confided in him of our plan to marry. His thought was that the best plan would be to say that Bashir, along with the other two wished to be posted back to Libya. In that way all the final settlements such as money in lieu of shipments, air tickets etc. would be paid. This was especially important as money was going to be tight in the future. Nothing about the plan, however, was to be smooth sailing.

Was Nairobi the best place we ever lived? Until now I cannot answer that. Everywhere we lived was different but the joy was that we were always together and life was never boring. Nairobi certainly was where we probably had the least worries and where we made the decision to spend the rest of our lives together. Soleiman still lives in Nairobi and I have an open invitation to visit Kenya but I think going back would revive too many wonderfully happy times that can never be relived.

Nairobi, was also however to cause the death of Ahmed. The embassy would eventually be closed due to similar reasons to those that occurred in Sierra Leone and Liberia. Ahmed returned to Libya and it was apparent that he was desperately ill. He too had contracted AIDS and was sent to Paris for treatment but at this time the disease was incurable. The good from Nairobi had died and the snake had survived unscathed.

Iyat was to be sent to Kampala, Uganda three years later. His humour and kindness to both of us were always remembered and treasured. The Libyan and French embassies had offices in the same building and in a case, it is believed, of mistaken identity Iyat was getting out of his car one morning when he was shot. He died immediately. He bore a resemblance to the French ambassador. Whether this was the case we do not know. Perhaps it was a revenge killing for Gaddafi's interference in countries making Libyan diplomats vulnerable. His body was flown back to Tripoli but the sole compensation that his wife received from the Foreign Ministry was a sack of rice, a sheep and a pitiful pension. Iyat would be proud to know that today his son, certainly at the beginning of the revolution was an up and coming career diplomat.

Five

The next part of our story returns to London where we naively thought we were going to spend the rest of our lives together. My cosy little, attic flat in Frognal Hampstead was rented but the tenant's lease still had a further four months to run. I had hoped that she would be willing to break the lease early, but she declined, leaving me back in London homeless. If someone were to ask me what the ingredients are for a good life setting aside financial considerations, I would say a loving partner, supportive family and amazing friends. Without a doubt I have been blessed with all three. Time after time in my life it has been my friends, Penny and Steve who have come to my rescue and they did so yet again this time, finding us a temporary home.

Across from their house was a rather strange squat. Unusually in the kitchen there was a shower with water lasting no more than two minutes; one had to be quick, soap before going in and then quickly showering before the water cut out. In the sitting room was a sofa and in the bedroom a double bed thankfully not a single. Returning from a place where so many lived in shantytowns in absolutely appalling conditions, we had no right to complain. Plus, reflecting on the first place we lived as a married couple, it was home and when you start at the bottom things can only improve. It certainly made us far more appreciative of everything that we managed to achieve in the future.

My memories of then are of a time filled with excitement. Bashir arrived from Nairobi and our first port – of – call was to put up our wedding banns and book a wedding day. That registration day turned out to be prophetic, but at the time I found it insulting. Rather than ignoring the advice I was given by the Registrar on marrying a Muslim and the necessity of a prenuptial agreement I should have thanked him profusely. In 1983 pre – nuptial agreements were just coming into vogue for the rich and famous but for people such as us it seemed irrelevant. At that time I was not advised of Sharia Inheritance law marginalising women rather, I was informed only on my divorce rights. Today I urge all women to have a prenuptial agreement whether they are to be married to a Muslim or to a person of any other faith or culture. I brought inherited wealth to our marriage and I was to suffer the consequences of not heeding the words of the Registrar. 9/36 was far away from my thoughts at that wonderfully happy time.

I can never forget our wedding day it was heavenly. It was done in haste and only Penny and Steve were present as witnesses. It was a gloriously sunny, summer London day. Bashir wore a newly, bought suit and I a plain white cotton dress that was the fashion in 1983. Penny added a spray of large, fragrant, white roses. It was a quick and simple affair but just perfect I was Bashir's bride and in paradise. He had escaped Libya and hard to believe we were together in London, husband and wife starting out on a new life. How foolish we were to think that it would be easy. Neither of us had any business contacts and in reality if we had stopped to think there really was little that a young Libyan diplomat could offer an employer.

On work prospects one idea had been that Bashir could do translation or interpreting but of course he needed qualifications. He enrolled on a course at the University of London and initially was enthused by the subject matter and his tutors. In the meantime applications were made to international oil companies operating in the Middle East, UN agencies and the BBC world service. What we had ignored or failed to anticipate was the plummeting reputation of Libyans due to Gaddafi's now persistent meddling in African, Asian and South American politics. Worse still was his silencing of opponents abroad by assassination. Given the choice a Libyan or any other nationality, why at that time would anyone employ a Libyan, especially one who had been a diplomat? Why had he left his job? What was he doing in London?

The second problem we faced was a residence visa for the UK. This involved visits to East Croydon and Lunar House, known aptly as Lunatic House. Bashir had no wish to claim political asylum, just wanted to go through the normal process of being issued a visa by virtue of his marriage to a British citizen. In fact our marriage was unrecognised in Libya as it was illegal for a Libyan to marry a foreigner. At the beginning of 1984 the law was changed.

September saw an improvement when we moved back into our Frognal flat. We had a place we could call home, a permanent address, a telephone line and a feeling of normality. Many idyllic evenings were spent in that flat over dinners either cooked by Bashir or myself with friends arguing over how best to repair the ills of the world amidst much laughter and cheer. However, it was not all cheer as rejection letter after rejection came through the post. The one ray of light was from the BBC world service who called Bashir for an interview and he returned believing the interview had gone well.

During this period I saw him at times at one of his most pessimistic wondering if he had made a gigantic error and if there might have been alternative options if we hadn't acted so hastily. In addition, his eldest brother Ibrahim refused all phone calls on learning of our marriage. His mother sobbed *"Oh my son what have you done?" We had arranged for you to marry your first cousin Awasha, and now you are in England married to a foreigner Oh my son, my son what have you done?"* Ibrahim probably whipped her up into hysteria. Bashir was ever the dutiful son, who adored his mother and would have done anything for her. Also as is the Arab tradition he had always respected his eldest brother. When I first met the family they endeavoured to make me feel welcome but I have no doubt today that this brother always harboured a deep grudge against me for our marriage.

Bashir's lack of a British residence visa meant no travelling and we felt trapped. In the three years that we had been together we had become so used to flying here and there spontaneously with no visa problems; Amsterdam, Prague, Geneva or out to Africa. Being born British I had never quite realized until this point in time just how the luck of where one is born is such an essential factor in where one can go and what one can do in this world. From 2006, we increasingly saw boats being openly built in huts beside the road between Tripoli and the Tunisian border. Gaddafi never one to miss a political chance saw the double opportunity on how to bargain with the West on people trafficking whilst at the same time allowing his cronies and supporters to make money from it by turning a blind eye. This was typical of his rule of law. Never more so has this been further highlighted today as one sees overloaded boatloads of Africans dying in the Mediterranean having being exploited by greedy and ruthless Libyan human traffickers; yet another legacy of the Gaddafi era. Yes to be born British is by many an unacknowledged blessing.

Thankfully, by February 1984 the residence visa was issued and we were able to travel to Vienna and Paris in the hope of Bashir perhaps being able to find employment in one of the UN agencies. Obviously competition was fierce and repeatedly the refusal letters were found in our mailbox. Prospects were not looking optimistic. Bashir had brought all his savings from Nairobi but these would not last indefinitely and he never saw himself filling shelves in a supermarket. Life needed to be demanding and with some level of job satisfaction. He had tasted the fruit of international life and anything else would seem sour for my former diplomat husband. His career had been intensely interesting and absorbing up to this point so by comparison he was going to find it extremely tough to accept the ordinary. The one letter he had been waiting for finally came through the post asking him to do a voice test for the BBC. He was thrilled. The test went well and he felt positive of the outcome, but on the 15th April 1984 all our expectations and hopes were shattered. Libya's international standing changed almost overnight and the country became a pariah state. Once Gaddafi's nose was put out of joint he became extremely vengeful. This led to some of the worst of his atrocities, his association with the IRA and Libya's total isolation.

It had been one of those bright, mild, sunny spring mornings and unbeknownst to either of us the Libyan National Salvation Front (LNSF) were holding a demonstration outside the now named Libyan Peoples Bureau in St. James Square. The protest was against the execution of two students who had criticized Gaddafi in Tripoli. The British Foreign office, aware there were going to be problems, called the embassy for a meeting having intercepted a communication between Tripoli and London. One of Bashir's old school friends from his same intake at the diplomatic institute, Hamada Zlitni, went to FCO, Kings Charles Street. For Hamada, perhaps it was fate, luck or chance, but he was not in the embassy on that ill – fated morning. What I have learnt is that Gaddafi had been informed the previous evening that the demonstration was to take place and gave orders that the embassy was to rent a crowd to mount a counter demonstration.

Roughly 75 protesters arrived by coach from the North of England and the police kept them and the LNSF apart with crowd control barriers. There were a few career diplomats working in the embassy at that time but the majority were from the revolutionary committees, loyal, gung – ho followers of the Green Book and their Leader. In their enthusiasm they played loud music, it is believed to try and drown out the shouts of the protesters, displaying their banal and infantile mentality in how to deal with dissent.

I remember so distinctly seeing the headlines at lunchtime and desperately calling the flat to discover if Bashir had heard the news. The 'Yes' of despondency that I heard in his voice was the confirmation that I had already realised; this event would dramatically alter not only the lives of those directly involved but for all Libyans.

The crime came from the second floor window overlooking the square where Matouk Mohammad Matouk, Abdulmajid Salah Ameri and Abdulqadir Al Baghdadi were believed to have been and it was from there a volley of shots was fired into the group of protesters. Why did they fire? These three were among the most noted of Gaddafi's revolutionaries. They were so indoctrinated with Gaddafi propaganda and so full of their own self – importance that I think they might have believed that even in London they could behave as they did in Libya, by shooting anyone who challenged the authority of their leader. It was also an exhibition of their arrogance and belief that Libyan oil wealth enabled them to buy, sell, kill and maim as they wished in order to enforce the Gaddafi word. This indoctrination of a people for 42 years is a legacy causing the continuing mayhem in Libya today, even after the death of Gaddafi. Of the three, I was only to meet one.

In 2006 I had the misfortune of being Salah's English IELTS speaking examiner at the British Council Tripoli. I had no idea who he was and the exam went through normally and he left the room. Less than a minute later he returned closing the door and saying we needed to talk. Immediately I asked him to leave at which point sternly he answered 'don't you know who I am?' I repeated my request again for him to leave the room or I would call the guard. He gave me a pretty gruesome stare but did leave. Subsequently I questioned my colleagues about the man and rather alarmingly was informed he was one of the men suspected of killing Yvonne Fletcher. Even worse he was a powerful member of the hit squad and revolutionary committees. On arriving home and recounting the incident with Salah to Bashir he was concerned and prayed that we did not receive a visit from the hit squad that night. Thankfully Salah had probably forgotten my name and had better things to do than threaten people to enable him to pass a British English Exam. For obvious confidentiality reasons I am limited in what I can write of this meeting but he was very evidently a man who expected to get his own way and was unused to having no for an answer. I came across Salah indirectly on one or two other education projects but that one direct encounter was enough. He is a short, tubby man with a mean looking round baby face; people were always wary and frightened of his power.

On that April day in St. James Square the volley of bullets fired from an embassy room struck eleven people including a young unarmed police officer whose name is etched in many people's memories Yvonne Fletcher she was only 24. Tragically she died of a stomach wound an hour later after arriving at the hospital. Of those working in the embassy they were to remain surrounded by armed police for eleven days; it was in fact the longest police siege in London's history. In the meantime the three suspected perpetrators had left by a side entrance knowing they had no diplomatic immunity and were on planes arriving back safely in Libya. In Tripoli, Gaddafi expressed 'disgust' that his diplomats' immunity was not being observed and ordered Libyan soldiers to surround the British embassy in Tripoli in response. The UK government eventually resolved the standoff by allowing the Libyan embassy staff to depart the bureau and then expelling them from the country. Britain then broke off diplomatic relations with Libya but maintained a British interests section in Tripoli, as did Libya through the Saudi embassy in London. The Americans seem to slam the door shut in such situations but British diplomacy uses the device of an interest section to leave a crack open to return and talk.

It was at this time I remember seeing the wife of the then British Ambassador leaving Tripoli bemoaning the fact that they had been forced to leave Honeybun an adopted pet rabbit behind. She led the embassy wives and children out to the waiting aircraft whilst singing God Save the Queen, rather like one of the colonial wives of the past. How embarrassing.

For British people, the murder of a young and conscientious female member of the police force by a gunshot was headline news and this was not a time to mention that you were Libyan. British people are very proud that their police are unarmed, so their fury was understandable. The perpetrators have never been prosecuted or named by the British courts and there are many conspiracy theories still circulating to this day. Sadly this must mean no closure for those who were there and especially for Yvonne's family, who must still feel utterly outraged by the lack of justice.

Since leaving Nairobi, Bashir had had no contact with any Libyans, especially those colleagues in the embassy. Later when he was working in the United Nations department back in Tripoli with several colleagues who had been in the siege, he was to learn what they related had happened that morning. They confirmed that the three aforementioned men were all in that upstairs room. During the siege all embassy personnel spoke in hushed whispers not knowing what would be the outcome and the frustration at their inability to talk to their families. At the end of the siege they were encouraged to speak to the British police but naturally none did for fear of what could happen to their family members in Libya. On returning to Libya two of the three men in that upstairs room were promoted to ministerial level posts and Salah became the head of a Graduate University with an unlimited budget. All three were always protected.

Where are they today after the 2011 revolution? Salah tried to escape to Bulgaria through Tunisia and was filmed in the airport reputedly carrying bags filled with US dollars. He was refused entry to Bulgaria and soon after it was discovered that he was in England. An online petition was raised to have him expelled and when I signed there were more than 70,000 names demanding he be removed from British soil immediately. November 2015 saw him arrested and interviewed for money laundering and the murder of PC Yvonne Fletcher. He is living in the South of England and claiming political asylum. His wife and son were also arrested on money laundering charges. All three have denied the charges against them and have been released on bail. The Police have stated that they wish to interview those who were outside the embassy on that fateful day. Perhaps those who can confirm or verify who were in that room when the shots were fired are those who were inside the embassy that morning. Possibly since the death of Gaddafi people might be more willing to come forward and speak out.

Of the other two, there are rumours that they are either dead or hiding in Egypt. Those in the embassy who were expelled in 1984 were issued with new passports with different names. This, I am sure was done frequently by the Gaddafi regime. The procedure was simple; if your name were Mohamed Ahmed Ibrahim for example, it would be changed to Ibrahim Mohamed Ahmed. They all received generous compensation for the possessions that they had left behind in London such as cars and other items. Even the glorious and prestigious posting of London had not proved to be quite as glorious as first imagined. Life as a Libyan diplomat was becoming uncomfortable.

Very recently I received a friendly warning from Libya proposing that I still must not talk openly about these three people. The caller suggested that as long as these men are at large one has no idea who might be a supporter, and revenge attacks continue to happen all the time. "Killing has become almost as easy as saying good morning" he said. I was shocked that after all this time and since the revolution these thugs are still able to frighten and intimidate people. My reply was that I am alone, living in London and cannot foresee a time in the future when I will be able to go back to my adopted country of Libya. My feeling is that I can write as a foreign wife who lived in Libya on and off for 33 years. I have a story to tell and I am going to tell it. However, I am grateful for the concern of all those who are thinking of my safety. I have subsequently received another warning, this time from London, which has made me somewhat skittish but I won't be silenced after everything that Bashir and I went through.

We were mesmerised by the TV as these events unfolded, hardly believing that circumstances for Libya could have taken such an incredibly bad turn. No surprise, therefore when the letter arrived from the BBC stating that with regret, they would not be offering Bashir a position. This had really been Bashir's last effort in the job market. Mere mention of anything Libyan was leaving a bad taste in the mouth to most. With little choice the decision was reached that as the law had reverted and Libyans could once again marry foreigners that we should relocate to Tripoli. Bashir would try and re – join the foreign ministry. This had never been in the plan and suddenly our marriage was taking an unexpected, unwanted, different route.

Tribe and family were and are still of paramount importance to survival in Libya. Having a contact, cousin or sibling who was within the system and could help in a moment of trouble or beg someone in a high position was how people survived. This may seem difficult to understand for people who come from a society free from corruption and cronyism, but that was and is the only way to get on and survive in Libya. However, much one hated the system one still needed to have people contacts. Bashir called Taher, his former ambassador from Nairobi, and told him of an accident in which he had hurt his back and had been receiving treatment in London but hadn't contacted Tripoli. Taher understood the message and amazingly wrote to the Human Resources department describing Bashir's circumstances and saying that he would be returning to Tripoli shortly. I took a piece of headed notepaper from a hospital where I had recently received treatment and asked Celia a friend who was a nurse to write a medical report for the Libyan authorities. At the time I found it amazing that we were believed and got away with it, but today knowing Libya as I do I am unsurprised. As luck would have it, Iyat, the administrator from the Nairobi embassy was back in Tripoli working in the HR Department. Thanks to Libya being so sluggish in terms of filing, and people not caring about their work, he was able to date and stamp the letter and slip it into Bashir's personnel file as well as false sickness certificates from London to cover the time he had been away. Here was an incidence of how, thankfully, everything was possible in Libya. Anything written in English at that time in Libya was believed and no confirmation was asked for in the form of translation or verification. What we did then would probably have been impossible today or perhaps it is still possible?

Six

Libya had certainly never featured in any of our plans, ever. My feelings were very mixed on relocating to what I believed to be a desert dictatorship. We had left Nairobi optimistically with no thoughts other than Bashir finding an interesting, engaging, well – paid job, residing in Frognal and the two of us living happily ever after. He had strong moral and religious beliefs one of which was that having promised for richer, poorer, in both sickness and in health he would never waiver and I too shared these beliefs. I had absolutely no doubt as to how awful it was going to be with no expectation of *anything* being enjoyable, but I truly loved my husband and with that belief knew that somehow we would survive. We had the hope that with various manoeuvres he would be able to return to the Foreign Ministry and in the future we would be able to live abroad. It was all going to be highly risky, after all Libya was a complete unknown for me. I used to wake in the night after bad Tripoli dreams. It was far removed from anything that I knew a country that was ruled by a monster able to destroy anyone or anything in the whole territory and beyond at a whim. We were about to enter the lion's den.

It is still hard for me to fully realise just how wise and knowing my husband always proved to be; he had incredible foresight. He knew his people well and had seen in the post King Idris years how Libyans had changed and what they were capable of doing to each other. In this respect every decision he made was to anticipate and be just ahead of the game. Those who knew him well recognized these qualities, but he always hid them in a belief that when he was at the negotiating table it gave him an advantage over his adversaries even to sometimes showing limited English language ability. This was proven wise, time after time.

Our first task to be completed before moving to Libya was to be married in a mosque. It would be our second wedding of three. The exquisitely beautiful, golden domed Regents Park Mosque was chosen and the day was set for July 23rd. One of our favourite songs at that time was the old Beatles number 'Here comes the Sun,' as it always gave us hope that things would be fine in the end. We played it dancing and singing round the room before leaving for the mosque. Coming from two different musical cultures our common choice of pop music can perhaps be perceived as corny but we found these songs fun and good, easy listening.

It was another glorious, hot, sunny day, which we felt was auspicious. Prior to the ceremony there had been a hiccup on the necessity to have two Muslim witnesses. Our Egyptian friends Farid and Hudda had agreed to take on this role but the Imman at the mosque reminded Bashir that Hodda's contribution was only worth half a witness as a woman, thus we had only one and a half witnesses. As I was beginning to learn this was yet another instance of gender discrimination. It was also unusual for the bride to actually attend the wedding ceremony; normally the father would represent his daughter. This posed a problem where to find a male witness or another female half? Neither of us knew any other Muslims and the suggestion made was that we should approach someone in the mosque or on the street outside. I grin as I recall that day arriving at the mosque with us running here and there trying to find a random male Muslim to be our second witness.

As ever dear friends came and supported us and the photos I can only describe as being bizarre as none of us had any idea on how to tie a hijab for entering the mosque, resulting in an ill – assortment of headscarf fashions on that loving, memorable day of fresh promise. The Imman enquired how much Bashir was going to state as a dowry, or rather in a pre – nuptial agreement. Instead of taking the matter seriously we treated the subject with bravado as it could have saved us in the future a great deal of heartache. Not ever having considered the matter Bashir asked the Imman what would be reasonable? The response came that it was entirely his decision taking into account also how much his bride was willing to accept. The fee for the wedding was twenty pounds, which was exactly what Bashir unimaginatively wrote into the agreement. I do so wish he had written a million pounds. The Egyptian Imman smiled his cheeky smile *'You have a real bargain if you were going to marry a Libyan bride it would cost your weight in gold, yes this lovely bride is a good deal'* . I had never thought of myself as a bargain or a good deal but this was yet another Islamic tradition I was to learn when living in Libya. Afterwards at the Frognal reception with our friends our hilarious attire, the witnesses and the gold were a great source of laughter. I have a lasting memory of Rose, the mother of my friend Kathy from our Sierra Leone adventures. She took on board everything that we were doing so supportively and intermittently chipped in with her little bits of funny wisdom.

On hearing that we had been married in a mosque and that Bashir was returning to Libya, Ibrahim the eldest brother, who had remained silent for a year, called to offer his congratulations. I am unsure whether it was truly an olive branch or if it was just given in the hope that once Bashir was back under their control in Libya that the family could break us up. Certainly I believe that they never liked me, but on my arrival they showed kindness and a wish to help me integrate but always only according to their rules. My acceptance nonetheless gave Bashir happiness, and the call he received from his mother was the most important.

I have to say that without his family's contacts it would have been impossible for Bashir to reclaim his job or my initial visa to enter Libya. It was an extremely tense period for both of us and it was nearing Bashir's time to leave and we hadn't effectively settled or confirmed anything. I could read the thoughts of some of the doubters around me wondering if I would ever see him again, but those who knew us well never had any doubts of Bashir's commitment to our marriage. I was not on a red, silk carpet going to Hollywood but rather on a dirty, dusty rug to Libya, and I understood their worries for my safety and wellbeing.

I will digress here to relate how life can come full circle and certainly has done within my family. My father had been a Brigadier in the Australian army during World War II and had fought in Libya. Here I was, his daughter returning to the country which he had helped to liberate from the Germans and Italians. At the time when he met Bashir his physical health was declining but thankfully his mind was still sharp. One evening he told a story of a military operation to capture Derna a city in Eastern Libya. As the commanding officer, when looking at the reconnaissance maps and aerial photos he spotted a large building with a white cross painted on the roof. Trying to discover whether the building was a hospital or a school, no one was able to verify the reason although obviously the cross had been painted for a significant purpose.

He gave orders for no bombing near the house and care was to be taken should there be any fighting in the area. When Derna was captured my father became the Governor of the city. Out of curiosity he requested to be taken to the house with the white cross in order to unravel the mystery. A very distinguished Libyan dressed in a traditional white robe greeted them on their arrival. To my father's amazement he spoke excellent, educated English and on being asked the reason for the cross he invited my father to enter and see for himself. To my father's astonishment, two impressionist masterpieces, a Van Gough and a Degas featuring his signature ballet dancers adorned the inner walls as did others covering the length of the room. Apparently this gracious, cultured Libyan enjoyed visiting the galleries of Paris and London to make art purchases annually. As he pointed out, if his house had been bombed then these remarkable paintings would have been lost and consequently he had put the white cross on the roof hoping it would be a recognized signal. The man was rare since generally the walls of a strict Muslim home will only be decorated with calligraphy and certainly not paintings of people. Derna was where the Senussi royal family originated from, as did many of the old Libyan elite families, which might explain the man's western education and knowledge of art. My father was unable to remember his name. Bashir asked that I not repeat this story in Libya, as it would evoke memories of foreign troops, which was considered to be part of the colonialism that the revolution had overthrown. It was to be yet a further secret.

To this day I wonder what happened to the man and his paintings, especially after Gaddafi came to power. I feel sure he could not have remained in Libya. I also wonder if his paintings were saved from the ruthless destruction that was demanded in the early period post 1969 when Gaddafi ordered all western artefacts and books to be destroyed. How strange that my father should have been the governor of a Libyan city and protected this man's property that housed those famous pieces of art. Now I, the next generation was leaving London to live in Tripoli to complete the circle. Perhaps someone will read this book and I will discover the end to that story.

Bashir came to a further realisation that Gaddafi was a tragedy for Libya when his family too felt it was unsafe to have any books in the house and it was wiser for them to be burnt rather than be discovered in their home. The danger of being marked as opponents to the revolution was just too great to risk keeping books on their shelves. He had also seen huge bonfires of library books at the university carried out by cheering pro Gaddafi supporters. Reading had been his great love with a large part of his salary always being spent on books. In 1984 the only bookshops in existence were the 'Green Book' centres selling Gaddafi propaganda.

I return to preparations for our Libyan departure. Our marriage in a mosque had been one of the factors prompted by Bashir's foresight and another was my becoming a Muslim. By this time Bashir had returned to Libya while I remained in London. Perhaps being back in Libya he realized the importance of this decision much more than I did at the time. We had discussed the proposition before he had left and I had agreed to convert by taking instruction at the Regents Park mosque. I disliked the pushy women, so keen to embrace me, telling how wonderful my new life would be with them as my sisters. I neither felt they were my sisters nor did I want them to be; perhaps this was ungracious as I know they only meant well and in point of fact *sister* was only a figure of speech. What I did love was the absolute peace obtained from prayer, which for me in fact was a form of meditation. Additionally, I garnered some benefit from the obligation to help the poor financially during and specifically at the end of every year.

I was not about to wear a hijab and Bashir had absolutely no wish for a scarved wife. In fact he wanted me to continue living in exactly the same way as when we had first met. Nevertheless I had to go before an Imman and swear the five tenets of Islam. I knew that my Arabic was appalling and I have a dreadful memory for rote learning, so on my first try the Imman declared I was unable to become a Muslim. Speaking from Libya Bashir had emphasized how imperative it was that I had this certificate, but it wasn't until 2013 when I fully comprehended and discovered the significance of the decision. The first Imman was from Saudi Arabia and I think he was a little bit of a misogynist, reluctant to have women in the mosque at the best of times and certainly not a woman from London. Through nerves I completely fluffed the rendition and the Imman turned me away not being either kind, gentle or offering advice. Tears welling up at my failure, I walked along the Finchley Road where I was found by my friend Tim and brought home crestfallen. Both he and later Bashir gave me all the encouragement I needed and I was successful on the second attempt. On this occasion it was an Egyptian Imman to whom I explained the details of my previous failure and with his encouraging, welcoming smile I was able to recite the five pillars of Islam correctly. I look at that certificate today hoping that I have not let him down in his judgement; I was now a Muslim.

A further step in preparation for my move to Libya was to commence learning Arabic both at London University and with an Egyptian tutor. I found the language fascinating so cleverly created with its suffixes and prefixes, dual plural but the difficulty is to decide whether to learn standard or a local Arabic dialect which can be quite different. I am ashamed to say I have never mastered either or even come close. In some ways I think it was an advantage as in later years my understanding was good but my ability to reply was as a four year old, so inevitably I kept quiet. This meant that I never had a dispute or argument with anyone and most people thought I was 'nice'. Without a doubt if I had spoken the language well I would certainly have opened my mouth inappropriately, so perhaps my inability was good. I do, however, wish I could read and write Arabic as it is a language I know to be rich and melodic and would add to the interest of looking at ancient monuments with Arabic calligraphy. It goes without saying it certainly would have eased the necessity for expensive translators when struggling with endless legal documents.

I return now to Bashir's departure as it was monumental and was the moment that had been causing those nightmares those long sleepless, restless nights. This airport goodbye was it going to be just that or was it going to be a final farewell?

Seven

ꓦ

All I remember of Bashir's departure is that we had decided that he would return to his troubled homeland immediately after his 34th birthday. Again perhaps it is selective memory loss but I have absolutely no recollection what we did which is unusual; we both loved making a fuss of each other's birthday. All that I do remember is Tim driving us both down to Gatwick, which was really noble given that he then had to drive a sobbing wife back to Frognal. I sat for the next few hours staring out of the window into a nothingness waiting for the phone call to know that Bashir had arrived, not been arrested at the airport and was safely in his Gargaresh home. Once more, lack of communication was to lead to many hours of waiting for phone calls and excessively large telephone bills. The difficulty of the phone was to prove a major problem in the first years of our arrivals in Libya.

Bashir had four brothers all of whom in their own different ways would cause and give us grief in the future. The third brother Mahmud, eighteen months older than Bashir was unmarried and living alone in the family house. I think probably he was bipolar but of course in Libya there was no such diagnosis then or now. He had joined the Foreign Ministry two years earlier than Bashir and had been posted to Prague around the same time as Bashir went to Sierra Leone. Both were good musicians and played the oud but whereas Bashir had studied English, Mahmud had studied Philosophy and was more studious. Bashir's year group was outgoing and fun loving and had enjoyed language courses and trips to Malta and London whereas Mahmud's course had offered no such travel opportunities. Thus Bashir became the social side of the duo although he always tried to include his brother. When living together in Tripoli Bashir had frequently had problems waking up his brother and bullying him to go to work. Being alone in Prague without Bashir's constant chiding and encouragement he rarely went to work or was late, and eventually the Ambassador requested that he be transferred home. The lack of a telephone in the house in Gargaresh was caused by Mahmud continuously phoning his girlfriend in Prague for hour upon hour with begging calls not to leave him and to come to Libya; all of which she was unprepared to do perhaps realising his instability. As the bills stacked up unpaid, the phone was finally cut off. Unfortunately, the telephone had been installed in Bashir's name to enable his mother to talk to her sons while they were living abroad. The result was a two thousand pound phone bill, which needed paying and without which there was no phone line. During his stay in London Bashir had been living on his savings from Nairobi but now there was little money remaining.

On arriving home Bashir discovered that the family house had been totally neglected. It was an open, Arabic style, one – storey house beside the sea and certainly would need upgrading before his rather westernized new bride arrived. To start with, an outside Arabic toilet with a hole in the ground and a bucket for flushing was probably the most important aspect of the house that needed modernising. He knew that I was resourceful and that I would suffer for one or two weeks but especially in the winter it would have just been a bit too difficult even for me. I was ready to deal with anything to be with Bashir, but he was determined that I should enjoy at least some of the creature comforts I had grown up with. Besides which, he had grown rather accustomed to them himself after his years away on foreign postings. Money was tight and the priority was to use the last of his savings to put the house in order with nothing left to pay the phone bill. If Mahmud had been in the UK he would probably have been diagnosed with some class of psychiatric disorder but the family put it down to his somehow having been given an evil spirit. Certainly part of the evil spirit was the still he had in his bedroom, the brewing from which he sold mostly to the local Gargaresh mafia, leaving the rest for himself. It was evil hooch that I am sure was addling his brain, adding to his deeply disturbed disposition. It was during this time that I learned that if you are together and know the problems, you can deal with them together, but a phone call to try and explain problems and difficulties sometimes just increases the worry. There were times when it would be a week before we managed to talk to each other and I felt stressed and tense.

On his return first and foremost Bashir needed to resume working at the Foreign Ministry without questions being asked about his one – year disappearance. Secondly, he needed to secure my visa so that I could come to Libya .Added to this was the trouble and expense surrounding the rebuilding of the family home. Finally there was an extremely serious worry concerning the war in Chad where Libyans were being conscripted or effectively press – ganged into fighting against their will. If Bashir was unable to return to work there was a strong possibility that he could be conscripted to Chad. It needs to be remembered that he had not lived in Libya since 1979 and things had moved from bad to worse. There were shortages of everything: food, clothes, medicine, building materials and cars and their spare parts. One needed a contact for all and everything and even with money things were still unavailable. For the new bathroom the toilet had to be bought on the black market and it took three weeks to locate a hideous, bright maroon, pedestal toilet. We were lucky to have found one the ascetics or of it fitting in with the décor were never a consideration.

In those early days of his arrival Bashir was truly bowled over at the situation in Libya coupled with the mountain of things he had to accomplish. Being fit, healthy, determined and resourceful that we would be together against all the odds, he battled on. Certainly on his arrival there was a family intervention to try and convince him how easy it would be to get a divorce and forget about me in London. They were also keen to describe every aspect of how problematic it was going to be having a non – Libyan wife in the foreign ministry. Undeterred by all their negativity and thanks to the help of Iyat and Tarah from Nairobi, within a month he was working again. International Organisations Department as it came to be known although in 1984 as United Nations Department was the place, when on a home posting he would always work for the rest of his life. He never lost his enthusiasm, passion and belief that through the United Nations he could do some good for Libya whilst working within the country rather than as an opponent abroad.

It is hard to imagine or believe how Gaddafi with his Green Book ideology managed in just a few years to absolutely destroy the country. By 1984 there was no public transport and the only way to get around was by taxi or to own a car. The next problem to solve was to find a car. No cars were being imported into the country and one was extremely lucky if able to find a second hand car to buy as the prospective buyers far outnumbered the vehicles for sale. Fortunately my brother was in the process of returning from his posting in Vienna. His right hand drive car was unsuitable for London so we did a deal knowing that it had been well looked after, had a low mileage and could be shipped from London to Tripoli easily. One of the few perks for diplomats was that they could import a car tax free into Libya, so this car was a huge bonus, we would have wheels.

After finishing work at 2.30 Bashir was back in the house to continue the rebuilding. For the really big jobs such as filling in the middle roof, the rewiring and plumbing, he had to employ builders but the rest he did himself with the help of his youngest brother but money was truly tight. Lamin was born when Bashir's mother was 50 and his father 70, some fourteen years after Bashir's birth. Lamin was thrilled that the family house was being rebuilt as it meant that he and his mother could return from living with his eldest brother. The picture that Bashir painted of his family and their living arrangements was worrying but he wanted that I was well prepared with no exaggerations as to the situation. The Libya I discovered on arriving on the 8th December 1984 was not as bad as he had led me to believe. He had over stated the difficulties so that I would have no false ideas but what I found was pretty grim.

Today I read in the newspapers and see on the television stories of young British girls going to Syria to join IS (Islamic State). They are leaving the safety of the UK to go to an unfamiliar country, to marry an unknown man, to live in a war zone under strict sharia law. I am astounded at what they believe they will find and how they have the conviction that they will keep body and soul together. I was 36 when I went to Libya, I had lived and done many things and was satisfied to give up my current way of life to be with the man I loved. Having lived through everything that I have, I cannot imagine the life that these extremely young women are going to and how they will survive happily. It will be no bed of roses and neither was it for me. It was tough but I do believe that with love one can endure most things. These girls will be without the love of a husband, family or friends.

Until now the experience of my arrival in Libya was so strange that it seems like some misty dream. Right up to the last minute there were doubts as to when and how I was going to get my visa. This I was unaware of thank goodness as otherwise my nerves would have been completely shattered. All that I had was a tentative departure date. In the meantime I bought a huge metal trunk and packed it with all my clothes, bedding and towels along with boxes of Tampax, soap and shampoo, everything that was unavailable in Libya, and the trunk was shipped. Finally I heard those magic words the house was ready, the car and trunk had arrived and were awaiting my arrival and my visa was ready. That just left buying my ticket and then to fly. In fact I was to learn later that the visa part was not exactly true. In Libya people say 'IBM,' an acronym for 'Inshallah bukarah malesh' meaning 'God willing tomorrow, but perhaps not.' The truth is that tomorrow can mean tomorrow, next week next month or never. Without a telex from Tripoli immigration to confirm that my visa would be waiting on arrival the airline would not permit me to fly. Bashir remained calm. I never heard any doubt in his voice but apparently had it not been for the intervention of his cousin's husband who worked in the Intelligence department, the visa would not have been issued at 2pm. My flight was at 4 pm. This highlights the reality that if you do not have contacts in Libya, you are a ghost. How glad I am that I was unaware of these goings – on; it was bad enough going into the vipers' nest without such worries.

Having said my sad goodbyes to all my friends the one that was especially hard was to my father who was now living alone facing the onset of Parkinson's disease. When I look back at that time I realise that I have been blessed with a good education and a strong inner sense of purpose. I am not a complainer; I just believe that one has to get on with whatever is dished out. These were some of the qualities that were essential for survival in Libya at that time. I had added one more string to my bow and that in the future proved to be my lifeline in every sense of the word. In late 1983 a friend and former colleague asked if I was interested in doing a one month and evening follow up course with Camden Council to teach adult literacy and survival English for immigrants. It had proven to be both motivating and extremely rewarding and was my first introduction into the world of education, EFL and ESL. I never could have imagined at that time what a lifesaver it was going to be, not only financially but also mentally.

As I waved goodbye to Tim and Mary who had brought me to Gatwick, there is no denying I was filled with absolute trepidation. It was probably the first flight I had taken for many years where I refused a glass of wine. I noticed that the majority on the plane were drinking inordinate amounts of alcohol, some with miniature bottles stacked up on their tables. This was the reality of last drinks on a flight into dry Libya.

On first seeing Bashir waiting for me at the exit to the plane I hardly recognized the man I had married. He looked awful and had probably lost 5 kilos; he was skeletal. Yet there was, as ever, that smile and those eyes inviting me to believe in him, reminding me that he had told me he would bring me here. "I love you" he whispered. An immediate cultural change was in the air; responding to those words, we had to solemnly shake hands. There were no kisses or hugs, how alien it all was beginning to be. I was introduced to man after man, not truly taking in who anyone was and of course there were no women to welcome me. This was Libya.

As I write our story I continually wish that it was Bashir writing as he knew so much more of the intrigue that was occurring at that time. My foremost wish of course would be that as he writes we are reliving those early days together. I think the family looked on us in later years and felt we were their honey pot. They had either forgotten or never realized the mental anguish that we went through in those first few years in Libya and how they offered no help. I have no hesitation in writing that if I had come to Libya in my early twenties I would have been like the vast majority of western wives married to Libyans whose marriages ended in divorce. I was one of the lucky ones. I had a husband who did not change his spots and when I was on his sand he became stronger in ensuring that I was not compromised in altering my personality or appearance. However the gift he gave me was the encouragement to evolve into directions that I had never expected my life would lead.

The sun always seemed to shine on us on auspicious days and that evening of my arrival was no exception. I had left London on a gloomy, cold, winter afternoon and arrived in Tripoli in an unseasonably hot early December of 30C. As we passed along Gargaresh beach, the one that Bashir had so lovingly described, all that I could see on the shore were heaps and heaps of plastic bags filled with rubbish along with broken bits of furniture. The beach was just a rubbish dump. Bashir explained that his beloved beach had become one of the places in Tripoli where people put their refuse as there were no longer any garbage collections. This is a further example of Gaddafi's lack of progress in building the Libyan infrastructure and destroying the environment. I was never to see this beach return to the glory of Bashir's childhood and on my last visit to Tripoli it was worse than ever. We drove down a sandy track with dense Hind cactus on either side and into a large open area surrounded by more modern looking houses and nestled in the corner could be seen my new home in front of which was a gigantic mulberry tree. As the cars stopped, women emerged from the gate shrilling their ululations of welcome, all of their faces covered by their traditional Libyan striped garments. I was introduced to woman after woman, all kissing me a million times on either cheek and at the same time gripping my hand. Of course, everyone from the area wanted to be there out of curiosity to see why Bashir had married this English bride. I was something of a novelty in those days. The young children touched my hair, perhaps in Gargaresh I was the first blonde they had ever seen and my hair colour to them was strange. As I went inside the question that I was to be asked repeatedly in those early days was whether or not I was a practising Muslim and prayed. I could not believe what I was hearing; I would never have been asked this question in England. In fact I think that most British people would not be remotely interested in another's religion. To us it is a private matter. I found it extremely intrusive and it is one of the things I immediately missed and continue to love about England, how one's beliefs are a matter of an ever – respected personal choice.

People may think when describing Bashir's family that I am unduly harsh when recounting the first years of our co – existence. They and I were so far apart in beliefs, culture and way of life. I had seen and travelled the world they knew Gargaresh and Saudi Arabia. I have to admit that I was the invader and as such I always made an effort to accommodate their beliefs and wishes. However, I drew a line when it came to socialising as I was to work hard and long hours and at that time the Libyan working week was six days and so Friday was sacrosanct. I needed and wanted time to relax and enjoy myself and was reluctant to spend my day off gossiping, eating and drinking tea with female relatives and their friends. If we had had children possibly it would have been different. I had resolved before leaving London never to open my mouth on sensitive subjects and I kept conversation to basically 'hello' and 'goodbye' with a smile and a wave. In that way I hoped that everyone was content to accept the alien, new wife.

My most vivid memory of that first night was meeting Ibrahim the eldest brother. It is difficult for me to write about him today with any kindness and that night he swept into the outside sitting room like a sultan visiting one of his subjects. The Libyan, like all African national dress makes the man look much larger and intimidating than their true stature. Ibrahim was wearing a Libyan hat and holi, all of which increased his size. The last time we met I realized what a small man in fact he was but on that night he scared me. There was no welcome in his face or eyes. I was the invader the intruder; he would tolerate me and that was as far as he would ever go. He was the head of the family and he expected my deference. Bashir never changed in his respect for Libyan family values of respect until right up to the end when he could no longer stand their lack of compassion and cupidity.

One of the things I loved about Bashir was never to be afraid of being different and standing his ground. His mother wanted to have a large Libyan wedding, which would have lasted seven days. We had no money and were not about to go into debt paying for something that we felt was a complete waste we had much more important things on which to spend our hard earned money. Finally his mother's tears persuaded him to accept a simple one night, one day wedding with no gifts. Why was he so adamant about the gifts? It is amusing to call them gifts when the reality was that they were not. Whatever was given was recorded and was then to be returned as another gift at a celebration for that particular family with 10% interest added to the value of the original gift, a sort of insurance policy. Culturally gifts were opened in private not in front of the person as in Japan and a number of other countries I have come across. I quite like this idea as it saves the response of 'thank you so much' when in fact the gift is a horror but under no circumstances can that show on one's face.

Bashir's only demand was for a special Hadra of prayers for his father before the Friday lunch. He was to repeat this ceremony on several occasions for his father. No one else in the family ever replicated this gesture. I was unable to discover why. Bashir had been in Sierra Leone for only three months when his father died. His family persuaded him not to return for the funeral as they were concerned that being of the right age he could be conscripted into the army and sent to Chad. Whether or not that was a right or wrong decision it was the reason I am sure for his being so adamant on having the Hadra. For his mother the loss of her husband was still quite recent and I think she wanted to celebrate some good news in the family. Libyan news at the time was all about austerity, the war in Chad and the isolation of the country.

71

When I commenced this book I had my memories and they were what I wanted to write, but on several occasions I have asked myself questions and then felt the necessity to research a gap. The Hadra was such a point wishing to ensure the correct name, spelling and its origins. I was to discover that the Hadra is a collective supererogatory ritual performed by Sufi orders. The term in Arabic literally means 'presence.'

Hadra features various forms of remembrance (especially devotional texts particular to the Sufi order) and in the Gargaresh Hadra, ritual drums were used with religious poetic chanting, centred on praise and supplication to God. Bashir was most certainly a Sunni Muslim but had no connection whatsoever with Sufism. Having originally thought that this celebration must have come into the culture during the Ottoman colonialism, I have subsequently discovered that in fact it was much earlier in the history of Libya. The Haj pilgrims travelling from Morocco to Mecca passed through Libya and others from Tunisia and Algeria came to live in Libya bringing their Sufi beliefs. In the 14th century the Isaouia, who have their roots in Morocco, came to Libya, settling in Tripoli and Ghadames on the Libyan/Algerian border. In Tajoura, a Tripoli suburb, before the revolution there was the tomb of Sidi Andulsi, which has been desecrated by IS followers since the revolution. What I believe was important is that when the prayers were said also poor people in the mosque, family and friends were fed in memory of Mohamed Shkuka. Today much of the Muslim religion is unclear or has not moved with the times. A ceremony such as this one must be positive rather than negative and had become a part of Libyan culture. Since the revolution whether or not it is still practised or covertly, I have no way of knowing.

I have never been one for wanting or having jewellery, yet this is a huge tradition and a requirement in Libyan society. My sisters – in – law wanted me to borrow their gold which I thought looked completely over the top ugly but I did accept reluctantly though politely a gold set from Bashir's mother. I wore it the once for our Libyan wedding and later it was sold as we needed the money. I wore the simple white dress I had worn on our wedding day in London, I think to the absolute shame of the family. Perhaps if I had realized what Libyan women wore to weddings I might have changed my mind, as I was certainly the most underdressed bride there has probably ever been in Libya. I continually heard the word 'maskina,' poor one. Neither Bashir nor I really cared, we were starting as we meant to go on and buying hugely expensive silk traditional clothes for weddings, along with gold jewellery was not and never would be part of our lifestyle. I have to admit that the women looked absolutely gorgeous. The Libyan national dress both for men and women is ravishing. It makes for a celebration of richness coupled with the hypnotic drums and singing. It was the latter two that I have always loved and regret their steady disappearance as in later years they were gradually replaced by ear splitting Arabic disco music and European style white wedding dresses.

The one advantage of the wedding celebration was to enable Bashir to reconnect with his old friends and relatives. This was essential in Libya, no contacts no survival. As luck would have it a cousin worked at the National Oil Corporation (NOC). I had to find a job as we needed money not only for Libya but also to maintain the upkeep on the Frognal flat. Furthermore, for my sanity I could not see myself sitting alone in the house in Gargaresh with my mother – in – law and busybody sister – in – law who lived opposite; that would have been a living nightmare. Probably it would have meant my Arabic would have resulted in being passable rather than dreadful. Oil companies were in reality the only place that I could work because of my lack of Arabic language. More importantly we thought I would be able to earn a good salary.

The National Oil Corporation's (NOC) Libyan HR Manager Khalifa Al Magreghi was a well – educated and very good – looking man, with a great sense of humour. He advised that there was a job opening in the Maintenance Department for an English Secretary. The boss would be Ahmed Doghman, a gentle and kind man who empathised with my situation as he too had a foreign wife. Thinking that I was going to be offered a salary similar to those I had seen advertised in London, I was horrified to discover that the absolute top that I could negotiate would be LD400 a month, approximate to 250 UK pounds. Apparently if you were married to a Libyan, by law one had to be paid at the same rate as a Libyan. There was a salary scale for foreigners, which decreased according to nationality with Americans at the top then in descending order Canadians, British, Australian, other nationalities and finally Libyans. Khalifa's tongue in cheek answer was that the best thing to do would be to go back to England and get a divorce. Thereafter, he suggested, I should apply for a job in the UK and then return to Libya. That way I would have been entitled to a substantial salary, two return tickets to London and to

Malta a year plus accommodation with all service costs covered. It was an extremely attractive package, but not one that we were willing to consider. We had taken the difficult step for me to be in Libya, so we had no choice but to take the copy – typing job. Khalifa welcomed me 'on board.'

It was extremely fortunate that I took this poorly paid position at NOC, since through it I met Moira, who knew everyone in the British expat community. Bashir came to call her *'the Dean'* (this is a diplomatic title given to the longest – serving Ambassador to a country who is given a high position in the order of precedence). It was she who gave me some of the best tips on how to survive in that rough and tumble environment also becoming one of my closest friends from Libya and we remain firm friends today.

It is important to understand how the Libyans were being paid based on grades from 1 to 13. There was meant to be an annual salary review but this was dependent on Gaddafi's whim which at times was not given for two or three years. Bashir, a second secretary, was grade 7 and I was slotted in on the same grade although at a slightly higher band. His salary was LD350 a month and at this time the average Libyan salary was roughly LD100 with the Oil Minister – Grade 13 in theory earning a salary of LD750 a month. The exchange rate was one US dollar to a Libyan dinar. Libya an oil rich country with a low population where my compatriot oil secretaries were earning a minimum of two thousand pounds a month, and yet Libyan managers with doctorate degrees were restricted by virtue of their nationality to a pittance. The majority of Libyans never saw a single dinar of the Libyan black gold; the country made expatriates wealthy but was miserable for the majority of Libyans.

There are many stories I could tell of those early days, they are so numerous but the one that will always remain in my memory that made those first months so unbearable, was the reaction of Mahmud to our wedding. As mentioned he was unbalanced either through drink or drugs, his mental state or evil potions. The Libyans believe in the evil eye and Bashir was surprisingly no exception to this superstition. Gaddafi himself wore amulets, which he had sown into his arm for protection and often visited an old Egyptian lady behind our house in Gargaresh. Bashir forbade me to eat or drink anything in a Libyan house for fear that they might have doctored it, even in his brothers' houses. I am unsure what to believe but I have seen some pretty strange happenings which have been attributed to the evil eye. Whether this was the case with Mahmud I remain sceptical but feel sad at his lonely demise. Personally, I think it was a strange sort of jealousy, perhaps egged on by other members of the family to make our life a living hell. He was initially pessimistic about Bashir being able to return to his old job so then to see him successfully working in a department of his choice despite everything, must have been hard. Once again it was Bashir the socialite having success and he as always reduced to being the loner. Probably also the family and we two lovebirds moving back into the house that he had inhabited on his own for eighteen months must also have been tough and unwelcome. However, the barrage of hatred that was to ensue was truly frightening. We endured the most dreadful abuse being shouted at incessantly through the night for hours and hours in different sounding voices. Uncooked, bloody meat being thrown at our bedroom door and horrific writing in blood over the walls of the house to be found every morning night after night relentlessly.

I had been prepared for most things but certainly not for living in someone else's psychotic nightmare. Mahmud was crafty not to carry on his antics on nights when his mother was sleeping at the house. Lamin was truly horrified, especially when Mahmud took to attacking Bashir with a knife needing the two of them to restrain him and leading him back to his room with the quietly spoken words 'Mahmud remember Bashir is your brother not your enemy'. Bashir could have been seriously injured during these attacks on a number of occasions but quiet words seemed to work after an outburst. The family were unwilling to believe what was occurring almost nightly and offered no reassurance or help, in fact probably hoped that this would make me hot foot it back to London.

Not only was there the human nightmare but suddenly the elements turned against us and the Indian summer turned into an Arctic winter. The house of course had no central heating, no fires and there were no electric fires for sale in the shops. Desperate shortages were thanks to the Gaddafi failed plan of large government supermarkets where the shelves were empty apart from tins of tomato paste and spaghetti. An urgent phone call to my father resulted in a fan heater being dispatched from London plus two hot water bottles. This was how we kept warm with my London duvet wrapped around our shoulders. Living by the beach, the sand managed to creep in through any tiny gap in the building and a fine, sandy film could always be seen on everything despite the daily dusting chore. The newly constructed roof leaked, causing a flood in the house, which was like having a lake lapping at the bedroom door. It just couldn't get any worse – I prayed every night that this seeming hell would end.

I never could have imagined that I would go happily to a boring typing job but at least my office was warm and I had the company of the sweetest Libyan secretary, Wasila. Luck was doubly on my side in that job as Wasila gave me lots of advice on how to survive in the country and where and how to find food. There was no meat unless it was bought on the black market, and there were few fresh vegetables or fruit. Additionally, there was no fish as the fishermen were no longer allowed out to sea as Gaddafi feared that he could not control the security of the coastline. I do not know what happened to Wasila, but I heard that she married a man much her senior who already had children. I do truly hope that she is safe and happy. I have a lot to thank her for helping me in those early days. We were yet to live through a very frightening experience together from the office.

Our goal, thanks to our nightmare with Mahmud, was to try and find somewhere else to live but we had no money as the last of Bashir's savings had been spent on renovating the old family home. Added to which there was a severe housing shortage. Gaddafi had initiated Law No. 4 which was to increase the problem and its legacy will somehow or other still need to be unravelled today. His goal was to try and equalize the society and one of his solutions was this law that stated that a house belonged to whoever was living in the property and no one could own more than one house. This resulted in Libyans legally jumping houses that were rented by expatriates when they were away on leave, and then putting the house into their names legally under Law 4. Those Landlords, especially those from the old elite who opposed Gaddafi and had left the country to go into exile, all lost their houses to unscrupulous house jumpers. Many have now lived in these valuable properties for more than 40 years and seem to have forgotten conveniently that the house was a land grab. Today, the old owners want the return of their property. Bashir was desperate to find a solution to our housing problem and begged everyone he knew for their help.

On one occasion, his brother Ibrahim who could easily have helped as Head of the Sahara Bank said he had found a government flat which we could rent. We went with high expectations but I think it showed exactly how little this elder brother was, in truth, prepared to help find a solution. It was a derelict building, stinking of urine and obviously used by drug addicts and dropouts; the walls were damp and covered in mould. Ibrahim felt no shame in making poor Bashir grovel, he had gone against his big brother's wishes and this was his penance. Implicit in this move on Ibrahim's part, was the suggestion that this was all Bashir deserved.

When spring arrived, the weather warmed up and life was somewhat easier as a result. In many ways I think that despite the scrapes that I get myself into when life becomes truly unbearable, I am given a let out and someone special does love me and gives me a lifeline. Khalifa El Megrahi, on hearing of our plight suggested an old terraced house in another part of Gargaresh. An Indian accountant working for NOC, who was currently occupying the house, was found alternative accommodation. Our new house would become available in the September. In fact, we were lucky as the property was owned by Gargaresh council and rented to NOC which meant in the future we could apply through the council to own the house. It was the same old story one needed to have a contact to achieve anything. Best of all we would be free of the family. Although only 100 sq. metres it had a little, open courtyard that was to become our outdoors spot of freedom. It was in a filthy state but we could see the potential and knew we could make it home. Khalifa commented that he found it difficult to understand why Bashir was bothered over such a small, badly, maintained property. For us it spelt freedom and immediately, gratefully accepted the offer. Finally, we had something to look forward to, our own place, and beggars cannot be choosers. We were once again the lucky ones and smiles returned to our faces.

I am not going to describe our social life but thanks to the Dean Moira we had an entry into the expatriate community and we started going to parties and developing friendships. Sometimes we came up against antagonism from those expatriates whom we learned to label *'the desert rats.'* They were abrasive and arrogant oil workers who felt they were superior to the Libyans and found fun in insulting Bashir and his nationality. I had never experienced racism before but being married to a Libyan I encountered this not only abroad, but also in Libya, Bashir's own country. This was to prove very trying, unjust and completely unwarranted especially in Bashir's case as he was always polite despite the insults hurled at him by these ill – educated people. The wonderful long – standing friendships certainly made up for the few horrors. We also encountered racism in reverse by the Libyan authorities, especially when coming home from parties late at night. It was quite scary as we had been drinking and at that time there were road blocks/checks everywhere trying to find deserters from the Chad war. We would be stopped by the military police and had to produce our papers but then the quiz would begin. Who was this woman? Where had we met? Why had Bashir not married a Libyan woman? Were they not better? It would have been amusing if not for the fact that one ill – chosen word could have landed Bashir en route to Chad or prison. Those were hard, unfriendly times and one did not challenge; one zipped one's lips. My new life was proving to be anything but easy but then I had never expected it to be otherwise. After all, you make your bed and then you have to lie in it and mine was with a lovely Libyan man. Though in this climate of fear there was continuous compromise.

Eight

I have had to be selective in what I have included in this account of my life. It could become a monotonous tome if every little episode were told. I have tried to include events that both reflect our life together but at the same time give a flavour of Libya during various periods under Gaddafi. 1985 for young Libyan men was terrifying. Families were receiving body bags of husbands or sons who had been killed in Chad. The only compensation they received was a sack of rice, bags of spaghetti, tins of tomato paste and a sheep. We were beginning to see veterans in wheel chairs and small mobile cars, although I rather gathered that these were only for the few as no one in authority seemed concerned at the plight of the war wounded. There was a hospital in Janzour on the outskirts of Tripoli that had been newly opened to cater for victims who had lost limbs but the numbers were far too great for what the facilities could provide.

Due to Bashir's job he was exempt from being sent to Chad but not from having to join what we termed 'Dad's Army.' Right up to 2010 there was a compulsory requirement for every Libyan male under 50 to serve one month, annual military service. It is not difficult to imagine how hard it would be running a business when all one's staff would be unable to work for one month in the year complying with their national service call up. Add to this the holy month of Ramadan, when in theory everyone had to work but in reality very little work was achieved with high absenteeism and very low productivity. All of these factors combined with national holidays resulted in a workforce that in effect was only working nine months of the year but being paid for twelve. Not an economically sound government work plan.

It was at this time and in the four years previously that those who had the financial wherewithal sent their sons to study abroad or set them up in a business overseas rather than have them play Russian roulette in Chad, or serve in Libya. The latter was an equally distastefully tough experience where there were endless tales of sexual abuse of these young men. With the deaths of so many and the large numbers escaping to live abroad, a sizeable imbalance in the numbers of marriageable age males in Libya resulted. Perhaps this is a reason why I was not the most popular bride on the block as it was felt that I had taken away one of their boys. In fact when Bashir was going through my vetting process at the foreign ministry, this was one of the accusations fired at him by the intelligence officer.

Yes I had married my Gargaresh man but we wanted to do things together that no Libyan woman would have considered, I feel sure. By 1985, The Underwater Club was open to all Libyans. This was the club where on the night of August 31, 1969, Bashir had seen the Libyan elite and expatriates enjoying themselves. Now the beach and club were open to all and we took full advantage of the tennis courts and became regulars, enjoying the freedom of being outside in the Libyan summer beside the Mediterranean. In its heyday it must have been a perfect spot and although it had become run down like so much else in the country, for us it was a sanctuary of near normality. I realized that Libyan men did ogle European women and as a result I always tried to dress simply, but this did not deter the comments and looks. It was hard for Bashir and certainly infuriating to have to hold one's tongue since many of the members at the club were the new Libyan elite, namely Gaddafi's cronies. It was unwise to cross them despite their wholly inappropriate ogling and comments. After only one day on Underwater's beach wearing a one – piece bathing costume I decided that it was not worth the aggravation and that was the beginning and end of my swimming excursions in Tripoli. It was frustrating, living beside the sea and yet being unable to enjoy its delights. There was to be one more swimming excursion, which resulted in an absolutely harrowing experience.

Libya has the most remarkable Roman and Greek ruins that have ever lain in the sand. They are virtually untouched, unexplored and unvisited. I was anxious to visit Leptis Magna, having seen the awe – inspiring Sabratha ruins. For those unfamiliar with these names I urge you to Google and see for yourself, in order to understand the remarkable splendour of these places and my resultant enthusiasm for them. I am incapable of describing the size and beauty of these extraordinary ruins situated on the shores of the Mediterranean. My first Ramadan in Libya, if I remember correctly, was in June and the days were long and extremely hot, especially for those fasting. We had no air conditioner as there were none for sale in the shops, just small fans which moved hot air around the room. This time I longed to go to work to be in the cold. Thankfully, Bashir's brother Ismael had agreed and persuaded Mahmud to move into his large house until we had ownership of our new home in the September. We finally had the peace to sit in the garden under the old grape vine and enjoy the balmy summer nights and have trouble free sleep.

I wanted to explore and get to know Libya but I think neither of us really understood exactly the extent of the deterioration of the country at this time. A trip was planned to visit Leptis over the four – day Eid holiday. People looked at me in utter amazement when I excitedly told them of our plans to stay in a hotel in Homs and then drive on to another hotel with the wonderful name of Gouzertik, meaning sand dune, just by Leptis. We had included in our itinerary for day one, a beach called by the expats *Paradise beach*. The Dean had given us a photocopied booklet entitled 'Libyan beaches east of Tripoli'. This little gem illustrated the ingenuity of some expats as it gave directions to about ten beaches along the coast off the beaten track. The instructions read 'go along the Tajoura road, past the doughnut shop, continue on until you see a mosque with a green dome on your left and turn left, drive a further 200 metres and there is a bent tree, turn right' and so forth until one reached a remote beach. Each beach had been given a name reflecting the atmosphere or look of the place, for example *Pigeon Island, Tintagel, Tahiti, Dead Cow* to name a few I can remember. This guide was to take us to Paradise beach. The beach was everything that one could imagine of a deserted white sandy bay with crystal clear, aquamarine blue sea. The air was fresh and pure and absolutely deserted, or so we thought. We settled down to enjoy the day swimming and eating the picnic we had brought for our adventure; this was how we wished to spend our time in Libya. I changed into a pair of my favourite turquoise, towelling shorts and a bikini top and suggested we walk along the beach. I don't drive and never have but Bashir wanted his siesta after lunch. With no cares in the world I wandered off down the beach alone at what was the first opportunity for a solitary walk since arriving in Libya the previous December.

I felt absolute contentment paddling in the warm sea, listening to the sound of the waves and walking on soft warm sand on that hot summer day. It was perfect. I was lost in my thoughts until suddenly I saw a group of youths running down the cliff brandishing sticks and hurling rocks. Absolutely terrified I charged back towards Bashir but I had walked far from where he was sleeping and quickly I was surrounded. One pushed me from one side and then another and another whilst another in the group tried to pull off my bikini top, all the while I was yelling 'leave me alone, get off, leave me alone' and trying to run back to Bashir or at least alert him to the danger I was in. Without warning from the cliff top the crack of gunfire rang out and I could see two Libyans with rifles. I was to learn after that they had in fact only fired into the air. The young men attacking me were probably only 15 or 16 and this was sufficient warning for them to take flight. Thankfully Bashir also heard the gunfire and came hurtling along the beach like a Bolt. I am unsure how it would have ended if it hadn't been for those two intelligence officers on the cliff and for once in my life I was overjoyed to see them. These youths were apparently deeply conservative Muslims, typical of people in the area. To their way of thinking I was dressed inappropriately and suffered the consequences although thankfully on this occasion, it was just a rather unpleasant wake up call. This became my second and last time to experience Libyan beaches.

What a shame that the Libyans could not follow the example of Tunisian tourism and exploit this natural resource for economic gain. The reality is that Libya was and is not the less conservative Tunisia and is much more radical in religious terms as I was to discover repeatedly. Gaddafi acted as the buffer for this festering extremism albeit in the most hideously draconian manner. He was to prevent the spread of Islamist terrorism during his brutal reign. The West very much failed to recognize this when aiding in Gaddafi's overthrow and their post Libya policy.

Shattered by this experience, we drove on to find our hotel in Homs for the night. No wonder people had looked at us in amazement. In all my travels in Africa I had never seen or spent a night in such a dirty and unwelcoming dump. Metal hospital style beds with broken legs, a dirty sheet and moth – eaten army blanket on the bed were meant to be our comforts for the night. The Arabic style toilet stank beyond belief. As soon as it was dark cockroach armies emerged out of every nook and cranny. Needless to say we slept the night in the car. By Libyan standards, this was apparently a four star hotel. We moved onward the next morning to

Leptis undeterred. Leptis can never disappoint whatever the time of year, whatever the weather and whatever the mood it is without doubt always uplifting. We were the only people at the site and one could almost hear the chariots rumbling down the cobbled streets or imagine the fights as the crowds shouted in the circus.

It is with great fear that I am deeply concerned today about the safety of this place. It is a United Nations Educational, Scientific and Cultural Organisation (UNESCO) world heritage site and as such is a world treasure. It has always been poorly protected and as early as this visit one could see recent cuts on statues where marble heads had obviously been removed. The perpetrators were carrying out this vandalism purely for profit. It was not only the Libyans but also expats and foreign diplomats who used diplomatic cargo to smuggle antiquities out of the country. Later more remote sites became a source of income for high – ranks in the army and today my greatest fear is from IS. I pray that these fears are unwarranted and that these Roman, Greek and prehistoric antiquities in Libya can be protected for future generations and for the world to marvel at their splendour. I am thankful that a few friends and my brother were able to visit me in Libya, travelled to Leptis and can attest to its magnitude, beauty and unique position on the Mediterranean.

In 'The Immortal Dinner' Hughes – Hallett gives details of Warrington arriving in Libya in 1814 in the service of the Foreign Office and becoming friendly with the Bashaw, Yusuf Karamanli. Apparently he managed to 'coax' the Bashaw to send a gift of a temple from the ruins of Leptis Magna to the Prince Regent which now can be seen on the shores of Virginia Water. Apparently many more looted antiquities followed which went to the British Museum. I quote this as an example of the historical looting of antiquities which is not a new phenomenon for Libya.

The Sand Dune Hotel was marginally better than the one in Homs but after one night and a further day exploring Leptis we returned to Tripoli early. We were bitterly disappointed at the experiences we had on our expedition and apart from a remarkable trip to the desert city of Ghadamas on the Algerian border that was the total of our Libyan exploration trips from 1984 – 92.

An additional problem curtailing our trips of exploration was that our imported car was now giving us problems. There were no spare parts in Libya and without a car life would have been extremely difficult, so sadly trips to the eastern Libyan Greek sites were never made. One always has regrets and one of mine is missing out on seeing those ruins. Given the situation in the country today I very much doubt if my wish is ever going to become a reality and remains only a bucket dream that probably will never come true.

Finally September arrived and it was time to take possession of our new home. It was in a dreadful state with a large family of mice living in the sitting room, the ceiling in the bedroom stuffed with plastic bags to keep out the rain, the walls in the kitchen covered in layer upon layer of black grease and hordes of cockroaches. We were undeterred; it was going to be fun making it into our home. Nothing could be worse than the nightmare we had lived through for the past ten months. Finally we had a project with a worthwhile goal, at the end of which we would be the owners of a house.

Before starting, there was a birthday to celebrate and as usual we planned something special for Bashir's 35th birthday, a trip to Malta. A further reason for the Malta visit was the necessity for shopping; paintbrushes, bolts, nuts, screwdrivers, electrical wire and everything we needed to renovate the house. Of course the inevitable car spare parts also had to be purchased. The word Libyans used for shopping was *shortages* or *unavailable,* the latter generally being the case. This was Gaddafi's new Libya, something he was trumpeting as a great success, and the same was touted for sub – Saharan African countries, which he claimed, should also adopt the theory.

I am certain that unless one has lived under a dictatorship or suffered true austerity it must be hard to understand or imagine the feeling of release when landing in an open country such as Malta. Taking a taxi to the hotel, we were to see advertising hoardings, something never seen in Libya as of course there were no companies to advertise because there was simply nothing to buy. Our clean hotel room was wonderful with its crisp, starched sheets and a view out over the sea. Having lived in Libya for all of those months one felt like a pressed down spring repressing feelings and ideas, having to carefully think about whatever one did or said. The passion of making love in absolute freedom was almost beyond belief. To be able to walk down the street holding hands and to kiss each other in the open without fear of arrest or abuse was sheer ecstasy. I recall vividly the feeling of absolute happiness during that first birthday night of eating out in a restaurant, sitting and drinking a glass of wine and not being ogled or talked about. It couldn't have been more perfect. We had come through the nightmares of the last year together, we knew there would be more problems but we had found a place within easy reach of Libya where we could be ourselves. At that time it was affordable and had everything that we needed or wanted. It was going to be hard to return to Tripoli but there was the goal of home building waiting to be started and that was the inducement.

Nine

9

Our communication with the outside world for news was through a tiny smuggled FM radio on which we picked up the World Service, listening to both the Arabic and English programmes. The alternative would have been Libyan TV, which advised everyone daily of the greatness of the leader and showed endless scenes of adoring, mawkish crowds who had seen him on that day; it was pure, unmasked propaganda. As I reflect back to those simple days without all the modern gizmos we have now I remember that our entertainment was talking to each other, playing backgammon, reading, tennis and learning how to play bridge. We had to be inventive and for the bridge the Dean, whose mother was a bridge teacher, formed a friendly bridge school. It was fun, despite my wanting to be the dummy after bidding, as bridge for me was a social event. On the other hand for Bashir, ever competitive, his motivations at the bridge club were to win. Perhaps he imagined himself as the future Omar Sharif of the Arab bridge world. My experience with bridge is not to play or learn bridge with your partner as it involves too many disputes on the homeward journey on what cards should or shouldn't have been played.

Life was simple, Bashir was back in the job that he loved, I had work even though it was tedious and we had our own house. Money was tight and becomingly increasingly so in order to pay the outgoings on the flat in London and our daily living in Tripoli. However, we were satisfied that we had made the right decision to return to Libya. Make no mistake, given the choice we would obviously have wanted to be living elsewhere. Tripoli was a series of daily compromises but then moving had in reality been a no choice move. Gaddafi policy had dictated our departure from London and again his policies were about to compromise our lives and choices. Storm clouds were gathering and the warmongers Gaddafi and

Reagan were heading for a confrontation, which would personally impact on our lives and those of the Libyan people disastrously.

One reason for writing this book has been to show that not all Arab husbands are monsters. When one wanders around any English language bookshop one sees endless titles all of which detail the trials and tribulations of living with misogonist, abusive, Arab husbands. I have yet to find a title based on the happy experience of being married to an Arab. Admittedly my life would have been very different had it not been for the fact that Bashir was a diplomat, but then I would not have married him if he had not been open and outgoing. One marries the man and in my case also the job. The majority of young British women had met their Libyan husbands in northern night clubs and had been bowled over by their good looks, generosity and exaggerated lies and embellishments of their Libyan lifestyle. These young brides, on arriving in Libya found themselves whisked off to the countryside, living with the family who expected them to wear Islamic dress and live their way of life of gender separation within the family. In many, many cases, these men changed their spots very quickly, UK was one way of life and Libya was another and once that step had been taken, any thoughts for their wives to be living as Europeans were immediately terminated. Once I was told by the British Consul that the average British woman married to a Libyan had at least six children; these women were trapped with no independent lives whatsoever.

I worked at NOC with a very pretty woman, Marlene from the north of England, who had one daughter. Her Libyan husband was abusive to the point that at times she came to work with a black eye or bruises on her arms and worse still bits of her hair had been wrenched out of her scalp. This was the abuse we could see. It had reached such a level of literal torture when I started working in NOC that she had decided to escape. Almost dayly she would bring some item of her possessions to the office and hide them in either the Dean's cupboard or mine; this continued for nine months. Her husband had agreed she could visit England to see her mother although forbade her to take her daughter, probably knowing that if he agreed that neither of them would return. Marlene came to the momentous decision of leaving the country without her daughter. The Dean and I took her to the airport with the suitcases and their contents that had been stowed at the office for all those months. I cannot image leaving one's daughter in the knowledge that one would never see that child again but for Marlene there was no other choice. As we waved goodbye at the departure gate I wonder what was going through her mind. We never heard from her again. This is a common story, of a Libyan man who had been a human being in the UK and became an abuser and tyrant in Libya. Marlene had in fact left right before the storm hit but she could not have known this when her plane took off from Tripoli airport to the freedom of London although I have no doubt with a life of wondering about her daughter.

Gaddafi was always firmly anti – Israeli and supported violent organizations in Palestine and Syria. There were also worrying reports that Libya was attempting to become a nuclear power. He had also been using former CIA operatives to set up terrorist camps, one of whom was Edwin Wilson, known as Ed to his friends. He had left Libya by the time I arrived, but the Dean had bought his VW car that she continued to drive around Tripoli for years. Where or what he had been doing in Libya I do not know but I believe those who did have contacts with the Libyan Intelligence service were probably up to no good. All the aforementioned were causing alarm bells and much irritation in the Ronald Regan camp. This came to a head in 1985 with the bombings in Rome and Vienna airports with the suspected support of Gaddafi. He openly admitted to backing terrorist groups such as the Red Army Faction and the Irish Republican Army.

A further escalation of tension in the spring of 1986 was when Gaddafi attempted to take the entire Gulf of Sirte as Libyan waters, as he stood on the bridge of a ship, heckling Reagan and of course wearing his signature sunglasses. Reagan claimed this action was an illegal incursion into international waters. As tension began to be retched up we had begun by this time to watch and listen to Libyan TV and radio. Nightly there was the Gaddafi tirade openly challenging 'the cowboy Reagan' as he liked to call the US President. Tension was further heightened when Reagan ordered three carriers from the US Sixth Fleet to enforce the standard twelve – mile limit of territorial waters. At this point we began to feel extremely anxious as to where all this rhetoric was going and how it was to end. My feeling was that Gaddafi relished this opportunity for flamboyance to flex his muscles at Reagan. Additionally it was an opportunity to show the Libyans his personal might. Bashir was working on the UN Security

Council Desk during this period and was on 24 – hour shifts due to the emergency. From what he heard and read he was becoming extremely concerned. On the 23/24 March there was an altercation between the US and Libyan navy resulting in the sinking of a Libyan corvette patrol boat as well as hits on selected ground targets by the US.

I have always been unsure of Gaddafi's psychological profile but those strikes on that day were taken as a personal insult to his dignity and probably he felt weakened in front of the Libyan people and that could never be. His days of endless uppers and downer drugs were probably just beginning, so perhaps his actions were more rational than in later life. However, for his skewered mentality those strikes needed retaliation and his policy always was and would be an eye for an eye. Reconciliation was not in Gaddafi's vocabulary. He called for Arab assaults on American interests. This resulted on April 5 with Libyan agents bombing La Belle disco in West Berlin, which was frequented by American servicemen. Two US soldiers and one civilian were killed and 229 people were injured.

The whole of Libya was on alert as a result of this bombing and the stand – off in the Gulf of Sirte. We knew these events were not going to be taken lightly by the Americans but we like Gaddafi were unprepared for the outcome that did occur. Thankfully on the night of the 14th April, Bashir was not on the shift and we spent our usual evening together and went to bed never dreaming of how we were going to be woken that night.

I learned some years later through an Italian student whose husband was a diplomat that the Italian politician Bettino Craxo had telephoned Gaddafi and forewarned him of the bombing, giving him and his family just enough time to rush out of Bab Al – Aziziya a few moments before bombs were dropped on his compound. Our alarm bell was an indescribably loud, low, rumbling and a violent shaking of our windows and doors. We thought initially it was an earthquake. When we heard the sound of a series of explosions, we knew it was a bombing. The anti – aircraft base at the end of our street began firing tracer bullets and goodness knows what else into the sky, the earth was rumbling and shaking. I am incapable of adequately describing the feeling or the sound, but it was more than petrifying. We realized we were in a war zone. The Libyan radio was dead but by some miracle the BBC world service had a correspondent down by the harbour, who was giving a minute – by – minute account of what he could see. That man became our lifeline and without him we would have been unable to gather any idea as to what was happening and who was bombing the country. It was not a coup; it was the Americans bombing Tripoli and Benghazi.

It may seem surprising but in all honesty I have to say we were thrilled. A superpower coming to our rescue, doing what the Libyan people had been unable to achieve; get rid of Gaddafi. Bashir was jumping up and down on the bed in delight laughing and saying 'we did it, we did it' and wanting to run out into the street. I cautioned, holding him back by his shirt as in reality we had absolutely no idea what was happening and what the result might be. In fact the bombing was said to have been only eleven minutes; it seemed like an eternity which was followed by a few minutes of complete, absolute silence. A short time after we heard car engines being revved up followed by crying women and children then voices yelling to each other to leave and driving off. Thereafter there was an eerie silent stillness which would remain for the rest of the night.

The truth was more people died or were injured that night whilst trying to escape from Tripoli in their cars than from the actual bombing. Our experience told us that the best option was to stay where we were and to run and fill up the bath with water. Since the Nairobi coup attempt we always had large containers of drinking water, candles, batteries and canned food stockpiled for any eventuality. There was a blackout leaving us to listen attentively to the world service, supping early morning tea and having no idea of the whereabouts of Gaddafi. Was he alive or dead? Who was in charge of Libya? Without those brave BBC correspondents that night we would have been completely in the dark and for the forthcoming days our radio was never off. I am eternally grateful for those correspondents' work at times risking their own lives in order to ensure that the truthful story is transmitted. During those days and nights when the bombing took place, without the BBC we would have been completely left in the dark. The following day it became clear that even the correspondents had no idea as to Gaddafi's whereabouts. Libyan radio and TV just played endless military music and old photo footage of the leader.

Our street and area was completely deserted since everyone had run for the mountains for safety as likewise we were to learn later did those living in downtown Tripoli. This seems to be a trend on many occasions when sensing danger, Arabs leave and do not stay to fight. Why did Reagan not finish the job? He quite obviously had Gaddafi on the run, it appeared that parts of the army had deserted and the majority of Libyans wanted Gaddafi to go as they were fed up with austerity and the Green Book theories. Perhaps the Reagan administration thought that the short, sharp, shock treatment would be enough to bring Gaddafi back into line or perhaps even into the fold. A further suggestion was they believed that the Libyan people would complete the job. If these were really their thoughts' they were very ill judged. Gaddafi was a desert Arab, a megalomaniac and his pride and dignity had been seriously dented. He slunk off to the desert like a wild, wounded dog only to return emboldened.

Tears come easily when I am frightened and I had difficulty holding them back when Bashir told me he was going to the office to find out what was happening as perhaps there he would be able to discover fresh news. I disliked being left alone but he felt there was no immediate danger, as all seemed quiet. He was to find only himself, Ali Mdored, now head of the International Organisations Department and one other colleague. On driving through Tripoli he saw little had changed except the total lack of cars and people on the streets. What he did learn was that the French embassy had narrowly missed being hit but a nearby civilian house owned by a colleague had been hit by a stray bomb. Thankfully all suffered only slight injuries or so it seemed at the time. Later the colleague and his daughter were to contract various forms of cancer.

As I write this in the safety of my London flat I realise that whenever I was with Bashir in critical situations I never felt that I was going to be harmed or afraid, but alone it was different. He never showed his fear and I think that it was his belief in fate; he would always say 'when God decides your time has come, there is nothing you can do about it. That is the day of your death'. People may think that I always write of Bashir as if he was an angel, but he was not. There were times when he drank heavily, drove when he was frighteningly over the limit and there were occasions when he was too blunt or unprepared to soften his position. Especially in the early years he would misunderstand a point and get into a heated argument due only to a poor English listening skill. Despite these faults he was my absolute angel. I am sure and know he could number many of my faults as well.

By the end of the day a short announcement was made informing all to return to work and their military units. That night the anti – aircraft base at the end of our street was hard at work firing at what seemed like an empty sky. We were never able to discover where and what were in fact their targets. It was alarming, as we had thought the US bombing was over but perhaps that wasn't the case or perhaps there was an internal Libyan uprising. Strangest of all were the rumblings underneath our house. It sounded like muffled car engines and heavy things being dragged along a tunnel. These sounds continued for over a week. We knew that Gaddafi had a relaxation compound on Gargaresh beach and had heard of there being a maze of escape underground tunnels throughout Tripoli, and perhaps this was one of those. We never discovered whether our speculation was correct or otherwise. We were advised not to talk about these tunnels by people who came to the house and also heard the rumblings. Until this point in time we had not felt personally threatened but day two was going to prove otherwise for me.

Perhaps most worrying was how I had been unable to telephone my father as we were still without a home telephone line, thanks to Mahmud. If I had been listening to the news of the bombing in London I am sure that I would have been convinced that there was total panic and devastation. In point of fact apart from Gaddafi's compound and the area around the French embassy, little structural damage had occurred. We went down to Gargaresh beach and saw divers out to sea. It was only later that we learned this was the area where one US plane had been downed.

On driving to work on that second day, there were only a few people and cars in the streets and to the untrained eye things seemed relatively normal. I felt it was essential to make a call to London and hoped that a phone with an international line would be working in the office. We had arranged that I would come home with the company bus and had said goodbye at the NOC gate with a pathetic grasping of each other's hands, no kisses. The company was dead apart from expats but of course dutiful Wasila was sitting at her desk. It was good to chat to another friendly face. Having a father who had been a Brigadier, I should have known better than to think he might have been worried about me. He asked in his usual measured, calm matter – of – fact way questions that he knew would not compromise my safety and on hearing my voice this was all the reassurance that he needed as to my wellbeing. Mission accomplished in terms of contacting London. I am sure that I was far more concerned, worried and tearful than the old warrior seemed to be.

The next task was to head straight to the Dean's office, to see how she had fared during the bombing. Similar to us the noise of the planes had been harrowing but all was calm and well on the expat camp where she lived. I have to say that I did chuckle at her story of the American desert rat. He was the one who had previously been full of American bravado and was now refusing to leave his room. The only way he would communicate even with other Americans was by passing notes under his locked door. He had been one of the extremely brash individuals who had insulted Bashir and his nationality and was now truly hiding like a little mouse in his room. One note read 'get me a ticket to anywhere out of this hell.' Even when he received his air ticket, this too had to be pushed under the door. Everyone was a threat and he went to the airport under a blanket – all talk and not much balls. His action was totally unwarranted as at no time were American or British expats threatened by the Libyans. In fact their presence was appreciated as enabling the country to be run with their expertise and without whom oil production would probably have come to a standstill.

On leaving the office that day I, along with my Indian colleagues came out into bright sunshine and started walking along a narrow back street towards where the company bus was waiting to drive us to our homes. It was at that moment I came the closest to possibly losing my life. Something whizzed into the wall just an inch in front of me and then I heard a hail of bullets coming from either ends of the street. I could see no one firing I just heard the crack of gunfire and could see and hear a volley of bullets ricocheting off the walls around us. I immediately discarded my heels for bare feet and ran for my life. I spotted a doorway and felt somewhat safer cowering in its relative safety. Seeing my Indian colleagues just standing transfixed in the road I screamed at them 'run, run for cover' and something must have clicked as they too started to race towards me. My poor colleague Sinha, a rather rotund, middle – aged man waddled as best and as fast as he could towards my doorway. I grabbed his hand and pulled him in next to me. The others had also found doorways in which to hide from the storm of bullets. Time stops still when one is terrified and everything seems to move in slow motion so I have no idea how long the two of us sheltered in that doorway. Urine was running down poor, gentle Sinha's legs, soaking his trousers, his face was completely yellow and he was shaking madly in absolute fear. My thought for some bizarre reason was that I had to reach the bus, so when there seemed to be a lull in the firing I grabbed Sinha's hand and pulled him down the road onto the bus screaming for the others to follow. Why they followed my instructions I have no idea as probably my plan was completely foolhardy but all I wanted was to get back to Bashir and the safety of our house. I yelled at the driver 'yellah yellah yellah go go go quick NOW' and again for some reason he too obeyed the instructions of a screaming English woman and drove off down the street in a hail of bullets which had once again resumed. That driver was brave and did not stop despite bullets hitting the bus but just put his foot down on the accelerator and soon we were out into the main road and free from that current danger.

I was never to discover why we were caught in that cross fire or who was firing at whom or why; all I did know was that I had never felt as threatened as when running to that bus. Bashir likewise could not comprehend what I had landed in the middle of. Whether it was part of an uprising or whether in fact it was a planned revenge ambush on expatriates, nobody will ever know. One can be offhand many years later after such an event, and I find it a good safety mechanism. Looking back at this incident I am always surprised at how I do not crumble. Thankfully I do have some inner spirit that enables me to just get on and try and beat, survive the challenge. I had remarkable parents in terms of tolerance, kindness and bravery and I must have learnt some things from them despite my ever – rebellious, independent nature.

So where was Gaddafi and who was controlling the country? No statement had been given to the Libyan people on the situation. It was assumed he had disappeared to one of his desert retreats to sulk. Why the Libyan people did not mobilise at this point against him I do not know but think that by 1986 he had managed to instil such fear of his authority in the people that they were helpless and had no spirit left to fight, no one could blame them. Nobody knew if their neighbour was a friend or foe, intelligence or informer, therefore no sense of unity. The opportunity was missed both by the Libyans and the western powers; Gaddafi would remain in fact strengthened. He announced that he had 'won a spectacular military victory over the United States of America' and that just as Britain was Great so too was Libya, he then renamed the country, 'The Great Socialist People's Libyan Arab Jamahiriya.' He additionally announced that so long as the cowboy Reagan was in the White House there would be no chance of reconciliation, and screaming as only he did in speeches 'he is mad, he is foolish, he is an Israeli dog!' He continued that Reagan's goal was to kill him, as the attack had been concentrated on Bab Al Aziziyah, his home. The building that was bombed was to remain in that state and became a shrine as the must visit place of all Heads of State when meeting Gaddafi. On being asked by a correspondent if he was in danger of losing power he replied 'Really these reports and writings are not true. As you can see I am fine and there has been no change in the country'. Of course this was contrary to now known reports of an internal revolt that was eventually quashed with the resultant arrests, kidnappings, imprisonments without trial and hangings. The reign of terror was going to become more intense. The gunfire we experienced on that day when leaving NOC could perhaps be explained by this speculation of a revolt.

I have mentioned little of life in general in Tripoli at this time. Shopping has never been an activity that I would spend a lot of time on, but due to Gadddafi's theory of co – operative shops there was nothing to buy in terms of basic necessities or even simple luxuries. For those wishing to shop for something special the only option was visiting one of the black marketers, business was booming for these people. Treats would be brought back to Libya such as a box of chocolates, a tin of tuna, jam, meat, clothes and so forth. Directly after the bombing things went even further downhill. Having come from the land of choice, abundance and advertising it was strange to find nothing. I remember on one occasion going to one of the huge government supermarkets and finding toilet rolls; these were like gold dust and I bought 40. Later I would take them as a dinner party gift, which illustrates just how desperate things were that we should be reduced to such a gift. Expats were an inventive bunch and recipe books were written, copied and distributed on cooking favourite dishes using Libyan supplements. After a dinner party, delightful notes would be written and posted through one's door, or a telephone call received saying thank you for the dinner. As time passed and things became easier, this happened rarely, just an unimaginative text. At that time there was always the most wonderful sense of pulling together. I have an absolute terror of rats and mice and early one morning discovered a mouse glaring at me in the bathroom, sitting on the basin. It did scuttle away as soon as it saw me but that was enough, no shower and moaning how awful life was in Libya with a mouse in the house. When I arrived at work obviously looking quite shell – shocked (pathetic really), the Dean sent around an SOS message for mouse poison, since there was none in the shops. By lunchtime I had a box of pellets and the following morning three other alternatives, two of which had come in on the AM plane. Our network was brilliant and we all helped each other. This was a time of hardship. By the 2000's, when things had become easier, the shops were full and this same comradeship seemed to have diminished.

I wish to show how the Gaddafi doctrine affected Libyan morals and cupidity in my life story with Bashir. Through Bashir's family I include here one more tale that reflects the mentality of many Libyans grabbing at any opportunity. Up until the bombing I had not considered teaching but when Ibrahim, Bashir's brother came after the bombing asking if I would tutor his eldest son Mohamed and daughter Nafissa for their secondary school English exam I willingly agreed. I felt this could be an olive branch and a way of gaining some respect from the family. The two came for a number of weeks until one evening Ibrahim arrived and informed me that it was no longer necessary to tutor Mohamed as he had arranged his exam. I did not really understand this euphemism for cheating nor could I understand why it was just for Mohamed? Two points come out of this story. Ibrahim, professing to be the most devout Muslim saw nothing wrong in using his position as Head of Sahara Bank to blatantly bribe someone so that Mohamed would pass his exam. Personally it was impossible to understand how a father could show his son that cheating was fine in order to achieve something dishonestly. Secondly, there was the gender question; why Mohamed and not Nafissa? To which I was told 'it is not important whether she passes or fails, she is a female and we are not interested in further education for girls'. There was, however a good outcome to the story in so far as I continued teaching Nafissa and without intervention in the actual exam she passed on her own and went on to a teacher training college, despite Ibrahim's position on women. As he rose higher, opportunity for corruption and greed increased and it cascaded down to the rest of the family.

Tragically this use of power and corruption was to be replicated in many other Libyan families seeing no wrongdoing in abusing the system. After all, they were just abiding by the leader's rules. On the subject of the corruption of the Gaddafi family and its cronies, I think what is forgotten is that corruption did benefit a few but the knock on effect was many times worse as a result for the Libyan people. It prohibited such benefits as aid and development projects being awarded to a country that was perceived as being rich. The reality was, in Libya's case that many were living on the breadline. No infrastructure projects were being built and education and hospitals were neglected. The country was on its knees.

Nothing can emphasise this more than the pathetic reward that Gaddafi offered the Libyans after the bombing. As mentioned, there were only basic commodities in the shops. Due to the fact that the border with Tunisia was closed with the Tunisian agricultural workers having been expelled this left the Libyan farmers unused to working their fields and orchards. As a result the vegetable shops were filled only with seasonal tired looking vegetables and fruit. Gaddafi made an order of bananas from Nicaragua and the shelves of the government stores were filled with boxes of this imported fruit. The Libyans rushed to the stores to acquire a box and in the ensuing mayhem it is said that two women were crushed to death and many injured. It was a source of pride to offer people bananas when guests came for tea. People wanted to give their children a treat by letting them taste and see an actual banana and for that they had to queue for hours and fight.

Since meeting Bashir in just five years I had lived through an attempted coup and now a bombing. We had managed to survive these harrowing events but what was to come next was to prove much more insurmountable.

Ten

After the experience of being in the crossfire of (presumably) someone else's battle on the day after the bombing we continued to hear rumours and speculation on what was happening in Gaddafi's fiefdom. The rumblings under our house and the nightly firing from the anti – aircraft centre at the end of our street resumed, both of which we had grown accustomed to and came to regard as harmless; the tracer bullets were rather like a free fireworks show. Our neighbours trickled back from their mountain hideaways and life resumed to what seemed almost back to normal. It had been a terrifying time and when I went back to England that winter I asked Maeve, my mother's friend, how she had lived through those long months of the Blitz. 'We just got on with our lives, it was the only way we could get through it' and I suppose that is simply what one has to do when living in a conflict zone.

We had learnt how to live with the Green Book, cope with austerity and now we had to learn how to adjust our lives once more to a Gaddafi regime after the bombing. The renaming of the country seemed infantile and almost laughable but the other, similarly juvenile new edict was the banning of all foreign language teaching. It was not until the mid. 90's that it was partially reinstated for scientific secondary schools, and a further four years until the Faculty of Education was able to once again teach English, French and later German. It was then also when English was reintroduced into all schools, arts secondary and primary. English also become recognized as the country's second language.

The far – reaching implications of this ban, I do not believe were initially understood by Gaddafi and his cronies. I have not followed a timeline but I am sure that there is a correlation between the time when Gaddafi's children were attending the military scientific secondary school in Tripoli and when English was reintroduced. It certainly was the time when Tarek Ibrahim's third son, who was at school with Saif Gaddafi, came asking for English lessons to pass the secondary school exam. Perhaps cheating was not quite as easy by that time. For those who had been caught up in the ban and had not had the opportunity to learn English elsewhere, the lack of English in a globalised world was to be a major hindrance for their generation in every aspect of employment opportunities and further education studies. For me, this was an opportunity, sadly on the back of yet another travesty for the Libyan people. I could teach English. Gaddafi, this megalomaniac, ruined many lives unnecessarily through his rants, raves and egotistical ideology surrounded by his sycophantic and murderous followers.

Personally one niggling outcome of the bombing was the stone throwing and name calling of Bashir and myself by the youngsters in our neighbourhood. It was tiresome and hurtful being called Reagan and Thatcher, neither of whom either of us liked or respected. It must sound funny nowadays and at the time I did not blame the children. This was what they were being taught at school and were watching nightly on television. This reflects the fear even within families of not doing or saying anything that could be perceived to be against the regime. There was a lovely open terrace at the front of our house but we were forced to build a protective wall in its place in order to be safe from the rock throwing. This is all the Libyan children knew, how to imitate and do as those in the regime did, never to be reprimanded as to the rights or wrongs of their actions by their parents. We were a very easy target. When it came to their using catapults, getting in and out of the house quickly was always a danger. I, as Thatcher and a woman, was the primary target, and of Bashir as Reagan, I think they were a bit more wary. What Gaddafi sowed will take decades and decades to change until there is a good harvest. I am forced to keep repeating this pessimistic outlook and I wish I could feel more optimistic.

We went to England that Christmas little realising it was to be the last time that Bashir would be able to visit for many years to come. I had found a lump in my breast and wanted to see a consultant in London urgently; I was not going to stay in Libya to be mauled by incompetent surgeons. I had been paying a BUPA contribution but money as always was very tight, especially getting foreign currency as at the time there were strict currency regulations over what money could be taken out of the country. Ibrahim had by this time left his job at Sahara Bank and his new position was as Head of Foreign Currency at the Central Bank of Libya. There were exceptions to the rules on foreign currency, one of which were medical reports. Bashir went to his brother asking for help with my medical bills. His brother disdainfully refused once again to offer us any help. Bashir was truly shocked at his brother's obvious inhumanity and dislike of me, his sister – in – law. Over the years we should have recognized this hatred but at the time we put it down to his stubbornness. How wrong we had been, it would be discovered in 2012. I had my operation and thankfully found the lump was benign, so we began to enjoy London.

Getting a visa for the UK had started to become harder and more time consuming as there was no embassy, only the British Interests Section in Tripoli. An interview system had been introduced and there were always long queues of applicants wanting visas. Many times in the future we would go over and over again the sequence of events during that January visit. Before leaving for England, Bashir had bumped into a friend who asked him to take a jumper to England for his brother. Purposely, Bashir had had no contact with Libyans in London but knew the recipient and although in retrospect it was a strange request Bashir agreed, met Shawish and gave him the package. Being cautious we had opened to check the contents before taking it to London. It is here that the beginning of what I shall call *the Spooks* part of our story begins. There were many Libyan informers working for the British Intelligence services and perhaps Shawish, needing a name and having just met Bashir gave him up, we were never to discover. This is just speculation, but a later event was clear as day.

One morning the telephone rang in Frognal and the caller announced himself as a friend of Willie. Alarm bells should have rung immediately as my brother hated that shortened form of his name and neither friends nor the family ever used Willie. The caller continued that he wanted to come and talk in order to help facilitate Bashir's visa applications. Also he mentioned he was from the Home Office and as a friend of my brother we saw no reason to refuse only a possible benefit. We naively let this man into our house who asked question after question which we answered openly and truthfully. When I thanked my brother for the contact he told me that he had no idea who the man was, and he had certainly never spoken to him. This man called later and returned saying that all was well and in the future things would be much easier regarding visa applications.

We were not to learn until some two years later the reality of these visits. That was Bashir's last visit to London for a decade. The country that he loved, where he felt at home and had visited so many times since the 60's suddenly, without warning, blocked him from returning. Personally that decision, along with a similar one to be made by the Libyan government put an unbearable strain our marriage.

By this time my father had decided to remarry so I decided to put my flat on the market as I saw no reason to continue coming to London as frequently since he would be happily settled. It was the perfect flat but I could ill afford the upkeep as it was putting a strain on our finances. This was exacerbated by the difficulty transferring money from Libya with the new currency restrictions and the total lack of help from Ibrahim. The flat was sold almost immediately and I returned in June to pack up all my possessions and have them shipped to Libya. It was a huge wrench; I would now have no roots, no bolthole in London where I could escape. This was when I totally committed to Libya. On the plus side it was wonderful seeing my pictures on the walls of our Gargaresh house, to have my books and treasures. The Gargaresh house had truly become home.

That winter with my father happily remarried and settled we decided on a beach holiday. Although we lived beside the sea we were unable to enjoy its delights so we pondered excitedly on where to go and what we could afford. The destination that we chose was Cuba. One of the reasons was that it required no visa for Bashir and was a cheap destination winter break. We flew via Madrid, meeting a former Libyan colleague who had left the foreign ministry and was living in Madrid with his Spanish wife. This was followed by a rather lengthy, uncomfortable flight with Cubana airline onto Havana. How wonderful it was to be in a country where nobody knew of Gaddafi or even the location of Libya. Castro had no wish for Gaddafi's theories to be known in his country. We both loved the beaches, enjoyed eating the sea food, drinking the Cuban rum, going on trips round the island and meeting the people who despite their hardships seemed to be able to enjoy life. As a child I had loved the book 'The old man and the Sea' and it had been on Bashir's reading list at university and he too enthused over the story. How delighted he was when he caught a quite sizeable marlin on a deep sea fishing trip.

We returned to Libya revitalized it was just the medicine that we needed after the events earlier in the year. What we failed to realise that perhaps this was to be yet another nail in our coffin in the future. Many had questioned as to why on earth we wanted to go to Cuba, a communist country. What they didn't understand was that we were odd balls and we were adventurers wanting to visit somewhere new; we were beach lovers and we had limited resources and that was the reason for our choice, nothing in any way sinister. Bashir at this time was also looking for possible places for a new posting. However, we realized by the end of the stay that Cuba was perfect for a three – week holiday but not a place to live for four years. Rather like Israel, when visiting Cuba they did not stamp one's passport. They just gave visitors a white slip that was returned on departure. I am sure that had they stamped our passports, our next destination in 1988 would not have happened.

Eleven

Bashir was enjoying working under Ali Mdored and increasing his knowledge on the workings of the UN. By being in the United Nations and International Organisations Department he was able to seize opportunities to obtain United Nations Development Programme (UNDP) funding for projects in Libya which would help employment and contribute to the well – being of Libyans. In later years he would call this Department his second home. There was fierce competition to work for IOD as there were endless opportunities to go on missions; this was a way to supplement the meagre salary at this time of about $350 a month on Bashir's grade.

He had been involved in a UN funded project for developing fish farming in Sabratha a coastal town 40Km west of Tripoli. Gaddafi, fearful of opponents and a US invasion had banned all sea fishing so although we lived on the Mediterranean, there was no fresh fish. There was little in the shops apart from absolute basics. People were even down to driving to Sarage (a Tripoli suburb) to fill up containers of fresh drinking water. There was no bottled water and the mains water was brackish. All of these things which I had taken for granted in London had disappeared under Gaddafi and daily living was getting extremely hard. When fish began being sold through this UNDP project, it was a real achievement and Bashir had the enjoyment of knowing that he had been partly instrumental in its inception.

I was fortunate despite my complaints in having somewhere to live, a job and could afford to buy black market food unlike many Libyans who ate meat once a year. The country has enormous wealth so it is in this context that criticism of the regime is just, since the situation for many Libyans was pitifull; they had so little whilst Gaddafi and his cronies lived indulgent, opulent lives. This inequality was so much more than even the regime they had toppled, supposedly in the name of equality in 1969.

I was becoming more and more frustrated in a tedious, copy typist job with a new Libyan boss. Fickri Al Allam could see no reason why he should not smoke his pipe in my office despite my obvious allergy to smoking. Constantly sending me up and down for another cup of coffee, speaking to me as if I were a fool and most unpleasantly he regarded himself as something of a lothario so a little grope on the bottom for him was absolutely acceptable. He was the most appalling misogynist. We had been back in Libya three years and seemed to have achieved a great deal – a house, jobs and wonderful friends but I was bored, so much so that every day I couldn't wait to leave the office. I was there only for the money although the pressure, now having sold the flat, was lessened to a certain extent. We had managed to put a little in the bank and I suppose that was why I was able to snap and quit. Fikri went just too far one morning. I have no recollection what it was he said or did but I do remember packing my things, leaving the office and handing in my notice on the way out. It was a rash thing to do as we did really need my earnings, but the tedium combined with aggravation with Fikri had caused an eruption. I called Bashir and he was at the gate by the time I left. He as ever, in his tireless belief in fate, reassured me that everything would be fine. I was not to know on that day quite what a momentous decision I had taken in my own favour. It would completely alter my life, our lifestyle and financial situation.

The jungle drums of the expat community banged pretty quickly around Tripoli notifying others that I was back in the job market. It took exactly one day to hear of an opening at the British School and for me to have a new job. Russ Sparks was the Headmaster, the man with a quiet American, west coast accent, amazing smile and a wealth of knowledge that he was always so willing to impart to others. Most importantly, his love of teaching and enabling children to learn was always apparent. He will always be my mentor and the one whom I have to bless for opening my eyes to the world of teaching. Without his enthusiastic support and encouragement I do wonder what my fate would have been.

After the bombing, the numbers in the school had dwindled to around 14 but by 1988, parents felt able to return to Tripoli with their children. The name British School is a misnomer; in the case of Tripoli the school was run by a Board of Governors, voted into their posts by parents who held British passports with the Ambassador as Patron. There was no funding or inspections as to standards from the UK. Children with British mothers and also British passport holders, but with a Libyan father were banned under Libyan law from attending the school. I think that this somewhat suited the expatriate parents, as it meant no Libyan interference. Although small, the school delivered the best education available in Libya then and at any time. Children passed easily into schools of their choice at 11+ and went on to attend top tier UK universities. The foundation they were given was exemplary. Classes were small with a maximum of 15 students compared to up to 40 in Libyan schools. Well – qualified expatriate staff that enjoyed teaching in an educationally conducive atmosphere staffed the school, overseen by Russ. My new post was as School Administrator, everything was new and I loved the daily buzz, excitement and joy of seeing the children learning enthusiastically. The team spirit was inspiring in an effort to rebuild and improve the school, aided by the parents. Russ is one of those remarkable men of whom one only hears praise in every aspect of his life. One of his passions was fishing off his Canadian Texada Island and his love of the sea set for an immediate bond between himself and Bashir. They were to become firm friends and there was always the promise remade annually via a Christmas card that they would go salmon fishing together. Up to this point in time our social life had principally been involved with expat singles through the Dean, but now another social network opened, that of foreign and British families living in Tripoli.

At the school we occasionally used to receive calls asking for English lessons, and one day such a call came from the Japanese embassy asking for someone to teach the Ambassador's wife. Russ kindly and generously recommended me for the job. Misa, an astoundingly glamorous and gracious lady, was my first student and Russ and his wife Joyce gave me guidance and support material to teach my first Japanese student. My lessons must have been successful as I was then approached by the Consular Minister's wife, followed by the Manager of Mitsubishi's wife until I was teaching every evening after school. The word had spread there was a competent English teacher despite the English ban. This was good, I loved the work, obviously the money was extremely welcome and I had a waiting list. Of course there were the usual Libyan detractors who warned us of the dangers of teaching English due to the ban but we were cavalier in some things that we did and this was one of them. Those courses taken in London were now coming to fruition aided by those working in the school, great colleagues always ready to offer advice or help. This was followed by Russ periodically asking me to give support teaching or be a substitute teacher to cover for sick or absent staff. I could see that teaching was to be the career I had always longed for but it had never been apparent. What I needed was a further teaching qualification in English as a Second Language (ESL) but I had to wait for that opening.

Twelve
١٢

Perhaps the greatest perk of working in the International Organisations Department was that annually diplomats' names were put forward by the department head, Ali Mdorid to the Foreign Minister to be included in the Libyan Delegation to the General Assembly (GA) in New York. Competition was unashamedly cut throat and fierce, even to the point of the unscrupulous Ali receiving gifts slid over his desk as diplomats attempted to increase their chance of selection. Ali's wife was Danish, Irene, who he was intent on taking to New York along with his daughter. I think that he had enjoyed working with Bashir during the bombing and the fact that Bashir had a foreign wife swung a place in Bashir's favour. Getting onto the initial list, however, did not guarantee a place on the final list to the General Assembly.

Dr. Ali Treki had been the Foreign Minister since Bashir joined the ministry and had been instrumental in implementing Gaddafi's Africa policy of zealously promoting the Green Book theory and supporting international terrorist organisations. He always surrounded himself with a coterie of his favourite young diplomats, even to the point of having them cook his favourite Libyan dishes at night and playing endless rounds of cards. Bashir disliked this type of climbing so he had never previously considered getting in on the GA list. It was always Treki's favourites who went with him to New York consequently there was no point even applying. Treki was a diabetic, wildly temperamental and suffered from poor health. Thus by 1987 he was probably quite exhausted with the demanding job of being Foreign Minister for Gaddafi. Like many, he perhaps also wanted a good education for his children and by going to New York this was a way of achieving that goal. He begged Gaddafi to be allowed to resign and be sent to New York as the Libyan Permanent Representative to the United Nations. His replacement was Jadallah

Azzuz Al Talhi from eastern Libya; he was a former Prime Minister. I always regarded Libyan men as being rather handsome in the main, but if people look at photographs of Gaddafi's ministers and ambassadors, not one of them could be considered typical of this; a shower of quite unattractive men. We always believed that this was deliberate on the part of Gaddafi the peacock.

Jadallah was an academic and was horrified on arriving at the Foreign Ministry to discover the low level of ability in foreign languages, the daily use of ugly, uneducated Arabic and near zero knowledge of widely accepted diplomatic protocols. The Diplomatic Institute had been closed in 1980 due to Gaddafi's theory that anyone could be a diplomat, regardless of education and background skills. Under Jadallah the Institute was reopened where he instigated compulsory Arabic, English and French classes with exams and the introduction of written CVs and support application letters for missions. He also stipulated that members of the foreign committees must have a Degree although I rather think that this was never enforced. This was Bashir's chance and he spent days drafting his application, passed all the required exams in order to go on missions and now was justifiably hopeful that he would be selected to go to New York. Many hated Jadallah, especially when he sent back memos marked in red with grammar errors. The only person in Libya allowed to use a green pen was Gaddafi, needless to say. Gaddafi had banned the wearing of ties in 1986 saying they were the hangman's noose of the West but Jadallah reintroduced suits and ties wishing his diplomats to look smart. He was a traditional diplomat and had zero tolerance for the usual barrage of predictable excuses. The Ministry had slipped into truly sloppy habits and he was going to up the bar, no matter what. Accordingly Bashir had the Jadallah signature for the GA and the next hurdle he managed to leap was the Gaddafi green tick, then a tick from Libyan intelligence and finally the US visa application. We were off to New York.

There was only one problem; I really did not want to resign my new job at the British school but this seemed the only option, as we would be away four months. I could go to New York with Bashir or stay behind and keep my job, but I knew that it would be completely impractical and unsafe for me to stay in Libya on my own. Fortunately, I had not taken into account Russ and his passion for enabling opportunity. He was absolutely thrilled at the prospect of Bashir being at the UN and immediately set about finding a substitute whilst I was to be away. I was in luck as a replacement was found and we were flying to New York to the GA.

Bashir was to work on two sections of the Third Committee: Social,Humanitarian and Cultural these were The Rights of Women and Children and Combating Drugs, which was always a slight source of amusement in the future with 'I did women and drugs in New York'. He was the only one in the delegation not to have worked previously in New York so had plenty of kind colleagues to show him the ropes. We were housed in a service apartment opposite the Waldorf Astoria and close enough to walk to the UN. It was like a dream come true for Bashir. When one first encounters the UN building, it is daunting in both its size and all the protocols and procedures that have to be learnt.

On the Libyan side there was the awkward dimension of Jadallah being the Foreign Minister and therefore the senior diplomat, and Treki as the former foreign minister not wanting to relinquish an ounce of his status. By their manner it was plainly obvious they disliked each other. Initially Treki mistook Bashir for his brother Mahmud (they had looked very similar in their younger days) and was dissatisfied that Bashir was even on the delegation. Furthermore, Treki saw Bashir as an invader; he was not one of his favoured young men. Treki was from the West and Jadullah and Ali Mdored from the East and Bashir was perceived as being in the latter's camp. Tribal favouritism was playing a huge part in internal foreign ministry appointments. If it *was* a case of mistaken identity once it was cleared that Bashir was not the member of the Shkuka family who worked in the Secret Department, Treki became more approachable. However, he was something of a tyrant in the mission and the work and rules were extremely demanding, as one would expect. The UN stint was not going to be a honeymoon. There were long hours to be worked and difficult negotiations, especially with the recent legacy of the 1986 bombing. There was also the additional balancing act between the two ministers, who at times were in strong verbal disagreement which added to the need to be on one's toes at all times. Jadallah only stayed long enough to deliver his speech and shortly thereafter returned to Libya. Treki soon had his realm back.

As mentioned the Foreign Ministry was and is an extremely competitive place in which to work. There was competition for missions, for postings and for ambassadorships. This situation is not unique to Libya; one supposes this competition exists in all the foreign embassies of the world. However, in the Libyan ministerial offices, merit was not generally the criteria observed for prestigious placements. Rather, it was consorting with Gadaffi loyalists and being signees to the Revolutionary committees. Working with Bashir on the Third committee was Musbah Allafi, a highly ambitious man who was forever fawning over anyone who might give him a career advantage. He was bright but lazy and it was Bashir's bad luck to be working with him. They were meant to share the workload but inevitably if Musbah could see personal advantage in any given situation he would lobby for it. There was no advantage in the simple day – to – day running of the committee so he would slope off and leave it to Bashir to complete the work. To add insult to injury, he was extremely good at putting his name to work that he had had no part in compiling. He was liked by Treki and shortly after he would be transferred to Cairo when Treki moved on to The Arab League. Many people from these days would reappear in our story and Musbah would be no exception. Throughout the periods when Bashir would re – encounter him, particularly during the 2011 revolution, he showed himself to be just the opportunist and chancer we had always seen, he never changed. However, his self – serving approach was not unique in the Foreign Ministry as there were many who had quite astonishing integrity. These people would form the backbone of those trying to work within the system, honestly trying to represent a country that had so many good things to offer. Alas they were always held back by the unbearable dictatorship to which they were shackled.

I had come from the culturally derelict void of Libya and to have four months in New York I knew was going to be bliss. There was no opportunity for me to work so the UN diplomatic wives' hospitality service was to be one of my sources of enjoyment. I was extremely fortunate with daily trips to everything from back stage at the Lincoln centre, platforms by artists and musicians, fashion shows, nightly receptions, theatres and concerts. We were invited to so many new and inspiring events. However, there was one downside. Our passports had been stamped with 'leave to enter the United States of America; limitation to the five boroughs of New York City'. This meant no visits to Westchester or New Jersey or weekend trips to Up State New York and a planned excursion at the end of our stay to the west coast had to be aborted. We not only had to deal with this hindrance, but we also suspected that our mail was being opened and our phone calls tapped. We talked to others in the delegation that also suspected the same. By being restricted in our movements we felt trapped.

One fun reunion was with my colleague George from Nairobi who had been transferred to New York. Perhaps best of all, Soleiman was also in New York and we spent many happy evenings listening to his poetry which he recited through his beautiful melodic voice. There was little that I could understand but there was always a seemingly sad lament for his lost country and friends. One evening we talked of our fabulous holiday in Cuba with Soleiman raising the question as to why we had gone there; he felt it might raise a question mark as to any future visa applications. We wouldn't realise how insightful these words were until sometime later.

There were marvellously frivolous things to enjoy in New York as the wife of a diplomat. Plus for me, there were the simple treats such as going to the hairdresser (banned in Tripoli) as well as having the freedom to walk along the streets free of sexual looks and comments. Sadly however, I was not able to enjoy the company of many other diplomats' wives as I was routinely ignored just as soon as they discovered I was not with a British or American delegation but rather with the Libyans. They would immediately move to the other side of the room. I was tarred.

Not being allowed to work, our movements restricted in what we could or couldn't do and where we could go were the major disappointments of the stay. One place that did have a mammoth, personal impact was a visit to an AIDS hospice. This was 1988 and the causes of the disease and how it was spread were still widely unknown. Sadly, we had personally had the experience of two of our favourite colleagues and friends having died of the disease, Gilban and Ahmed. I had not been to see Gilban in hospital because he had not wanted people to visit, but he did agree to see Bashir, as I am sure he knew that Bashir would bring cheer to his room. Bashir warned me that the visit to the hospice would be traumatic and distressing. What was extremely shocking was that we were in the city where the UN was located but were informed that we did not have to shake hands or have any physical contact with the patients, if that was what we wanted. These poor victims at this time were still hidden away like a dirty secret. Personally it raised awareness on my part of exactly what was occurring and for the sufferers we were I hope, friendly faces. I held one man's hand but was unable to tell him I couldn't make a further visit as we were about to leave New York. I just wished that I could have made more such visits. As far as Libyans were concerned the disease did not even exist and this denial would be the cause of the deaths of many eastern Libyan children in the future.

Obviously one of Bashir's duties was daily attendance on the proceedings of the Third committee but most importantly he had to write speeches on both women and drugs on behalf of Libya. He had a dilemma how to write about the Gaddafi regime, which he loathed, whilst simultaneously satisfying the keen eyes that were watching him from all sides. When Gaddafi seized power in 1969, few women went to university or worked and any suggestion of raising the status of women was frowned on by the strongly patriarchal tribes. One of the first laws that Gaddafi passed in 1970 was an equal work law. Unlike many other Arab nations by 1988 women in Gaddafi's Libya had the right to education, jobs, divorce, to own property and to have an income. This was perhaps one of the few areas where Bashir was in agreement with Gaddafi. The shame was that despite these laws it was a country controlled by men who were either reluctant or strongly opposed these rights. Libya was and still is a deeply conservative country.

The morning of his speech came and I took my seat in the gallery. I felt nervous as Bashir rose at the Libyan desk and started to give his speech. I shouldn't have doubted. Always so elegant and handsome he never hesitated or faltered; he sounded amazing, putting forward his points for the improvement of rights for women. There were no diplomatic relations with the USA or UK at this time but a delegate from both of these countries came and shook hands with him at the end as did many other representatives which was extraordinary given Libya's pariah status. I felt so proud and yet privately hoped that in the future it would be a female diplomat rather than a male giving the speech. By the time he had to make his speech on drugs it was his second time and with renewed confidence he was again congratulated by many delegates. Bashir said that working at the UN headquarters was one of the highlights of his career. The experience was truly motivating but the thought of working with Treki long term coupled with the US Government restrictions on living and working only in the city ruled out pushing for a New York posting.

The UN General Assembly is a huge financial burden on countries annually to run missions and to send delegations to New York for the GA for four months regrettably for some delegates it's just a bit of a jolly. The running costs of the UN are astronomical with many countries not paying their contributions; a continual problem. One wonders if anything is actually achieved. It does give a chance for diplomats to meet other diplomats and to have informal consultations between ministers and their counterparts in an international forum. A former Secretary General Dag Hammarskjold once said that the UN was not about taking us to heaven but about saving us from hell. The world has not yet found an alternative to the UN and therefore perhaps reform within the existing organization should be the way forward. The Security Council constructed in the 1940s is no longer fit for its purpose. The vetoes enjoyed by Britain, France, China, Russia and the USA in the Council should be replaced by a majority voting system that empowers smaller nations. The selection of the Secretary General must become transparent and democratic, not a secretive coronation by the permanent five. However, I am a firm supporter of the U.N. Agencies in the work they carry out and the bravery of their staff working in conflict zones. Without the work of these people the situations of so many human beings would be even more appalling and life threatening.

We had arrived in the summer and were departing in the freezing winter snow; it was definitely time to leave. Bashir's committee was one of the first to finish and there was no reason to remain in New York. We had seen and done everything that we wanted and the adventure was over. Additionally, by staying on it was costing us money so Bashir signed off with Treki and we were on our way back to Tripoli. We had decided that we wanted to spend the New Year away from Tripoli and planned to go to the island of Djerba in Tunisia. If we had stayed a few days longer we would have been in New York when possibly one of the worst of Gaddafi's atrocities occurred.

Thirteen

The late night view of the New York skyline as we took off for London was as ever powerful. We were to spend a few days with my father and see friends in London and then fly onto Tripoli. Bashir and I sat transfixed when those first pictures started to come through on the news channels. It was with absolute horror that we watched the scene unfold with its catastrophic implications.

Lockerbie is a town known internationally by many as the place where on the 21st December 1988, Pan Am flight 103 crashed. Eleven residents of the town were killed and all 259 people on the flight died from the bomb blast. The 259 victims were citizens of 21 different nations and the event was and remains the deadliest terrorist attack and aviation disaster to have occurred on UK soil. Not withstanding the tragedy for the families for Libya with Gaddafi at its helm this act was to put Libya into the dark ages.

Much has been written as to who was responsible and who actually planted the bomb and there are many conspiracy theories. There are people alive today who know for sure what happened, but of course Megrahi is now dead. One person who seems to have faded out of the picture is Lamin Khalifah Fhimah. When Megrahi was released on compassionate grounds and returned to Libya, Fhimah was the first to run up the stairs to embrace him. They had both been in The Hague accused of the bombing and had worked together in Malta. Yet nothing on the day of Megrahi's return was said of who he was and the part that he might have played in the bombing?

Today Abdullah Senussi is in prison in Libya having been sentenced to death by firing squad. He surely knows the facts as does Mussa Kossa, who was also a former head of foreign intelligence, currently in Qatar both having been given the nicknames of the Blackboxes. October 2015 the Crown Office in Edinburgh issued a letter to the Libyan Attorney General asking for permission to interview Senussi along with Nasser Ali Ashour an intelligence officer who supplied the IRA with explosives and weapons in the 1980s. Abu Agila Mas'ud also in a Libyan goal has been identified as being the bomb maker and has also been added into the mix. Undoubtedly there were papers found in the Intelligence headquarters after the revolution but as to their whereabouts who knows? After 27 years one has to question if this is going to be yet another of Gaddafi's acts where the truth will never be revealed. If Libya *was* the perpetrator of this abominable attack, then what was the motive? In 1986 there had been the confrontations with the US navy over the Gulf of Sirte, followed by the Libyan bombing of the West Berlin nightclub *La Belle*. These events were followed by the US bombing of Libya. In the meantime the US was encouraging and aiding the Chadian National Armed Forces by supplying satellite intelligence during the Battle of Maaten al Sarra. That attack resulted in a devastating defeat for Gaddafi's forces, after which he had to accede to a ceasefire ending the Chadian – Libyan conflict and his dreams of African dominance in that area. The result of this was Gaddafi's lingering animosity against the US and France that many believe led to the Libyan support for the bombings of Pan Am Flight 103 and indeed UTA Flight 722. The resultant embargo, no fly zone and sanctions were to preoccupy Libyan diplomats' work until the reproachment with the west in the 2000s.

We could not believe that Gaddafi had gone this far but then he believed himself to be the new lion of the desert; he had to roar. Gaddafi had a reputation for being revengeful by so many that there seemed to be no reason to doubt his complicity in this heinous act. Perhaps we as the general public will never know? Bashir was never involved in the negotiations on Lockerbie and therefore I am in no position to write on this subject and it has been well documented from the many court cases and appeals.

During this period fate was to do Gaddafi some favours and certainly the renewal of diplomatic relations with Tunisia in February 1988 was to be a lifeline when the UN sanctions and air embargo were in place. Earlier in 1974 Gaddafi had been hoping to create 'The Arab Islamic Republic' he was eager to see Libya and Tunisia merge. However, Tunisia's first president, Habib Bourguiba, having signed the official announcement, revoked Tunisia's membership after just a few hours. Gaddafi never forgave this affront and kept trying to topple President Bourguiba. Many of the agricultural labourers working in Libya were Tunisians and in 1976 Gaddafi expelled 14,000 Tunisian workers and in 1985 a further 30,000 suffered the same fate. The result of the 1985 expulsion was a lack of vegetables in the shops as the Libyans were unable or did not want to take the place of the Tunisian agricultural workers.

It is interesting to draw comparisons between Libya and Tunisia being that they share a border. The Bourguiba government was the most forward thinking in the Arab world passing reforms which included female emancipation, public education, family planning and a modern, state – run healthcare system. By 1987 aged 84 President Bourguiba's behaviour was becoming increasingly erratic. When in the November of that year he ordered a new trial for 15 Islamists and demanded that 12 of them be hung a week later this convinced both his opponents and supporters that he was no longer thinking or acting rationally. Zine El Abidine Ben Ali, the newly appointed prime minister of Tunisia had President Bourguiba impeached citing the President's old age and health making him unfit to govern. The removal of President Bourguiba saw the appointment of Ben Ali as the second President of Tunisia with improved relations with Libya. Their common enemy was political Islam and they agreed on a number of ideological points. It is easy to see today how the West appeared unable or did not want to realise quite to what extent these two dictators were in fact the guardians of North Africa. They held back the forces of what would become IS and other extremist groups in the region. If the two dictators had been more tolerant and not withheld basic human rights to their populations, perhaps they might not have been overthrown since history tells us time and time again that repression breeds dissent.

In February 1988, Gaddafi, ever the showman, drove a bulldozer to the Libyan Tunisian border at Ras Jadir and bulldozed the border crossing between the two countries, emphasizing that there were no borders between them. This now meant that Libyans could drive to Tunis, a ten – hour drive or holiday on the beautiful Island of Djerba, just four hours from Tripoli. Djerba had a small but busy tourist airport and during the days of the air embargo, apart from the ferry to Malta, this was to be one of only two exits to the rest of the world for the Libyans living in western Libya. Tunisia and Malta were both to make billions from the sanctions.

Gaddafi ordered and paid for the road between Ras Jadir and Bengardan, refurbished Djerba airport and of course the Tunisian shops benefitted from the influx of Libyans buying basic necessities. At the height of the embargo one could see a stream of ambulances and cars ferrying the sick to Tunis for treatment unavailable in Tripoli but I am moving a little too far forward in my story.

Leaving London and being back in Tripoli was good but we had planned to experience a Tunisian New Year staying at Club Med in Djerba. Lamin had been left in charge of our house whilst we were away in New York, and continued with the guardianship. Our route to Djerba was a drive we would do many times in succeeding years as the place became our bolt hole. At the time of this visit we were not to see the people trafficking boats being constructed along the way, this was to happen later. It was just a straight run through Sabratha, Zawia, Zwarah and then the border. What we had not anticipated were the thousands of Libyans who had a similar plan, to cross the border for a variety of reasons, be it fun, medical or just shopping. It was pandemonium. Now that the border crossing had been knocked down, all that remained were shacks for immigration purposes that were expected to deal with the vast numbers of Libyans wishing to leave the country. This was still at a time when no Libyan or foreigner could leave the country without an exit/re – entry visa, as Gaddafi's way of keeping tabs on his opponents. Luck was on our side as a Libyan official spotted me struggling, grabbed our passports and stamped them; we were on our way. It is not in my nature to queue barge, in fact I hate those that do but I am afraid on that occasion I was glad for the help. I have no excuse save to say that I am short and hate being pushed by crowds, and in this case there was a massive surge of people. During that year, a million Libyans visited Tunisia.

Club Med was a wonderfully relaxing time with no pressures, no decision – making and perfect weather for the time of year. This was the case whenever we visited this tiny, Tunisian island. We became quite regular visitors over the years due to its proximity to Tripoli and the easy drive. On our return we avoided the border chaos by returning early in the morning so missing the majority of the crowds. We had left the date of our return open and were surprised to see the car of one of Bashir's nephews' outside our house. On walking into the sitting room there was Haffad sprawled out on the floor with a young Libyan woman. Bashir and

I were absolutely furious that our house was being used as a knocking shop and probably had been by the nephews during our time in New York. I suppose I had to be grateful that they were not using our bed. Although on entering our bedroom I found my clothes strewn everywhere with many items missing and some of my jewellery had also been stolen. Nothing was ever returned despite begging the nephews to ask their girlfriends for the items. I think this shows how the family felt about us. Even to the younger generation we were useful but there was little if no respect for our position. We excused Haffad as being young and his parents were not told of his escapade. He like all of them never returned the good grace we had shown him after his appallingly disrespectful behaviour. They were all complicit in the 9/36 violation of our entire world.

Between 1988 and 1992 our lives under Gaddafi remained unchanged. However, on June 12 1988 the Green Charter of Human rights led to the release of hundreds of political prisoners. Furthermore, the Chad war was over. It was as if the cork had been removed from the bottle. The release of prisoners came with Gaddafi falsely claiming there were no longer any political prisoners in Libya. With the liberalizing economic reforms, life became somewhat easier despite the sanctions. I think by this time Gaddafi had realized that his experiment with the Green Book was only resulting in declining oil revenues, forcing him to make the announcement in 1987 of the 'Revolution within a Revolution' which began with reforms to industry, agriculture and the re – opening of small business. Restrictions were placed on the activities of the Revolutionary Committees in March 1988. For those in the Foreign Ministry the latter was to be good news as it meant that there would now be fewer of their representatives in the embassies. The reality was that Gaddafi was in trouble internationally and he needed competent diplomats rather than sabre rattling, incompetent brigades of psychopaths.

When we came to Libya in 1984 it was always with the hope that sooner rather than later Bashir would be sent on a new posting and we could live out of Libya freely. It was that word *freely* that we longed for we had learnt to cope with Tripoli living but it was always the restrictions which grated. The wait seemed endless while lobbying and hoping his name would surface on the list for a foreign posting. In 1989 we were hoping for a quick visit to London but this was when the reality of the pointers we had in 1986 became a reality. Bashir applied for a visa in the usual way but then surprisingly received a call to come to the consular section. There he was given a letter effectively stating that his presence in the UK was deemed to be a danger to the country and his visa application was declined with no grounds for appeal. Neither of us could believe the situation; with no appeal how were we ever to have this decision overturned. What would be the implications for travel to Europe and other countries, and would his name also be on their blacklists? We were to discover fortunately that the ban applied only to the UK. I was absolutely mortified to think that my husband was being accused of being a terrorist when I knew this to be a lie. Was this because of the home office visit? Was it as a result of delivering the jumper and meeting with a suspicious Libyan? Was it as a result of having been to Cuba? Or indeed, was it because someone in the Libyan intelligence had used Bashir's passport to obtain a British visa as this was a practice uncovered some years later? We were never permitted to find out. I began my search on how to solve this travesty, my husband not being allowed to travel with me to my home country. I was devastated; the place where we had hoped to spend our retirement was out of bounds. It was no longer our England our place of refuge.

Fourteen

١٤

Despite the visa blow life continued pretty much unchanged for us in Tripoli. We resolved to keep the problem between the two of us for fear that it could affect any future posting opportunities. The lack of a British visa was constantly on our minds with no way in sight of seeing the situation being resolved. It was black days and months.

Every day life for us and the Libyans remained pretty much unchanged, an endless repetition of mundane daily living while never murmering or mentioning anything against Gaddafi. I have never been interested in football but for the Libyan youth it was a passion so intense that it could and would cause full – scale riots relatively frequently. In 1989, Libya was due to play Algeria for a place in the World Cup Finals. Gaddafi saw this occasion as a means of furthering his dreams for greater North African integration using sport. Everyone was talking about the match and all TV sets were on with faces glued to the screens waiting for the game to start. No cars were moving on the Tripoli streets and all the shops were closed. It would have been the ideal time to invade the country. As the country watched to everyone's amazement before the teams had even come into the stadium an unknown man walked onto the pitch and blew the final whistle. I am sure that a murmur of astonishment could have been heard throughout Libya. Gaddafi not approving of spectator sports had ordered the cancellation of the match. In fact the cancellation was linked to yet another of his madcap ideas; he wished to see Algeria and Libya united. In a hope of persuading the Algerian Government of the merits of this idea, he announced 'the two teams are, in fact, one team' so there was no need for 'conventional competition'. What was unusual was hearing and seeing people chanting anti – Gaddafi slogans, triggered by the cancellation of the football match. Passions erupted in and around the stadium. As was the normal pattern, suspects were rounded up and at least twenty people were executed. Absolutely nothing was reported in the media although this was to be expected. Unusually, people were talking angrily being far more outspoken than had ever previously been heard in the streets. Football had been the trigger. Perhaps Gaddafi took it as a warning that his perceived stronghold on the country was in fact rather more fragile than he thought.

I digress again a little on the subject of football as it was to play a tiny part in our lives in the future when we were to live opposite Mohamed Gaddafi, the son of Fouzia Gaddafi's first wife. Mohamed's team *Al Ittihad* wore red and would be the main rivals to the team *Al Ahly*, wearing green of his stepbrother Saadi. Whenever there was a match between the two sides, expatriates carefully warned each other to avoid the stadium, as there was always a fear of riots and stampedes at these events Football was not only the beautiful game in Libya; it was also politics. On football match nights our street would be full of bodyguards with their Kalashnikovs and fireworks at the ready in the event of an *Al Ittihad* win. We would hear the hooting of many car horns on their return when there was a victory. When the team lost there would be absolute silence and long faces guarding the leader's son. Either way we didn't care; all we saw were the sons squandering Libyan money yet again, frittering it away on football when the infrastructure of the country had virtually collapsed. On football nights we firmly shut the front door and turned up the music.

Meantime Gaddafi designated 1989 as being a landmark year in the evolution of his Great Fatah Revolution i.e. the 20th anniversary on the lst September. There were to be massive festivities to show the world the success of his socialist theory as laid out in his Green Book. As the 1st September celebrations drew closer there was trepidation amongst government officials as to how the country would be able to cope with such a large gathering of dignitaries. The country had proved ill equipped to hold the failed OAU summit in 1983 and now Gaddafi was hoping to host a spectacular celebration with Kings and Presidents attending.

One such VIP monarch on the invitation list was King Hassan of Morocco. What a dilemma it must have been for him, knowing that he had to come to a potentially riotous and chaotic Libya after Gaddafi had tried to have him assassinated. During the 1970s King Hassan well knew Gaddafi's hatred of monarchies, which the Libyan leader viewed as in need of Libyan – style revolutions. The relationship between Morocco and

Libya was always lukewarm and capricious. In the early 1980s Gaddafi had been funding the Polisario Front of Western Sahara in their independence struggle against Morocco, which obviously caused friction between the two countries. In 1984, after the killing of Yvonne Fletcher, Gaddafi was in need of some respectability and he proposed unity with Morocco and the Oujda Treaty was signed. This benefited Morocco both in terms of its citizens being able to work in Libya and the repatriation of much needed dollar funds. Due to King Hassan's relationship both with the USA and Israel, the post – 1986 bombing period saw the union abolished. By the time of the celebration there had been moves by the regional partners Tunisia, Algeria and Morocco towards substantial trade and employment opportunities between themselves and Libya. Although this was not in the form of a union with Morocco, it was enough to bring King Hassan to Libya. He refused Gaddafi's offer of accommodation preferring to stay on his yacht in the harbor, presumably to better ensure his safety as well as a quick departure if needed. He indeed, took a quick exit after just two days, for reasons unknown.

Certainly no one from Europe would be attending; Lockerbie had dealt that blow. The running tap of black gold was the lure for many, especially those from minor African and revolutionary South American countries. They saw an opportunity to catch a few drops of some of the Libyan wealth Gaddafi was known to be generous to those that obeyed.

The Libyans were growing increasingly tired of Gaddafi's unions and investments in other nations, as they never saw themselves as the beneficiaries. There was a joke doing the rounds at the time, typical of the sardonic Arab tradition: Gaddafi, Egypt's President Mubarak and King Hassan were driving across the desert, only to find their path blocked by a lion. King Hassan was unable to persuade the lion to move out of the way, despite being a great king. Mubarak, the leader of the largest Arab nation was also unsuccessful in getting the beast to yield. However, when Gaddafi lifted the animal's ear and muttered something into it, the lion raced off across the desert. 'What did you tell him?' Mubarak and Hassan asked, 'I offered him unity with Libya' Gaddafi replied.

There were many disgruntled Libyans seeing their national wealth being squandered on enticements to foreign leaders to attend the celebrations as well as questions as to why he was never generous towards his own people. To this day this is an unanswered question.

All leave was stopped from May onwards with rushed preparations being put in place. Protocol Department had rusting old vehicles that were continually breaking down which were replaced by new Mercedes being imported into the country, as were suits and shoes for all the drivers. No expense was to be spared and the foreign ministry drivers were thrilled at this turn of events. The army had to be trained to march for an endless procession down the harbour road. There was to be an exhibition similar to one Gaddafi had seen in North Korea, of Libyan school children performing traditional dancing in the stadium. Parents sought every means to have their child excluded never knowing what might occur at such a Gaddafi gathering.

The celebrations were to be for three days and Bashir was allotted responsibility for the President of Madagascar. September 1st seemed frequently to bring sandstorms, which the Libyan people always felt was the weather showing its outrage at the state of the country. Chaos was Bashir's prediction in the main trying to ferry delegations around Tripoli, especially with Gaddafi never arriving on time and keeping Heads of State waiting for sometimes up to two or three hours. On top of this there were an inadequate number of people qualified to handle the operations, especially when it came to the catering and transport arrangements at Grand Hotel. His prediction once again proved accurate when King Hassan and President Ben Ali both left the proceedings early, no longer able to cope with the poor arrangements. Of course, many of the Africans remained in order to obtain their handouts.

It had been an exhausting time for Bashir and on the final day he couldn't wait to take his delegation to the airport and for the whole shambles to be over. He left early that last morning with sand flying and as a result, visibility was quite bad with a sweltering temperature of around 45C, it was miserable. On arriving at Grand Hotel he discovered there were no protocol cars to take the Madagascan delegation and their president to the airport. This was a time before mobile phones and therefore there was no way to contact the Protocol drivers to find out where they were and why they hadn't arrived at the hotel? Bashir's astoundingly bad luck was to be seen by a young Khamis Gaddafi, then probably aged only about ten, wearing military fatigues with guns on his belt and surrounded by his bodyguards whom he called his brigade. On demanding why the delegation was waiting in the lobby and wanting to know which diplomat was responsible for this mess, Khamis ordered his guards to arrest Bashir and take him to one of the Tripoli prisons. As mentioned, in Libya you were only safe if you had someone in the system able to give you protection. Thankfully on that morning Bashir's cousin, a Colonel in the CID, was on duty at the hotel. On seeing Bashir being led away by the guards he interceded saying he would take over and ensure that Bashir would be appropriately reprimanded. This story highlights how Khamis at the age of just *ten*, and all of the Gaddafi children, were now flexing their power and were able to do whatever they wished, whenever and however they liked. Bashir arrived home furiously swearing and spitting at not only the perpetual incompetence during these celebrations, but also at the obvious up and coming power of the young Gaddafi children with access to unlimited funds, backed by their thuggish brigades.

Fifteen

I shall repeat continuously our inability to obtain a UK visa for Bashir was utterly devastating. I had received bad news before but for both of us, especially Bashir, it was heart breaking. Not only did it impact on his mental state but it also had the potential to affect his diplomatic career. Being practical, we had to decide how we could attempt to unravel the situation. On my next solo visit to London I tried calling the so – called 'Home Office visitor' to Frognal using the number that he had given us if ever we should need any assistance. On phoning I was told there was no one of that name at the number, and on asking the name of the organisation the call was disconnected. So much for our first avenue of enquiry – blocked, spooks? No further progress was made with just the reality of deep disappointment and concern. Up to that point we had believed there *must* have been some kind of error. However, all contact with the Home Office and Consulate officials for an explanation were just met with a reiteration of the initial statement that we were unentitled to any explanation. It was a constant reminder that if the Libyan authorities became aware of the banning it could or would jeopardise a future posting or mission possibilities.

Yet again we had to keep another secret, the pile was mounting. This was a time when Bashir would go into periods of quite deep depression I found it alarming as I had never seen him so despondent. Before, even in troubled periods in our lives he had been ever the optimist but this time it was another country calling the shots. So many nights were spent asking ourselves how the situation could be resolved. He took it as a personal blight on his career as a diplomat with no clear resolution. As time went on we still came no further to discovering why he had been sanctioned in this way.

In the meantime Bashir moved from working on the UNDP

agency desk to the United Nations Educational, Scientific and Cultural Organisation (UNESCO) agency. A new postings list came out but it contained few names so all immediate hopes of being able to leave Libya were dashed. We tried with difficulty to keep our dreams and be optimistic, it was growing hard.

Libyan living was always a compromise but we continually told ourselves that despite everything we had a place to live which we could call our own away from the family. We both had interesting jobs and thanks to my ESL after – hours teaching I was earning an excellent salary even by UK standards. Plus we had made good expatriate friends. However the lack of places to visit at weekends with our self – imposed restriction on not going to the beaches made us feel terribly trapped. By comparison, however, to the majority of women married to Libyans, my life was perfect. Despite the hardships and worries, I knew I was blessed. I had a husband who was exactly the same man as when I had first known him. Importantly, I had a five year residence visa for Libya which meant I could leave whenever I wanted without the permission of my husband this was unknown to most foreign wives married to Libyans and is withheld to most even today. However, I still had to complete forms with Immigration every time I wanted to leave for the exit stamp a pushing, shoving process dealing with endless queue bargers. This was a requirement for both expatriates and Libyans as a way for the authorities to keep tabs on where people were going and stopping those they wanted to detain. On a personal level, with some exceptions everything was going well, but this *was* Libya. The ever – present restrictive Islamic influence plus having to watch my tongue whenever with Libyans all still felt unnatural. I appeared I am sure as a dramatically unconventional wife by Libyan standards especially due to my London upbringing.

My contact with Bashir's family was just the weekly half – hour courtesy visit to see his mother who I think despite my best efforts had been indoctrinated into believing Bashir should either get a divorce or take a second Libyan wife, much to his heartache. I was far too western and we had no children. Many people have asked me why? The answer was simple for Bashir; it was all down to fate or God's will. When we were in New York we both had numerous tests to see if there was any reason why I hadn't conceived and all of the tests came back positive. These were the early days of in – vitro fertilisation, which was expensive and would have required endless visits to the UK, which the visa ban had made impossible. We decided that we should leave it to God to decide. Personally, I did not want any further pressure on our relationship, which already had the strain of the visa problem as well as the stress of daily Tripoli living. A child never happened and in retrospect if it *was* God's wish, it was the right one. I have no doubt as to this, and neither did Bashir. I think for both of us we would have found life too unbearable continually compromising on the way of bringing up a child under the Gaddafi regime. When I see those who have succeeded I am full of admiration but for mothers with sons killed in the revolution I am unsure whether I could have dealt with such a blow. Today a friend keeps her son's room exactly as he left it before leaving to fight in the revolution. He never returned and died a hero. For her it is not only the loss but much more the waste when she views the chaos in Libya today.

When talking about Libya under Gaddafi one talks continually about waste and Sirte was certainly a project of megalomaniacal waste. Sirte was Gaddafi's birthplace and he had a dream, yet another one of the many, that it should become the flagship of his self – proclaimed revolution, the new capital of Libya. It had been a tiny coastal, sandy village but by the 1990s it had an airport and conference centre. As the new capital it needed new government offices, hotels, a parliament building, and housing for the new government officials who were to be located there. Those working in the ministries were horrified, as it would mean leaving Tripoli, their families and working in that desolate part of the country. All of the foreign embassies without exception stated their refusal to move, as did the oil companies citing the expense and the impracticality of such a move. Nevertheless by the mid 80s, Ministers had to drive to Sirte for weekly cabinet meetings. Minimal ministry offices were established, it is believed, just to placate Gaddafi with no intention of actually conducting any meaningful work. The road to Sirte is dangerous and there were numerous fatal accidents including one where 'the Dancer' Minister of Telecommunications from Nairobi days was killed. To be sent to Sirte to work was tantamount to being sent to hell but it was a constant worry that Gaddafi might get his way and every government employee would have to relocate. Gaddafi never saw the impracticality of his dreams; he had the money so he executed the order. Personally, this was a further additional worry as we realized that I could not be left alone in Tripoli if the Foreign

Ministry were moved to Sirte. Thankfully as far as the ministries were concerned it was just another Gaddafi dream even so huge, extravagantly expensive buildings were built which stood empty for the greater part of the year.

In Bashir's new capacity as the focal point for UNESCO he came home with the exciting news that he was to be sent on a one month mission to Thailand. UNESCO, UNICEF, the World Bank, UNDP and the UN population Fund originally launched the Education for All (EFA) Agenda. The declaration was to recognize education as being more than just access to primary education but also addressed the basic learning needs of all children, youth and adults. Education in Libya was in a pitiful state with children sharing one text book with three to a desk, broken glass in school windows so freezing in the winter and overpoweringly hot in the summer, inadequate instruction, and no English language teaching.

Neither of us had been to Thailand so this was an exciting new adventure and as flying to London was now impossible we flew to Zurich and then on to Thailand. We had planned to spend a day in Bangkok and then take one of the UN buses to Jomtien, the location of the conference where a brand new conference centre and hotel had been built. Coming from Libya, the contrast was so marked between the decline of Libya and the rise of Thailand, both as developing countries. Unlike in New York Bashir was fortunate as the Libyan permanent representative to UNESCO in Paris was a well – educated and charming man. He could easily have been a gung – ho Green book revolutionary, which would have been a nightmare. The work was divided up equitably and at the end of the conference both felt they had achieved some good lobbying results to take back to Libya. For Bashir it had also been useful to get to know his counterpart in Paris face to face rather than through telephone calls and letters. He was also anxious to push for the World Heritage Greek and Roman historical sites in Libya to take advantage of expert advice from UNESCO on restoration and preservation strategies. The EFA Declaration had many aspirations but today progress, despite numerous conferences, has been minimal. It was a wonderful place for me to visit, as I was able to attend many interesting talks on education and pick up publications that would be useful not only for my teaching in Tripoli but also for the British School. I returned loaded down with pamphlets and books. As we began to attend conferences so we developed life – long friendships with people in the agencies and foreign embassies throughout the world.

A small story at the conference was the invitation by the Princess of Thailand to a dinner and performance of a Thai opera for all the delegates. We arrived just before the start of the event to find most of the tables were taken apart from four empty tables as we thought at the back. We were led to one of these tables only to discover that the back was in fact the front and that we were sitting at a table one away from the Princess but with senior Thai military, senior UN officials and the Minister of Foreign Affairs. We had quite obviously been mistaken for a much more important VIP diplomatic couple. The dinner was sumptuous but an hour and a half of Thai opera was laborious and sitting at one of the top tables there was no retreat we had to sit it out. Thai opera was never on our future menu.

After that inspirational and fun break in Thailand it was back to work in Tripoli. I had been lucky that the conference coincided with my being able to find a substitute once again for my job at the British School. I enjoyed working with Russ and the school staff enormously; we were a happy, cohesive band.

One area of interest in our free time where we were able to become involved was in the Tripoli British Archaeology society with their monthly expeditions and meetings. Archaeological ruins had become a red hot subject for Bashir since our return from Thailand. On one occasion he arranged for the school to visit the Gargaresh catacombs. Coming from the area he had known this Roman burial site as a child although even then it had been unprotected. Now he wished to see their state many years later especially given his new role with UNESCO Libya. As the catacombs were inside an army camp it involved a great deal of bureaucratic toing and froing with the military. Finally with the paperwork completed the British School sixth form students, their parents, the teachers and the two of us all set off to see the site. We found the entrance to the catacombs covered over with a piece of corrugated iron and stooped down to enter into the chamber. The paintings around the actual two tombs are extraordinary but without protection, lying open to the air as a result I fear their colours will fade from the strong sunlight. All the parents tried to decipher the Latin inscription; as far as we could understand it was 'sacred to spirits of the departed' and that the person had lived for 60 years. For the children, here we were being real live archaeologists unravelling a text on a tomb and in so doing bringing their history books to life. I think for myself and particularly for Bashir, the fact that he had made all this effort for expatriate children served as a sad reminder of the lack of Libya's historical background being taught in Libyan schools. If he had tried to arrange such a visit for Libyan children he might have been accused by zealous Gaddafi intelligence officers of promoting colonialism; such was the bizarre outlook these people had on life. In fact, after the visit he was once again given a warning, this time about visiting these sites. Libyan history lessons in school only revolved around the Great Al Fatah Revolution. For those Libyans who had been brought up post the 1969 revolution, they had learnt nothing of their country's past and seemed to be generally disinterested preferring football and such froth. Add to this the fact that the only bookshops were Green Book shops by decree of the regime, and one can kind of understand the ignorance. These are the Gaddafi lost generations and it was a tragedy for Bashir to have to acknowledge, especially with his endeavours working with UNESCO. I am still unsure whether Libyans are simply unaware of the historical magnitude of their ancient remains, or they simply don't care.

Libya is overflowing with Greek and Roman remains many undiscovered and in the most surprising places. In 1998 close to our house a villa was being knocked down in order to be replaced by a new duplex. The excavators were busy at work when they suddenly hit a room at least 30 feet below the road. Inside the room were urns, all of which were filled with gold in various forms. On further digging the University Archaeology Department discovered the site had probably been a pottery works with ovens being unearthed together with what must have been the owner's wealth. Again, we asked if the school children could visit as it was just a five – minute walk to the site from the school. The chief archaeologist kindly showed what was being uncovered and each child was given a small roman pottery shard. It was a simply unique experience for these children to watch an actual dig. They saw these Roman wonders first hand rather than just learning and reading about them from a book; history had come to life. I always hoped when digging in my garden that I would discover gold but was never in luck, possibly I was not looking deep enough below the surface.

There are many expatriates who have contributed to archaeological and cultural research in Libya. In 2007 I was to meet Elena Schenone Alberini who had been with her Italian diplomat husband in Libya between 1994 and 1998, although our paths had never crossed at that time. Elena had researched the history of Libyan jewellery and produced a coffee table book full of exquisite photographs together with the story of the connection between customs, superstitions and secrets of Libyan jewellery. Due to the fact that in the book there was a mention of Jewish jewellers Gaddafi had the book banned, so for those who had a copy it was a well – hidden treasure. By the time Elena was in Tripoli in 2007, attitudes had softened and we paid a visit with our Bulgarian friend Ekatarina to the old souk in Tripoli. In one of the shops a rather wizened old jeweller said he could make any piece that was displayed in Elena's book. Immediately she told him 'I am the author of this book'. His face lit up in excitement and he ran out of his shop calling other jewellers in the area to come and meet Elena. They were all thrilled at this chance meeting and we were suddenly surrounded by perhaps fifty men praising her work. The jeweller thanked and blessed her for the book saying that without it, the history of Libyan jewellery would have been lost and that they had been relying on her photographs to replicate pieces. Although Gaddafi had tried to ban Elena's book, people realised its importance and this fascinating insight into the old culture of the region, with its picturesque traditions and practices now will never disappear thanks to her research and writing. My treasured copy has travelled with me everywhere and sits on my bookshelves in London today in pride of place.

The expatriate British community Archaeological society's monthly trips to various sites accompanied generally by a very able professor from the archaeology faculty who also spoke excellent English was an event we always looked forward to. There was also a group of enterprising oil exploration engineers who had access to satellite imaging and they used these maps to go on dinosaur digs. They would meticulously examine the photographs of an area and then set off in the search for bones. Any finds if I remember rightly were sent to the University of Bristol for carbon dating and research. Their main finds were primarily in the mountains up in Gharian and Khabow where fossilised fish teeth and petrified wood and trees were discovered and around Tahona to the east of Tripoli along the coast. Any excursion was potentially an exciting day out with a picnic. It is a sad fact there are those from the expatriate community who probably know the whereabouts and history of prehistoric, Greek, Roman and Ottoman Libyan history better than many historians and certainly more than the majority of Libyans. Bashir was more knowledgeable than most but never had the opportunity to go down into the desert to view the prehistoric rock paintings. Libya has so much greater wealth than just its oil.

Tragically in my opinion there are some people in Libya who consider any reverence for these ancient treasures heretical; fundamentalists in the region are troubled by examples of pre – Islamic civilisation. Worse others from this group wish to destroy these antiquities therefore it is of major concern that these sites and their relics may not survive these turbulent times. The country has such a rich heritage from the prehistoric desert paintings to the Greek, Roman, Byzantine and Italian remains. Libya is truly a treasure trove but a sadly neglected one that needs protecting.

In order to relieve the tedium of Tripoli living regular trips were made over public holidays to Club Med Djerba with groups of friends. The feeling of being free, normal human beings for us was indescribable. Djerba had taken over from Malta as our retreat as it was so much easier to reach. We were extremely lucky that we did have places to go where we could be ourselves, and thankfully I was earning enough to facilitate the trips. We had many blessings, the greatest one having each other.

With Bashir being unable to visit London other places had to be found and in this respect it was fortunate that it made us travel further afield. Of course we had never lost our spirit of adventure and with Egypt being on our doorstep a trip was planned for December 1989. I had been through the Suez Canal as a child but that was the closest I had come to visiting the country. Bashir always spoke extremely fondly of Egypt especially during the time when he was a student. Despite my intolerance he loved the Egyptian TV series, and movies. To go to Egypt with an Arabic – speaker I felt was really a golden opportunity. The plan was to join a British tour company in Cairo. Due to the news of a possible invasion into Iraq, tourism in Egypt was suffering. Foreign tourists were staying away perhaps not realising just quite how far Egypt was from Iraq. On visiting the Pyramids our little group of nine were the only visitors to the site and as we continued on our trip down to Luxor, Abu Simbal, across to Sharm el Sheikh, up to Mount Sinai and back through Suez to Cairo the lack of tourists was to be seen everywhere. The question always on the lips of the street hawkers was where were the tourists? Why were they staying away? The street traders continually begging us to buy their wares were truly feeling the effects of the likelihood of war. Tourism is a major contributor to so many Arab countries and any terrorist attack or threat of conflict causes people not to choose that country as a holiday destination. The losers are the majority of the population as the country suffers economically.

On our last night in Cairo was spent having a drink at hotel Safir (ambassador in Arabic). Bashir whispered not to turn my head as Omar Sharif was sitting a table away; that was irresistible I had to look. I found my bridge loving husband to be far more handsome than the King of the Bridge tables in Safir hotel. Sadly this famous Egyptian actor has passed away but I am sure his performances in Lawrence of Arabia and Dr. Zivago will live on in many non – Arab memories. For me Egypt was beyond all my wildest expectations another astounding journey with my other set of amazing eyes.

Finally the news for which we had both been long hoping for came through Bashir was to be posted to India. As soon as I heard the news I visualised all the places that we could visit from my childhood reading and the many films and TV programmes that have been made about the country. Always wanting to be surrounded by our personal possessions wherever we lived I suggested a small shipment. Bashir was reluctant citing that we could buy unique things in India so we took nothing barr a few pictures and books. On our return we were to find the consequences of that decision. In order to supplement our income we wanted to rent our house and were lucky, we thought, to rent to the Philippine Labour Attaché. I hadn't had the best of luck renting out my London flat, and our luck wasn't to change this time. The assurances that the house and its contents would be well looked after didn't prove sincere. Bashir's brother Lamin was asked to keep an eye on the place, which in addition, proved also to be a disastrous plan.

There being no direct flight we flew from Tunis via Zurich and thence onward to New Delhi, another adventure was about to begin. It had taken Bashir almost ten years since our marriage to be back to where he had been in Nairobi. However, now he was a First Secretary, with improved salary and status within the embassy. He knew the Ambassador, who was a career diplomat and also one other member of the Committee. That man too was a career diplomat but was also a revolutionary who had been imprisoned with Gaddafi just before the revolution. They were known as the Comrades and had immense privileges Gaddafi never forgot those who had been loyal to him. The Indian army slogan was 'Do you have it in you?' We were certainly prepared and rearing to leave for four years in New Delhi.

Sixteen
١٦

When writing about 'Incredible India' it is a place that I have hardly thought of since leaving. It was meant to be a four – year posting and resulted in only three. I wonder if it is selective memory loss or that I have seen other places that have been more significant. India was memorable, but not for good reasons. It was earmarked as a hardship posting due to the infamous health issues, the climate, the marked disparity between rich and poor and the unimaginable dirt and squalor. These hardships were exacerbated by our finally having to leave early, having been put on the Libyan black list. Perhaps I can be forgiven for not placing India high on my list of positive experiences.

I had flown to London before leaving Libya to say goodbye to my father and friends. It was no longer going to be a quick hop skip and a jump to London but rather a long haul expensive flight although I hoped that friends would take advantage of our being in Delhi and come and visit. When travelling to a new place I have one must – read book 'The Lonely Planet'. Having bought a copy in London it was read and reread, looking avidly at the photographs of places and sights that I imagined we would visit. We had decided to treat ourselves to a five star hotel for our first couple of nights, which proved to be another piece of good luck or fate. As is the protocol, Bashir sent a fax to the embassy advising them of our arrival time and requesting a car to meet us.

It was midnight when we landed in Delhi at the beginning of June. The monsoon had not arrived resulting in an unbearably hot heat just like an oven with people absolutely everywhere; you are never alone in India. We searched for an embassy staff member but no card with Bashir's name or a Libyan face. A telephone call to the embassy had equally zero result. Thankfully we had brought cash and decided that a taxi was the only option and on being asked whether we wanted an ambassador car or a scooter, naturally, we asked for the former. Waiting for the car, at one point I saw a rat climbing up Bashir's leg and there were beggars everywhere, sleeping on the concrete outside, a pretty grim introduction to the country. The car that arrived to take us to the hotel was similar to the one my father had owned in 1956 then named a Morris Oxford. This was certainly not the car we had visualised but with no apparent choice that was our form of transport to the hotel. We learned that the Morris car had been bought for production in India and renamed the Ambassador. It was an uncomfortable, gas – guzzler with no air conditioning. Thank goodness we had the reservation at the Oberoi Hotel, as it was a quiet, clean, luxurious oasis. I rushed to the hotel hairdresser to treat myself, something that was banned in Tripoli and came out feeling totally refreshed and ready for anything.

We knew we would be unable to afford the Oberoi for long it was therefore down to the recommendations of the embassy staff to help in finding somewhere to rent. The Libyan embassy was not responsible for paying our rent, diplomats chose how much or how little they wanted to spend on accommodation. People may have an idea that diplomats live in wonderfully opulent places and are well looked – after and this *is* generally true, however, one has to remember that Gaddafi was not in favour of diplomats, so Libyans were an exception to this customary rule. Things were changing slightly; since Lockerbie, Gaddafi had begun to realise the competence and usefulness of diplomats. Thus, we were on our own for organising flights, paying for the shipment of our possessions and selecting where to live. We also had to find medical and other services, always relying on established colleagues for information. The Libyan taste and knowledge in such things was generally rather sketchy but ask about a good shopping tip and they were winners. In fact as time passed we became the oracle for doctors, dentists in fact anything other than shops.

When looking through lists of Delhi hotels today I am absolutely astounded by the choice and number; Delhi has truly changed. We arrived in 1992 the commencement of the opening up of the economy but when still there were a limited number of mid – range hotels from which to choose. It was either a few luxurious five – star or numerous backpacker hotels to opt for, not much in between. The third day of our arrival and it was time to move to our new hotel which had been chosen on the recommendation of the embassy staff. It was going to be a come down from the lovely Oberoi, but on walking up the stairs to our room in the Rashdut, the stench of mouse urine was indescribable. The room was little better but on that evening we could not move as we knew of nowhere else to go. Bashir, putting on a brave face, said it wasn't as bad as it looked, which we both knew wasn't really true. It was a noisy night as we had numerous little guests in the room in the form of either rats or mice as well as the scuttling of cockroaches adding to this nightmare. Bashir left for the office in the morning and as I looked out of the window there on the balcony were three huge, ugly and mean – looking vultures pecking on the window. I was later to discover that the hotel was close to the Parsi temple. There was absolutely no way I was going to stay in this hotel so I pulled out my trusty 'Lonely Planet' and discovered Claridges. Obviously by no stretch of the imagination comparable to the London hotel of course but it met our criteria of being clean, central, with a lovely garden and helpful staff. It was to be our home for the next month. We found 33 Panchsheel Park to be our Delhi home but it needed painting and repairs and this being India what would have taken a week anywhere else, took a month.

It was finally the time to move in meanwhile we had had to buy furniture as rented property in Delhi generally came unfurnished. The embassy gave us a loan and thankfully with the money that I had from selling Frognal we were able to order a car from Dubai and we became license plate number *CD88 8* a lucky number for many. The Libyan foreign ministry either had no idea what a struggle it was, or did not care. I think also that diplomats were so desperate to leave Libya and earn a foreign currency salary that they were unwilling to rock the boat by complaining about their salary or allowances. Embassies were graded from being an easy posting to a hardship and obviously the latter paid the most. Additionally when it came to the housing allowance, this was related to the cost of living.

Bashir had a special philosophy when inspection units came to visit a mission. Most people wanted to put the inspection team in the best hotel and take them to the best markets and the top restaurants. Bashir's policy was to put them into a hotel guaranteed to have creepy crawlies and where they would get upset stomachs. It was rather cruel but then they would be sure to award Delhi a hardship posting which would mean a higher salary. All shopping also was to be done in the most expensive supermarkets.

It worked, Delhi was graded a hardship post, and a salary increase was assigned for all.

I could tell tale after tale of Delhi life but many of them would be similar to those told by so many travellers and Diplomats. For us Delhi would prove to be a hardship posting for both of us health wise. For Bashir it was continued bouts of giardia, amoebic dysentery and some kind of parasite that seemed to resurrect itself annually for over a decade. For me it was dengue fever, something I would not wish on my worst enemy. At the height of this mosquito borne infection, I was unable to eat solids, was only drinking through a straw, had a temperature of 40C and no antibiotic seemed to be working despite repeated blood tests. Thankfully once again the jungle drums came to my rescue and a friend managed to locate an American doctor who was in Delhi at that time doing research on dengue fever. He brought a new set of pills and almost immediately my temperature dropped. I was lucky; at one point Bashir was thinking to order my coffin. It took me six months to regain my energy levels. India is not for the faint – hearted, this was especially true at that time.

In order to understand what happened later, it is necessary to be aware of the makeup of the embassy. The ambassador was a career diplomat who enjoyed writing reports but disliked socialising. He was newly married to a much younger bride, whose brother was powerful in the revolutionary committees, probably the reason for his being posted as an ambassador. Then there was Abdullah, responsible for the Green Book Centre and all of its related perks, who as mentioned previously was a comrade of Gaddafi. The next in the scale was an old diplomat at ministerial level, El Gout. He was lazy, incompetent, had appalling English and was on his final posting. There was Ali Habat, the Financial Attaché and Nfez, the Administration Attaché and finally Fauzi the Vice Consul. The one who I would single out was Khalifa from the Intelligence, who was also responsible for visas as the Consul. He was ignorant, spoke no English whatsoever, and thought everyone was either a spy or a Gaddafi opponent. He was a colonel and powerful with Gaddafi and later he would become one of the butchers of Benghazi. Due to his presence all personnel were on their toes when he was around and we were especially careful to keep out of his way.

What dominated the first two years in Delhi for Bashir were Libya's attempts to prevent economic sanctions being voted in by the UN

Security Council as a result of the Lockerbie atrocity. The West was demanding the handover of Megrahi and Fhimah for trial while Gaddafi refused to acknowledge being complicit in the PanAm bombing. In April 1992 Resolution 748 was passed but with India abstaining. The resolution imposed a no fly zone over Libya, which was why our departure from Libya had involved flying from Djerba, Tunisia. There would be a succession of high – level special envoys from Libya to lobby India as they held a place on the Security Council at that time and an abstention could be critical in a resolution not being passed. In 1992, Umar Mustafa Muntasir replaced Jadallah as Foreign Minister. He had previously been a Prime Minister and was a tough negotiator and highly competent. Gaddafi for once was choosing able negotiators to head up his government. Muntasir was the first envoy to come to Delhi arriving on a private jet I was to learn later belonging to Tiny Rowland, the CEO of Lonrho

Gaddafi tended to catch all kinds of people in his net, but how and why Tiny Rowland should have been one of his fish I do not know. One has to suspect, as with everything involving Gaddafi, money was involved. This is only my personal suspicion. Tiny Rowland had been born in India to a Dutch mother and German father. His mother had nicknamed him Tiny because of his large size at birth and the name stuck throughout his life. At the end of the First World War the family moved from India to Berlin and from there to London. Tiny served in the British Armed forces during World War II and after the war in 1946 he went to Southern Rhodesia, later to become Zimbabwe, and began working for the London Mining and Land Company which was later to become Lonrho. The company had large controlling stakes in British newspapers, hotels, the textile industry and many other different lines of business. When and how he began his association with Gaddafi or even why, people can only speculate. In December 1993 an article in the Financial Times revealed that Hemar Enterprises had been responsible for the making of a documentary film entitled 'The Maltese Cross – Lockerbie'. Hemar was owned by Metropole Hotels, which was controlled by Rowland. The film stated Libya had no responsibility for the bombing. Shortly after this exposure, Rowland sold a percentage of his interests in the Libyan Arab Investment Company, controlled by the Libyan government. In 1993 he was forced to step down as Chairman of Lonhro; it is unknown whether this was before or after he met with Muntasir in Delhi. Whatever the intrigue and deals he had done by 1995 he was dismissed also from the Board of Lonrho due to conjecture surrounding his association with Gaddafi and the financing of the film. Many would learn during the sanctions era that there were huge profits to be made from association with Gaddafi, but by putting one's fingers in his pot one could just as easily get burnt. A Gaddafi connection was only for risk takers and gamblers.

How did I come to know of the Tiny Rowland connection with Libya? When Omar Muntasir came to Delhi with his wife I being the only female in the embassy that had learnt my way around the city, spoke English as well as a bit of Arabic, was nominated to accompany her. I have to say it was a great pleasure and although I never met her again after the visit, I have very positive thoughts on the three days and evenings we spent together. Muntasir took an immediate shine to Bashir who was ordered to accompany him everywhere. Talks were arranged with the Indian Prime Minister, Foreign Minister and secret meetings with Tiny Rowland, perhaps with his intervention in various quarters but this is only speculative. On the second day the Minister's wife and I were sitting in their suite when the phone rang and she asked me to answer the call. A male voice asked for the Minister and on being told he was unavailable I was asked to relay the message that Tiny had called and would meet him at some downtown venue at 4 pm. When the Minister returned with Bashir, I passed on the message and they left almost immediately afterwards. I later asked Bashir if I had spoken to Tiny Rowland. Bashir blinked but admitted yes, but that it was a top – secret meeting and I was not to mention it to anyone. Bashir commented that Tiny was quite intimidating, physically imposing with a real presence. Private Eye used to call him 'Tiny but perfect' as he was always impeccably groomed, Bashir laughed at this but said it was entirely accurate. Gaddafi always managed to have strange bedfellows. I am unsure of what Tiny's role was but people such as he always hedged their bets and had fingers in many pies, acting as intermediaries in countless deals.

Special Envoy visits were exhausting as the Ambassador always relied on Bashir. He loved this demanding work, especially at that high level. Once more the words of his former Head of Department had proved to be true; small embassies were the best training ground for young diplomats to gain experience. When Major Jalloud came the visit was completely different as he came with an army of his personal security sweeping all of the rooms for bugs, stationing his own guards outside the suite and demanding military precision, although always tempered with more than a couple of whiskies. The final special envoy was the Minister of Agriculture whose wife went on a shopping spree buying carpets it took two cars to take these to the airport. It seemed as if it was 'unto those that hath shall more be given' in Gaddafi's world of cronies.

UN sanctions imposing the no fly zone had caused innumerable logistical problems in running the country with the main beneficiaries being the Maltese and Tunisians. Gaddafi had absolutely no room to manoeuver and the Americans and British wanted to squeeze him even more. Gaddafi knew what was inevitably going to be imposed, hence the visits of Muntasir, Jalloud and finally the Minister of Agriculture, but by September 1993 the writing was on the wall that financial resources were about to be frozen. Billions of dollars were transferred to newly set up accounts with Middle Eastern banks and then transferred onto embassies with instructions to withdraw all the monies and hold the cash in the embassies.

Withdrawing the dollars and taking them to the embassy had to be one of the more bizarre tasks that Bashir was required to accomplish. He and the Financial Attaché drove to the embassy bank in two cars, and using diplomatic bags each withdrew a million dollars in cash. This exercise was repeated on three consecutive days. It was accomplished first thing in the morning so as not to draw attention as to what they were carrying or doing. If I had known at the time what was happening I would have been deeply concerned for his safety. I am constantly to repeat these words in the stories told in this book possibly ignorance was bliss at the time. It only would have taken just one tip off to lead robbers to hold them up. They had no protection whatsoever. When Bashir talked about it later he joked that perhaps he should have set up a heist and we would have been rich. He laughed and said if he were ever to take a bribe it would have to be for millions so that he could disappear and live a comfortable, incognito life. In fact India was an intrinsically corrupt country where bribes were commonplace, and there were some working in the Libyan embassy, especially in the visa section who took many sweetners. Bashir always returned every gift or gave it to embassy staff saying he wanted to be able to sleep at night and not fear someone coming to his door to arrest him. He always slept the sleep of the just.

On the 1st December 1993 despite all the lobbying under Resolution 883, all countries were required to freeze funds or other financial resources. The resolution did not apply to funds or other financial resources derived from the sale or supply of petroleum products. There was however, a prohibition on refining equipment and spare pumps, which would put increasing pressure on the Libyan oil companies. Libya had in a way escaped lightly; they still had their oil revenues untouched but the stranglehold of sanctions were beginning to bite.

Bashir's work was extremely demanding and time consuming. I am a natural fidget and like to be kept busy and to be just a decorative, hostess diplomatic wife was insufficient to keep me active. This led to my initial Indian teaching project. Our driver Ashok on being employed spoke no English. For the first six months he worked for us every morning I gave him a half hour English lesson and his progress was fast. He also learned how to guard the car and how to work for an embassy. We went on our first trip out of Delhi at Christmas and Ashok was instructed to report for duty on our return. He never materialised and on finally talking to him he told us that he had found a new, better paid job thanks to us having trained and taught him English. His newly purchased uniform did not fit our new driver. We later saw him driving a British expatriate banker with whom salary wise we could not compete. I did not learn my lesson as when a new driver started again I repeated the English lessons and was rewarded with that driver once more leaving for a better – paid job as he too had now acquired good spoken English. It was then that Gumbandra took over. He was an enormous man from Nepal and looked like Odd Job from the Bond movies. No one messed with Gumbandra; he was loyal and reliable and stayed with us until we left Delhi.

It may seem arrogant to talk about having a driver. I absolutely cannot deny it was for me one of the absolute luxuries in life and one of the few things I do miss in my changed circumstances. I don't know how to drive and have never wanted to, perhaps because of having been brought up in London. Tubes and buses of London Public transport have served me better than inching along London's busy roads in a car. There was, however, another reason for employing a driver in that both Indian public transport and the taxi drivers were very hazardous. By having our own car and driver we were assured of a better level of safety. I think also since Iyat had been killed in Kampala, Bashir was always worried about shootings and bombings. I was to have a driver throughout our life together commencing in Delhi with Gumbandra, followed by Yusif, Khalifa, Yahya, and Jericho who were all my guardians and companions for so many years and have been brilliant and loyal right up until today. I'm grateful for the care they took in protecting us both. We always did our best to make sure that the drivers that showed good character received the best training we could offer them. We endeavoured and thankfully were always successful in finding these loyal employees good jobs on our departure from the country. It was the very least we could do for them.

My second attempt at teaching was at the Japanese Embassy School. The Government had decided that they wished to introduce EFL into the primary schools and as a pilot scheme chose to use the Delhi school. I should have smelt a rat as after starting at the school I discovered that my predecessor had only stayed for a month. Perhaps one has a stereotypical picture of well – behaved and polite Japanese school children, but this was not the case with Japanese expatriate children who were in many cases lacking in discipline and extremely naughty. In the end on the advice of a colleague I had to resort to bribery games at the end of each lesson, and sweeties as rewards. It was not a pedagogically sound approach but it did work until such tricks were no longer necessary and normal teaching methods were adopted. The Ministry of Education arrived once a month to video my lessons and write a report. It was very demanding but a great introduction to setting up an English department in a foreign school. Sweeties were not dished out during filming needless to say and the children knew to behave themselves. The school gave me a wonderful reference when I left and that was to be helpful when applying for future posts. I came into teaching by chance and every new job that I have had has been a stepping – stone into a more involved and rewarding role. I do recommend it as a career to all women, at any stage in life, as a brilliant way to achieve financial independence with unaccountable rewards from the teaching.

This brings me to perhaps the most rewarding and worthwhile of the three teaching jobs in New Delhi. In 1993 Indian children without a permanent fixed address or birth certificate were unentitled to attend school and thus orphans did not receive any education. I had visited Mother Theresa's orphanage in New Delhi but nothing prepared me for what I found at the orphanage in Old Delhi. This was before the days of the new metro system and it was a nightmare to reach. A series of old decrepit buildings with perhaps five rooms housing cots with a majority of tiny mostly female babies, some of whom had been left at the gates of the orphanage. Female children were especially unwanted as they would in the future require a dowry and thus be a financial burden on a family. There were a few older children, probably up to the age of eight or nine, all of them were minimally dressed and infected with head lice. The place was very dirty and although the nuns did their best, the majority of local staff were neglectful and seemed to be uncaring.

I, along with two friends had come up with the idea that we could visit the orphanage twice a week and spend the mornings teaching English concepts such as colours, numbers, size, weather, nursery rhymes and songs through fun learning activities. By teaching concepts in English these would be understood later when it came for the children to learn the new language of their adopted parents. Initially we had few resources but each week we brought a new activity with which to teach the children. They knew our day and arrival time. Our cars were surrounded with their smiling chattering faces, delighted that here were people who were going to break the monotony of their daily lives. It was an overwhelming welcome. Soon they had learnt the songs such as *head, shoulders, knees and toes* and there would be special requests. We would then break up into three age groups, doing different activities. Leaving was the hardest as they would cling and beg us to take them to our homes. It was an uplifting experience knowing that we were helping these children in a very small way but at the same time feeling what we were doing was inadequate and minimal to their needs. This orphanage was visited by few expatriates being in old Delhi, unlike the one in New Delhi. I used to come home and go straight to the shower feeling dirty from the sweltering heat and the squalor of the orphanage. Old Delhi highlighted the injustice of how place of birth so marginalises one's chances in life.

We casually started talking about our project to friends resulting in people giving us their children's discarded toys and clothes and so our suitcases became bigger and bigger and we started to have better and better resources with which to teach. As word spread the numbers of volunteers working with us increased until we had teams working with the children five days a week. What had started as a small idea was starting to blossom as people also wished to give us donations to buy materials to better facilitate the learning of these children. One mother whose daughter was at Millfield public school brought her daughter for sessions during the school holidays. Millfield boarding houses were required to take on a charitable project and during the year raise money in support of their venture. The daughter took photographs of our teaching activities to raise awareness and through her school house we received further funds.

At this point we had a dilemma since we were no longer just a group of friends visiting an orphanage but had reached the level financially of being a charity and had then to declare ourselves as such to the Indian tax authorities. We had become too successful, people wanted to support us precisely because they knew that the money would not go into our pockets as did so much charitable funding. Many truly well intentioned donations were wasted on bureaucracy, squandered on charitable misadventure or demanded as bribes or simply embezzled.

I volunteered at the orphanage for eighteen months, came to know all the children seeing some go to European homes and others growing older with few hopes of any kind of future. They were protected and fed in the orphanage but there would come a time if they were unable to find a family, when they would be on their own. Our project had only taught basic maths and writing skills in English through fun with a little compassion. Hanging above my bed today is a print by Hussain, probably the most famous contemporary Indian artist. The husband of one of the three of us worked for 'The Financial Times' and had interviewed Hussain for his paper and told him of our project. Hussain had created a series of limited prints of a faceless Mother Theresa nun holding a faceless Indian child. We were each offered the opportunity to buy one of these prints at a heavily reduced price. It is a daily reminder that whatever my feelings are when I wake in the morning on looking at the print I know that there are millions of people who wake up to loneliness and suffering every day. I have lived a privileged and happy life, for which I am ever grateful.

I was never to see the outcome of our small venture. My driver Gumbandra, although having been told time after time not to tell anyone where I went or who I saw, had been threatened by the Intelligence Officer Khalifa, spilled the beans and accordingly my charitable work became one of two nails in Bashir's Indian coffin. The orphanage nail was one of the two that sent us to the graveyard for eight barren years.

Two of the teaching projects had been voluntary but due to the

Japanese school being an embassy school I was able to work there without the necessity of a work permit and received a good salary. Thus I was able to buy treats and surprises and also to help in building our savings for when we had to return to Libya and live once again on Bashir's pitiful government salary. Bashir's family always seemed to like the thought of my working and in 2011 I was to discover why. Bashir and I had joint bank accounts as we shared our money completely; we shared life and there were never disputes over any aspect of it. He encouraged me to be less cautious when it came to money. He believed in enjoying one's money and not dying the richest person in the graveyard. My birthday is in January and as a Capricorn I was compatible with Bashir's September Virgo sign. Bashir had his horoscope read in India and was told that in the near future he would have a comfortable lifestyle and buy a one – storey home facing south. Both these predictions would come true.

For holidays I went back to London to see my father and friends but of course always without Bashir this was impossible. It weighed heavily on his mind and at times he would become quite maudlin, not knowing how we could get the ban lifted. At one point, through a friend in the Tunisian embassy, Bashir was approached by the CIA and we felt, though dangerous, this could possibly have been a route to clearing his name. After many clandestine meetings he felt that the demands they were making were too great and they seemed to have little real understanding of the situation in Libya. The water was already muddy and it did not need to become even murkier with third party involvement added to which on both sides there was mistrust. He was also not a gambler and believed that they would buy and sell one as they saw fit and that was something that he did not need. He was a career diplomat, not a double agent spook.

During our whole time in India Bashir never went back to Libya as the government only paid for a home ticket once every two years for someone of his grade. It is quite incredible how poorly diplomats were paid when expatriate workers in Libya were given at least four tickets home a year. His non return to Libya during the posting would raise question marks with the Libyan intelligence as to why he did not want to go home. Surely there was nowhere as great as Libya? Unfortunately, during this period the Libyan working week was six days. This meant that we were restricted from going away for weekend trips but we had teamed up with our wonderful Swiss friends David and Tamara and regularly on a Sunday

145

we would go off on a cultural expedition be it to a gallery, local ruins, a concert or an event. We were also able to take two long holidays, both of which were memorable.

The first was to the obligatory golden triangle trio of Agra and the Taj Mahal, Fatepur Sikri and Jaipur and we added on a trip to Corbett in the hope of seeing a Royal Bengal tiger; we had not lost our love of wildlife safari quests. The tiger hunt proved to be just that as all that we saw were supposed footprints. We never met anyone who had actually seen a tiger there except in photos, reminding us of the comic Indian film on the same topic. The trip was in bitterly cold December and the rooms were unheated so we never took off our clothes the whole time; nights were totally unromantic. Never losing our adventurous spirit we returned to Delhi for a flight down to the Andaman Islands. After Seychelles we were horrified to see how the coral had been destroyed as well as the forests by logging. There seemed to be a total lack of care, attention or perhaps even awareness of the destruction of this astonishingly beautiful environment. It was a breathtaking spot in India that was later to be hard hit by the tsunami in 2004.

Perhaps one of the most luxurious trips that we took was to Malaysia. Bashir had been there in 1976 and was staggered at the development of Kuala Lumpur and perhaps it illustrated once again the lack of interest on Gaddafi's part in developing Libya. Rather, he chose to use the Libyan money to build grandiose palatial projects named after him in Africa and selected parts of Asia. I have always wondered again and again why he never developed Libya, his own country. I heard rather wild stories that as he had a Jewish parentage connection, that he had suffered racism as a child and that this was his revenge on the Libyan people. Personally I found this idea extremely far – fetched and typical of anti – Jewish Arab conspiracy theories. I think rather it was that his grandiose image of himself was indulged in Africa; he was an emotionally unstable megalomaniac, after all. This question needs an answer as to date I have never heard a reasonable response to the question.

After Kuala Lumpur we chose to visit the island of Penang, as this had been where my mother and father, like many Australians had visited in the 1930s. There were many pieces in our London childhood home of superb quality needlework produced on the island verification of which is that I am still using some of them today; delicate hand – embroidered towels and napkins. The island was still beautiful but one could see that without proper regard for the environment that this tropical island paradise could be severely damaged.

From Penang we moved to Langkawi and a chance problem resulted in us staying in unimaginable hotel luxury. Langkawi was the island where the 1989 Commonwealth Heads of State summit was held and a special village was built in traditional Malaysian style for the conference. We were thrilled with the village and after having had an enjoyable evening we returned to our room. On that evening and the following a drunken brawl strangely broke out between two of our neighbours. On the second night Bashir called Reception and asked for our room to be changed. It was just after the New Year so the hotel was very full but they assured us that by the morning we would be moved. A golf buggy arrived early to take us to the new room and we asked the driver if it was a good room. He just gave us a knowing smile and assured us that we would love it. We drove directly down to the beach and a row of large, wooden villas which had been built for the Heads of State attending the conference. Halfway along the beach our buggy stopped and we saw on a plaque 'this villa was occupied by the King of Swaziland in 1989.' This was where the management had decided to relocate us, a beautiful suite that was only to be charged at the original room rate. We joked that a drunken aggressive guest had turned into a week of living like a king. It was a more than memorable holiday.

After three years of living in India, we could afford to do things that would have been unaffordable elsewhere and Bashir decided he would like to celebrate my birthday with a party catered in the house by one of the five star hotels. This was the first time we had held such a party in India and we were full of excitement. On the night waiting for our guests to arrive the telephone rang it was to be the killer phone call. I could see by Bashir's face that something was desperately wrong and assumed immediately it must be his mother. On completing the call he turned ashen faced and said that he had been called to Libya for an investigation with the Finance Attaché, Ali and the Administrator, Nfez. I asked why? He kept a blank face and said it was nothing, just a formality. I really do not know how he managed to get through the party, always the perfect host and seemingly enjoying himself despite what he had just learnt. As ever, whatever the circumstances there was always the endeavour on his part to protect my welfare and feelings.

It has to be remembered that there was a no fly zone into Libya, therefore there was difficulty in not only choosing a route but even more difficult booking a seat on a flight. It was decided that I would go to London rather than stay in India and catch up with family and friends. We flew together to Jordan with Bashir flying on directly to Tunisia, from there to Djerba and finally a drive across the border into Libya. As my flight was late that night and having arrived early, I decided to visit Petra, something that I had wanted to do since childhood. The drive down through the Jordanian desert is quite unimpressive but Petra just left me astounded at the beauty of this ancient city. At that time there was just a sandy track into the city and inside there were only one or two other tourists, with no kiosks selling kitsch Bedouin souvenirs as we were to find in 2011. On my solo visit it was everything that I had imagined and more. I wish that Bashir had been able to visit Petra then and not in 2011 when it was so changed, in my opinion for the worse. Part of its mystery had been lost by commercialism.

Before leaving each other at the airport in Amman Bashir assured me that he would probably be back within a week and there was no cause for concern. Once again there would be the problem of no telephone communication as the bill for the telephone in the Shkuka home remained unpaid. It was not one week, not two but rather three and as each week went by I grew more and more concerned. This *was* Libya but at that time I had absolutely no inkling as to why he was actually in the dragon's lair. On his return I was to learn about the consequences of chatting casually against Gaddafi.

As mentioned previously, the Intelligence Officer in the embassy was Khalifa with his incessant reporting to his bosses on anything he perceived to be against the Leader or his Green Book beliefs. Apparently Nfez had been in Bashir's office along with Ali the Finance Attache the latter who had been talking against Gaddafi and was overheard by Khalifa. On the grounds that neither Bashir nor Nfez had reported Ali they were considered by Khalifa to be complicit and all three were called to Libya under suspicion of conspiring against the regime. This was horrifically serious and could have resulted in imprisonment or even far worse. Bashir told the other two to absolutely deny the conversation whatever the investigators tried to say or imply. Day after day Bashir was called to Tajoura, the headquarters of the Libyan Intelligence with them levelling accusations against him as were they also against the other two. Additionally a further major charge was my charity work at the Mother Theresa Orphanage. Bashir was accused of having a Christian fundamentalist wife of not having married a Libyan woman in the first place and of mixing too much with foreign diplomats. These were ill informed ignorant men who quite obviously thought that the work of a diplomat was to go abroad and sit in one's house and just go to the office between 8am and 2pm six days a week collecting the salary at the end of the month.

Concerning my visits to the orphanage Bashir pointed out that he had received orders from the Ministry to discuss bringing some of the nuns to work in Libya and that as this was the case I was hardly breaking the law by doing charitable work with the Mother Theresa order. Obviously the charge against Ali was the most serious and throughout the three long weeks of investigation they continued to strongly deny the allegations. At one point Nfez wanted to agree but Bashir prevented him, explaining that in doing so, firstly he would in all probability be sending Ali to an indefinite prison sentence or possibly worse and by not having reported the fact he could suffer an unknown fate. Nfez did not waiver and neither did Ali or Bashir although the outcome was that they were recalled to Libya with immediate effect and put on the 'Black List'. What I was not to learn until arriving back to our house in Gargaresh was that despite being paid to look after the house and acting as an agent, Lamin was as negligent as he was to prove time after time but as happy as ever to take our money. He was both greedy and self – serving.

Bashir and I reunited in Jordan and flew on directly to Delhi where I learned the details of those harrowing weeks and once again I could see it had taken a heavy toll on his health. Bashir was given one month in which to sell up and return to Libya. He was, in effect, a disgraced diplomat. As you may remember when we arrived in India the house rental agreement had been unfurnished and we had had to buy all the furniture and electronics. We did not wish to take any of the furniture back to Libya so were tasked with the unenviable job of putting advertisements in the paper and selling our things. Indians are tough negotiators when it comes to money deals and we were beaten down on every occasion and frankly we were in no mood to do anything but leave. The atmosphere in the embassy was completely sour and full of fear from Khalifa as to where his heavy hand would fall next.

Bashir tried through all of his contacts to have the order revoked but once again so – called friends and colleagues, perhaps understandably, faded into the woodwork. The die was cast and we were returning to Libya at least together but to an unknown future. Bashir was on the 'Black Lists' ironically now of both the UK and Libya and his mood was dark.

When we had first arrived in India and moved into Panshcheel Park the front and back gardens were bare apart from rough grass. With our joint love of gardening and flowers at the start of our tour we had brought the embassy gardener to ask his advice as to what to plant. He was given some money for seeds, bougainvillea and a couple of other trees. In the spring our garden was absolutely blooming amongst other things with huge poppies. In our ignorance we later discovered that the gardener was harvesting opium from slits in the buds and had created a little opium – growing field in our back garden. We kindly asked him to desist from such activity.

I wish to end our India chapter by mentioning when we left Panscheel Park we had created a small oasis of trees and flowers. This was our tiny legacy and would be repeated wherever we lived as our contribution to the environment.

Seventeen

١٧

Nothing was predictable living under the Gaddafi dictatorship and as a result subconsciously we only ever lived in the moment, trying not to focus too much on the future. This was something that was unspoken between us but it very much guided our lives and relationship. There never was or could be any long term planning. Being on the blacklist of two countries simultaneously made daily life just survival. In many ways it brought us closer, perhaps making us less ambitious and less willing to take any risks. It gave us a personal harmony. It is not really worth contemplating how life would have been if we had been together in a safer environment. There were never any *what ifs*.

It most certainly was not a happy homecoming in any sense. Just before I entered our home in Gargaresh, Bashir held my hand and murmured gently to be prepared for the house not being exactly as it had been left. This was one of Bashir's definitely understated diplomatic euphemisms for what was to come. I knew that the Philippine Labour Attaché had left after only six months, having fallen out of favour with the Libyans, but other than that had heard nothing. On entering, I found the wonderful collection of coffee table art books that I had acquired over the years strewn all over the hall floor with watermarks where there had obviously been a flood. Someone had thrown them out of the bookcase in an attempt to stop them being destroyed by water. In the sitting room there was no furniture, no pictures, none of my childhood knickknacks. On walking into the dining room we beheld the similarly miserable sight of bare, white walls just the black outline marks of where paintings had hung; every painting had been lifted as were the beautiful ebony and stone sculptures that we had bought in Kenya. Likewise in the kitchen every cupboard was empty. As I wandered through the house with tearfilled eyes I felt completely overcome with utter despair after all that had happened in recent months and now this theft of all of our belongs and the desecration of our home. The story that Lamin, our designated guardian gave was that the house had been burgled. How could heavy pieces of furniture have been removed without anyone noticing was beyond me but *everything* had been removed, even down to knives and forks, and the plastic garden furniture, nothing was left. Lamin apologized for the neglect adding that one night he had forgotten to turn off the water tap in the bathroom. On returning to the house some weeks later he found the whole house flooded, destroying my beloved art books and all of our carpets. I was absolutely mortified, we were not only back in Libya under a dark cloud but also our house had been ransacked. As we walked out into our walled garden there was yet a further shock. On looking up at the terraced house with which we shared a common party wall I saw the final disaster. Our neighbours had built up three storeys with a balcony overlooking our garden. The result of the building meant we no longer had the privacy of our little garden and natural light to our sitting room was totally blocked. Bashir had been reluctant to tell me I think, perhaps because he was afraid of my reaction, which was utter heartbreak. I was especially upset, as I had already been burgled twice in London and lost a great many personal possessions from my childhood. This would be the last time that I ever grew attached to possessions. I had thought what few treasures were left these I would be able to keep; even this was not to be. I became a minimalist; I would now only have my memories they could not be stolen. This was the second time our Libyan house had been invaded and robbed and from hereon I was hardened to it. I cried bitterly for two days non – stop until there were no tears left. Meanwhile I knew as ever I had to get on with the reality, rebuild my life yet again. In retrospect this was an extremely hard lesson although, I do think that perhaps all of us place too much value on our possessions and that there are better and more important things to value in life. One has good years and bad years and although the actual New Year in Delhi had started out in real style with us being upgraded to the honeymoon suite at the Taj Hotel, that was about as far as our good luck went that year.

Once back in Libya we were facing being on the UK and Libya black lists, the ransacked house, the ugly next – door building overlooking our garden and blocking out our light and Bashir's family once again urging Bashir to get divorced. They argued that I had been part of the problem with him being recalled from India. I was too strong willed and also we still didn't have any children. What they never asked, or wanted to know was whether we wanted children and if either of us had a medical problem which would prohibit us from having children. This once again was complete gender discrimination. It resulted in my having a very frosty reception when meeting them on our return. I think this was probably to lead in part to their justification of 9/36, since they never saw any reason why I should be part of their family, regardless of Bashir's wishes. At that time these thoughts never occurred to me. I remained true to myself, endeavoured to do the right thing, and always went with Bashir to visit his mother keeping, my mouth firmly shut. Bashir as ever, had a very fatalistic and karmic approach to those who brought injustice on others. He believed that the universe would bring their actions back on them in kind, and that God would take care of unresolved grievances on Judgement Day. Today all of the eldest boys in the three Shkuka families are childless.

Despite being on the Libyan black list, Bashir was allowed to re – join his old International Organisations Department. He was made Head of Agencies; a post he was to love. This put him in the teaching role with the young attaches in the section and he relished giving them opportunities to travel on missions and gain experience. I met a number of these young men in Libya and abroad and it was obvious how much they appreciated Bashir's guidance over the years and had taken it on board. How he could be on a black list and yet still be working at the Foreign Ministry was surprising but a common mantra in those days was that everything in Libya was possible, and nothing was impossible.

I returned to working at the British School sadly under the leadership of a new head; Russ having returned to Canada. With teaching qualifications and experience under my belt I taught years 5 and 6 English and gave support teaching to EAL children who needed help to come up to scratch. The latter helped build my reputation in the community, as when a child achieves success parents are mindful of the fact that a teacher may have been instrumental in enabling them to reach set goals. Within a very short time, I had a waiting list for private lessons at home.

Libya had changed to some extent in the three years we had been away. Perhaps most noticeable of all were the satellite dishes on the top of many of the houses. I am unsure why Gaddafi gave permission for these to be allowed after so many years of controlling the press and media. Suddenly the Libyans had access to 24 – hour news from all parts of the world. It was still only 1996, the early days of satellite TV, but stations were developing and for those Libyans who had never travelled beyond perhaps Saudi Arabia for pilgrimages, it was a window to the rest of the world. The Libyan youth saw how they were being marginalized by the Gaddafi regime, while the Leader and his family seemed to be living like royalty although we were all meant to be *partners not wage workers*. Something was very wrong.

Private shops were opening and the huge government shops built at the beginning of the 80s had turned into derelict, grey, concrete mausoleums. There were essentially three jobs in Libya: 1) Government worker / military service person. 2) Oil industry employee. 3) Black marketeer / small shop owner. Due to the sanctions and no – fly zone into Libya, the people adjusted to being self – employed suitcase vendors. I am continually amazed how these young Libyan lads, speaking no English at all, travel to all parts of the world where they believe they can source a product to make a profit. How they manage to negotiate, I couldn't even guess, but undoubtedly they reach a good deal and bring their wares back to Libya for sale. The Libyans are good business people and know how to strike a hard bargain. These enterprising youths unable to find employment in Gaddafi's corrupt system, were determined to make a life for themselves.

There did seem to be a more relaxed atmosphere in the country despite the sanctions. I am sure this was in part because the Chad war was now consigned to the past. Unfortunately people had short memories or chose to blank out the Gaddafi atrocities. The austerity of the 80s coupled with the realization of quite how isolated Libya had become due to Lockerbie, plus the hangings and disappearances of opponents resulted in people just wanting to get on with their lives as best they could within the constraints of the Gaddafi regime. They had learnt to live without freedom of speech and democracy and these had become long forgotten aspirations.

Generally when someone returns from a period abroad, friends and relatives would come and welcome the person back home. In our case this was not what happened, perhaps because the family had told people they were hoping Bashir would divorce me, which of course might open up the chance of him being a potential husband for one of their daughters. Probably, most likely was the fact that he had been blacklisted by the regime and people wanted to distance themselves from us for fear of being associated by the regime. Since Omar Montasir was still the Foreign Minister and had taken a shine to Bashir in India, Bashir wrote a memorandum explaining his situation and asking for an interview. The Minister agreed and was as affable as ever but explained that he was unable to interfere in intelligence matters, much as he wished he could be of help. His advice was not to worry and that in time it would blow over and be resolved. No one wanted to be seen treading on another's toes. The situation remained unresolved and we remained despondent.

Eighteen

I should like, if you will indulge me, to devote a chapter on the passing of my father and on attending his funeral alone without Bashir as a result of the UK visa ban.

I am ever thankful for my loving parents who created a home which nurtured learning. To my father perhaps more than anything, I still feel the warmth of his honesty and integrity. I shall thank him until the end of my days especially for the passion he developed in my love of words. Reading was my saviour, especially during the revolution. Wherever I may be if it is with a book I am content. On dark, cold, London, wintry nights now that I am alone books are my constant companions.

My childhood memory of books was waiting for my father to arrive home from work and then we would all curl up on one of my brothers' beds and the night's story would begin. First for William, followed by Anthony and then we would move to my room for my chapter. Stories were always stopped at an exciting point so we could hardly wait for the next evening to arrive to discover what happened, or sometimes we would even cheat and read ahead. The choice of book was my father's and many would be from his own childhood reading. Both he and my mother had somehow managed to keep many of these books which were magically or scarily illustrated making them even more enticing. He led us into a priceless library of different genres and all three of us have remained avid readers. No books were available in Libya, so whenever I went to England I would buy as many as I could afford or carry back to Libya and enjoyed giving them a first read. Thereafter they would be placed on the bookshelves waiting for my retirement. By putting them aside for later I knew I would always have a title to reread despite limited retirement finances.

One of the very few positive results on our return to Libya was that

Bashir managed to negotiate a deal with the Post Office on the dreaded telephone bill reducing it to approximately 1000 pounds; a heavy price to pay for someone else's futile indulgence. Nevertheless it meant that we were able to have a phone installed in the house, which was a lifesaver.

As a result of this breakthrough in August I received the phone call I had long been dreading my father had passed away peacefully. His Parkinson's disease had developed to such an extent that he had no longer been able to live at home with his second wife and was moved to the Forces Star and Garter Home in Richmond. I do believe in nature being kind as he had no quality of life. He spent his final days lying in bed, unable to speak and just looking vaguely at his visitors with his old, grey, tired, eyes. As his daughter my loss was to know that the quiet spoken, upright, honest, loving man, my father was no longer with us but equally there had to be the resolve that for him the leaving was a blessing. Another circle had been completed, since the Star and Garter was only a few houses away from where his two grandfathers had lived and Richmond – Upon – Thames, where he had been born. My brother lives in Richmond today on the same street where my Grandfather lived and the house we used to visit as children.

A quick solution had to be found to reach London without Bashir by my side for the funeral. It was on such an occasion that his presence would have been invaluable and comforting. He would have enabled me to pass through all the Libyan bureaucracy that one had to negotiate in order to leave the country. Now I would be on my own about to be pushed, shoved and jostled by the crowds, questioned by officials yet grieving for my father, and this just made it all the harder.

The implications of the no – fly zone made travelling from Libya a nightmare. There were only two exit routes from Tripoli, either to take an indirect 12 – hour road journey to Tunis airport or to take the ferry from Tripoli to Malta. My father died at the height of the holiday season and it seemed as if all Libya were travelling abroad. At every airline office there were queues trying to buy tickets for onward journeys. I have mentioned countless times if you do not have connections in Libya you are a ghost. The networking started by obtaining a berth on the ferry to Malta that night and an air ticket to catch an onward flight to London. On top of this there was still the exit/re – entry visa with its all important stamp needed to leave the country. This required a contact at Immigration. Thankfully we had Fawzi the former Libyan consul in Delhi and my visa was stamped in less than half an hour a miracle. Without his help it might have taken at least a couple of days.

That night I sailed to Malta. It was August and the sea was calm if not travelling for such a sad reason I could have imagined it being an expensive Mediterranean cruise. The reality was that the ship was old; it looked as if none of the lifeboats had ever been tested and the whole rusting ship was crawling with cockroaches. Nevertheless entering Malta harbour at dawn as the sun rose was a splendid sight. A taxi ride straight to the airport and a flight on to London completed the trip. I had to rely on my dear friends Penny and Steve once again for a place to stay. It was good to be with them as they had known my father since childhood and together we would be attending the funeral.

I think most people find it hard when a parent re – marries and my father had done so within two years of my mother's death. He had been lonely, he was not good at socializing without my mother and had little idea of how to feed, clean and look after himself, all of which had been done by Mummy. Olive filled that need and since we his children were living on three different continents were grateful that he had found her and she made him happy giving him a purpose in life once more. I actually wasn't hugely keen on her, but I had to respect her wishes when it came to my father's funeral, which was in a small church near where they had been living and then in a nearby crematorium. We had, however, made a stipulation that he had wanted his ashes to be spread around the old, yew tree where those of my mother had been scattered in what had been their local church for forty years. My mother was a devout Christian, my father an agnostic.

There were few people at the service as my father had moved away from our family home and he had not kept in touch with old family friends. My brother read the eulogy and he included one of my father's favourite poems and I quote from it. I often thought of these lines in my own life as being inspirational and a way never to lose hope. We knew them by heart as we had frequently heard Daddy read from the whole poem as children. This Autumn I travelled to Samarkand the desert heat, the clear, bright, blue cloudless skies beneath which were the astoundingly beautiful mosques revived my spirits. I heard his voice reciting this poem as I had so many times during his life time:

Hassan: The Road to Samarkand Ishak

We are the Pilgrims, master; we shall go
Always a little further; it may be
Beyond that last blue mountain barred with snow
Across that angry or glimmering sea,
While on a throne or guarded in a cave
There lies a prophet who can understand
Why we were born: but surely we are brave,
Who take the Golden Road to Samarkand.

– James Elroy Flecker

The Inheritance rights within families seems at times to result in family schisms. My parents had at no time shown gender differentiation when it came to their wills. The end of this book will show sharia inheritance law disbursement and how it affects women and particularly in my own case. When my mother died, her will had been written before the marriages of my two brothers. She requested that her estate be divided equally into three shares although she wished that I should receive all of her jewellery. After her death we found a draft letter for a new will, which wished for the jewellery bequest to include myself and my brothers' two wives. This letter was not a bona fide Will but in my mind it contained my mother's final wishes and so Sharman, Sylviana and I each took pieces from her collection. As far as the jewellery bequest was concerned I would have been absolutely within my rights to take everything, but I felt I had a moral obligation to do as my mother had written at the time of her death. When it came to my father's Will it was simple his estate should be divided between his three children. My parents saw no differentiation in our gender we were each to receive an equal share.

I write here about inheritance but it is interesting to remember that it was not until The Succession to the Crown Act 2013 in the United Kingdom whereby a first – born daughter could become queen, even if a younger brother is subsequently born. Cultural, social and economic changes take years, decades, even centuries but I do believe that when it comes to inheritance aside from the law there are also moral obligations. In 2014 The Law Society issued guidance, by way of a formal practice

159

note, on how to incorporate sharia law provisions in wills. This guidance details the following provisions which could be seen to discriminate against women, non – Muslims and "illegitimate" and adopted children. It states that male heirs in most cases receive double the amount inherited by a female heir of the same class. "Non – Muslims may not inherit at all, and only Muslim marriages are recognised." "..Illegitimate and adopted children are not Sharia heirs." It is a guidance and as such does not change the law, and in any case under the English law principle of testamentary freedom testators are free to discriminate if they so wish as long as they provide for their dependenants in accordance with the Inheritance Act 1975. By issuing this guidance the Law Society, whatever its intentions are offering politically neutral guidance and are not expressing views either way. Nevertheless it could be taken by those wishing for sharia enforcement to be an acknowledged as a way of gaining legitimisation and credibility. I write to raise awareness of this practice note as a warning to young non – Muslim women where marrying a Muslim could lead to inheritance according to the Islamic tradition rather than UK norms of fairness between children and the loss of their own wealth. The book title 9/36 reflects what was to occur in my future fight against the morale intransigence of the Shkuka family using the laws and edicts of sharia inheritance for their monetary gain.

Nineteen

My 1984 arrival in Libya had seen austerity and persecution but by the end of the 90s and up to the revolution in 2010 the country developed rapidly. It was the clandestine groups that grew during those years that have surfaced today who are the ones causing widespread turbulence and upheaval throughout the country and returning its people to those former days of terror.

Gaddafi's reign didn't end that long ago. It is easy to analyse it today with hindsight and speculate on what did and didn't happen and what should and shouldn't have been. Nonetheless, even with this 20/20 vision, there are elements of that 42 – year dictatorship, which remain puzzling. Perhaps more than anything, this period saw a growth in Islamist inspired opposition, which formulated into groups like the Muslim Brotherhood and the Libyan Islamic Fighting Group. Through his repression underground hornets' nests of extremism secretly flourished and today it is perhaps the most worrying factor of post – revolutionary Libya. Gaddafi had been the repressive guardian at the North African gate. Today he is gone and hell has been released throughout the country. This festering sore has developed into an active IS insurgency.

Examples of the deep – seated conservatism of Muslim Libya and its growth were increasingly apparent in Bashir's family through the years. His eldest brother Ibrahim had always been deeply religious, running his household with an iron fist. The second brother, Ismael had in the early 80s been a musician for one of the *Last Bullets,* Bulgassim Gangha, playing at his weekend parties where there was an abundance of drink, drugs and women. Ismael probably found it useful to be the court musician for this man as it enabled him to ask for favours. Later, on losing his job at the radio station possibly through being hung over and not going to the office, he one day claimed to have had 'revelations' and became even more religiously zealous that his fanatical older brother. Ismael's eldest son had always been deeply pious to a point of annoying Bashir to distraction, who found him ponderously dull. I remember teaching this son Ahmed English and on asking him once how he spent his free time he replied that the only activity he devoted any time to was reading the Koran. I was far removed from a life such as his and the increasing conservatism in the family was faintly worrying. I should add, however, that Ahmed is a well – meaning person; it was just that our lives were so *opposite* in every sense. I do respect his beliefs (as I do anyone's religion), but I also feel that it would have shown a little integrity, if he and his family were able to respect ours, which was never in their dictionary.

Much later in 2007, we met the HR manager for Emirates airlines in Malta. Bashir ever good at networking mentioned that Ismael's third son was working for a Libyan airline and perhaps there might be some openings for such a young man with Emirates? Her next assignment was to be interviewing in Tunis the following weekend and they exchanged business cards. Bashir was thrilled at this chance meeting and immediately called his nephew on our return. He was rewarded for his caring efforts with a dismissive, no thanks response that such a post was impossible because Emirates served alcohol on their flights. Bashir was hurt, both by the flippant rejection of his endeavours to help his family, and by the reason for it. This young man had no prospects whatsoever if he was to set such a criteria for himself; the global world, as well as the Middle East, had been moving on from such doctrines for a long time. I suppose, when considering our own revolution in England and the response of the Cromwellian Levellers, their parallels to the Muslim Brotherhood are significant. Both grew out of movements that stood out against what they saw as foreign occupation, both were/are religious puritans of a pretty rigorous kind, both were/are powered by grassroots activism and both were/are unsound on women. Perhaps it just needs time before a more stable and diverse culture settles across Libya and North Africa?

A further radicalization of the Shkuka family was the wedding of one of the daughters whose honeymoon was in Saudi Arabia. It was an arranged marriage and the groom was considered suitable because he attended the same mosque as the family. There ought to have been clear warning signs when considering such a man as a potential groom for a beloved daughter such as his beard, short trousers and callus on his forehead from zealous prayer but presumably these were all considered attributes, as was his choice of mosque. The bridal couple disappeared in Saudi Arabia and eight weeks later reappeared in Libya having been expelled and placed on a Saudi watch list. Apparently they had gone straight to a household inhabited by Islamist fanatics from Libya who were actively hatching plots against Gaddafi. On his return to Libya, the new son – in – law was repeatedly arrested and finally Bashir's niece was divorced from him as he was too radical even for Ismael's family.

I feel perhaps I have skimmed over my feelings on living with Libyans. I have commented on various political aspects that affected us personally but little on my inclusion into the Libyan social life, which was in fact virtually non – existent. I worked long hours, and therefore unlike the majority of Libyan women my social life did not start on Wednesday with the wedding Henna night followed on Thursday by the wedding night which would begin at 10 pm and finish at the earliest by 2 or 3 am, and then onto the Friday evening festivities at the house of the groom. These celebrations were solely for the women, the men being just the taxi drivers. Libyan social life revolves around visiting on special occasions for births, deaths, marriages, bon voyage on a Haj visit to Saudi Arabia or for an illness. There is also an element of paying back. If I were leaving or returning from holiday in theory people would have a duty to visit and I in turn would have to reciprocate with a similar visit. I remember well when I first arrived in the country, Bashir's sister telling me I had to visit Fatima because she was sick, or Aisha who had just given birth. Bashir strongly advised my not being involved in such visits as he knew I surely would not want a reciprocal visit when I was sick or about to leave on holiday. 'Start as you want to go on'; it was sound advice. We might have seemed anti – social to the Libyan society but a cheerful hello and goodbye were to become our way of living in Arab countries. Also I believe there was a secondary reason for not mixing or freely inviting people to our house namely the Gaddafi fear factor. If the country had been more open things might have been different.

Unlike in Tunisia, Egypt and Jordan, the other Arab countries I came to know, Libya had no culture of restaurants or coffee shops and it wasn't until the 2000s that these began to appear with the liberalization of the country. At this time it was still unusual for women to be seen in these places right up to the revolution. Those that frequented the coffee shops or restaurants would be considered by the majority as either quite loose or too freethinking; not marriageable attributes. This perception was such an important element within the society for women. There was a very negative stigma attached to women who had reached their 30s unmarried, who were labelled as spinsters with the sad, judgmental voice of 'maskina'(the poor one).

Likewise when first arriving in the country the shops were empty one just shopped for the necessities of life. The vast majority of women did not drive therefore men had no option but to shop. Once cars began to be imported into the country men could see the advantage of the female population driving themselves to work and the children to school and taking over the shopping thus another gender change took place within the society.

It would seem that by 2000, life for women in Libya had changed dramatically since my arrival in1984. The truth of the matter was that due to the abysmal wages paid to the majority of government workers being 80% of the workforce, families needed 'another tap' (translated from the Libyan Arabic to show a second income). Families too were becoming smaller from the days of Bashir's siblings, starting with his brother Ibrahim having the smallest number of children, only five to his brother Ismael who had eleven in the 80s when large Libyan families were the norm. The pendulum had swung with educated women having smaller families, having a salary and spending their money how they wished. They were also able to dictate to a certain extent how they and their children lived their lives within the confines of this deeply conservative country. The ratio of women to men in the universities saw perhaps the biggest swing with in some faculties a 75/25% ratio of women to men. However, despite laws to the contrary, Libyans liked the subservient role of their women. Their earning power was a necessity but any further rights were a red – light as the old cultural norms had not moved forward into the 21st century.

When my father remarried, Bashir suggested that it would be good if his mother were to think of getting remarried as he had been asked on a couple of occasions if his mother would like to be remarried to colleagues' widowed fathers. His mother's face brightened as she was so dependent on her sons for every aspect of her life. Libyan widowers remarried young brides but it was unheard of for older Libyan widows to remarry and Bashir's suggestion was met with outraged reactions from his siblings. Sometimes I do wonder if when the stork was flying over Libya it dropped Bashir in the Shkuka garden in error. Many of our friends and foreign diplomats commented that he did not seem like the typical Libyan; he had moved into the 21st century with his ideas on life, while Libyan society had remained in the dark ages. The Libyans liked to say that it was my influence that led him to be so different, but Bashir had always been his own master and he never did or thought anything with which he disagreed or found unacceptable. Nothing was further from the truth. Of course, we learned from each other, we either accepted each other's ideas and thoughts or rejected them. This was our marriage whilst each maintaining our independence.

Although perhaps it appeared that the country was modernising a number of assassination attempts on Gaddafi's life resulted in the security forces continually raiding mosques that they believed to be centres of counter – revolutionary preaching. The Islamists had launched an insurgency in Benghazi in 1995. In 1996 there was fighting in the East of Libya as the army took on the LIFG in the Green Mountains. Perhaps one, if not the worst of Gaddafi's atrocities was the mass slaughter of prisoners in June 1996 at Abu Salim prison. A large majority of the occupants were opponents belonging to Islamist groups. The appalling conditions in the prison and the attitude of the guards led to prisoners seizing one of the most hated guards, Khalifa al Magtouf, and demanding that they be allowed to talk to Abdullah al Sanussi, Gaddafi's brother in law and head of internal security. Sanussi was almost as feared as Gaddafi but he agreed that the prisoners' grievances would be met. The following morning the prisoners were ordered into one of the courtyards and ordered to lie face down. Some of the few survivors later recounted how they heard an explosion and on looking up could see soldiers positioned on the roofs of the courtyard, and Sanussi and other officials standing on the side of it. The soldiers on the roof then opened fire. Some say that Sanussi was heard to say 'No, not killing, not killing,' but orders must have come from someone. Between 11 am and 2 pm, the shooting in the prison continued without halt and 1,270 prisoners were killed. 500 were left alive. Nothing is secret in Libya and rumours of this atrocity soon leaked out, but foreign journalists were rarely granted visas to Libya and there were no tourists. The event was not reported either inside or outside

Libya. It took years for families to discover if their sons had been among the victims and where the bodies had been buried. These events saw a resurgence of the Revolutionary Committees who were re – energized to combat the Islamists. Terror was still endemic within the country; caution was as always the watch word.

One of Bashir's only saving graces with the Intelligence Service was that he was a drinker, didn't go the mosque and therefore could not be accused of being a part of the Muslim Brotherhood. Despite trying to find endless contacts to clear his name, it seemed always to be a dead end. These were the hardest years of our life together although many happy events happened and our lifestyle improved. At the back of both of our minds there was always this inescapable problem of being on the UK and Libyan blacklists. Bashir grew weary with trying and became extremely despondent at times, resorting to heavy drinking and black moods. Thankfully both problems were to be solved at a later date but the delay was testing on our relationship.

The sanctions were causing Libya huge revenue loss, which was becoming unsustainable. Many African States opposed the sanctions, probably having been encouraged to do so by Gaddafi sweeteners. In October 1997, Nelson Mandela, who was ever grateful to Gaddafi for the support he had given to the ANC (African National Congress) during the Apartheid Years, visited Libya. Nelson Mandela's world standing was unquestionable, and without a doubt he was able to help broker secret negotiations between the parties involved in the Lockerbie standoff. This resulted in Gaddafi finally agreeing to the extradition of the Lockerbie suspects to the Scottish court in the Netherlands with the Sanctions being suspended in 1998.

I had unsuccessfully tried every imaginable way to have Bashir's UK ban revoked. It finally occurred to me that perhaps one avenue could be to write to Glenda Jackson, my local MP, to enlist her help. The response to my first letter was that the ban was still in place and that unfortunately there was nothing more that she could do. I felt such utter frustration. If we could at least *know* the reason for the ban, then perhaps we could be in a position to challenge the claim. Initially I had not written in great detail to Ms. Jackson about the circumstances leading up to the ban and so my final shot was to write a lengthy letter concluding with the fact that we knew the Libyan intelligence had used the passports of men who had British wives and photographs should be checked. When we finally received Ms Jackson's and Keith Vaz's letters advising that the ban had been lifted and there were no longer any restrictions for a British visa to be issued Bashir was elated and champagne corks popped. I could see this was like lifting the heaviest tonne of bricks from his shoulders. We were never to discover what caused the years of anguish and despair. It had been so unjust but at least the system had finally rectified the error thanks to Glenda Jackson's intervention. We could now travel together to London, see our friends and finally we would be able to make plans for our retirement; all of which had been put on a back burner.

It seems incredible that one person could have been on blacklists for two opposing countries; nevertheless this was Bashir's lot. Sometimes it is the person who is on the lowest rung of the ladder who can make things happen rather than the one at the top. Gargaresh is home to the Libyan mafia and to low level Libyan intelligence workers. One such operative from the intelligence service was the secretary to Abbdallah Mansour, who was one of Gaddafi's cousins and also the Head of Internal Intelligence. Bashir drafted a letter to Mansour, detailing the circumstances of the ban and asking that the matter be investigated, giving it to this Gargaresh clerk to be delivered by hand. Mansour summoned Bashir to Tajoura for a meeting; at least some response was better than no response. Bashir knew that everything would hinge on such a meeting. Survive or prison there had to be some sort of resolution it was stifling his career and causing him almost daily grief. Bashir found Mansour surprisingly reasonable, believing that there had indeed been a miscarriage of justice and that the ban would be rescinded. Two days later Bashir received the news that he was off the blacklist. These orders had hung over our lives for eight years; it was especially tough for Bashir and at times I needed to be his crutch. I had never imagined that this would be my role in our marriage as he had always been so strong. His dream had been to be a diplomat and that had been squashed. Now he was back on the posting list, we had been in Libya for far, far too long.

Twenty
٢٠

Our return to Libya had found our house desecrated by the burglary, the flooding and the light into our rooms being blocked out by the next – door's illegal building extension. Furthermore, our neighbours had been using the area around our house as theirs and were irritated by our wanting it back, so the stone throwing resumed from the children. It might seem wonderful to live so close to the Mediterranean, but the unmadeup roads were decrepit, and flooded in the winter. There was always a thin layer of sand on every surface however much or little one dusted. Gaddafi despised Gargaresh, as he could never bring this area to heel. The independent Libyan mafia controlled the suburb, and as a result Gargaresh was neglected in terms of infrastructure projects along with Benghazi and many other areas of the country. I suppose also that we had lived comfortably in India and by contrast it was difficult to slot back into the compromises that one had to accept of Tripoli life. Having the cash from the sale of my London flat enabled us to think that the time was right to look and try to find a better home. By this time we had lived together in quite a few places and whenever the search took place, somehow we knew immediately just walking through the gate or front door when somewhere was right. Luckily, we were always in total agreement.

It was early one evening on entering an old, Italian villa in Hay Andalus and spotting a grape vine loaded down with bunches of huge delicious looking black grapes we saw the home that we had to have. It had everything that we wanted a large sitting room, a dining room, a bedroom, a study, a kitchen, a bathroom, a terrace and an area which we knew could be the garden we had always dreamed of nurturing. The owner wanted a quick deal and as most deals in Libya are in cash, this was no exception. We had saved money from India and this paid for one quarter and the outstanding three quarters came from the London flat money. With all the legal formalities and searches completed Bashir went to the bank to withdraw the quarter payment along with the owner acting as bodyguard. At that time the largest Libyan denomination note was LD10 so one can imagine the four heavy suitcases filled with cash arriving at our house all of which had to be recounted. The deal was done and we had a new home.

The house had been built in the 50s when the Italians were still living in the country and little if anything of the building had been changed since that time. It was therefore in need of quite substantial renovations. It had 2ft. thick walls made of solid white bricks to keep out the hot summer sun and the cold winter winds, and high ceilings. We had ensured that the property was not under the Gaddafi Law No.4 and so it was truly ours and could never be taken back by any of the previous owners in the future. If not for the owner wanting a quick deal we never could have afforded the property; Bashir had negotiated hard. This was yet another rich question of debate for Bashir and I over whether this was fate, luck or chance. Here was the confirmation of Bashir's horoscope from India which had foretold that within a short period of time he would be living in a bungalow facing south. A further perk it was located in the diplomatic area and only a five – minute walk from the shops, the British School and the main road. The latter being vital during the revolution when petrol became scarce.

The neighbourhood was quiet and those living opposite were Fathia, the first wife of Gaddafi, her brother and Gaddafi's first born son Mohamed. When I saw Fathia walking down our street simply dressed with a guard behind her I always wondered about her story. Hers had been an arranged marriage with Gaddafi rumoured to have been against her wishes. Shortly after the birth of their son Gaddafi left Fathia to remarry the woman who had nursed him whilst in hospital Safiya. It was amazing to observe how Fathia lived simply compared to the lavish existence of Gaddafi's second wife and her children who were always flaunting their wealth. For some reason I always felt sorry for her. I could recognize that she had a story to tell but I was never able to talk to her and ask about her true life. She now lives in exile in Oman with her son Mohamed and her grandchildren together with Safiya and her children, which too must be a strange existence. At the time we did not realise the drawback of having a Gaddafi in our midst, as they were always good and respectful neighbours.

In Libya there is something called *manwa*, meaning shared space to prohibit the neighbours blocking of air and light. On one side of the new villa such an area was shared by two other houses forming an E shape. The house with which we shared a wall was empty as it was a Law No. 4 house, the owners having disappeared. The *manwa* area was empty and overgrown, blocked off from the street by a wall. We had complete privacy. If we had known then what was to happen with this piece of land in the future, perhaps we never would have bought the villa. We were assured by our lawyer and the council that it was shared ownership between the three houses as the name indicated on the house plans. We both wished to have the property in our joint names but this was prohibited as I did not hold Libyan citizenship only Libyan/Arab citizenship. It was against the law for non Libyans to own property in the country. A resolution for this problem had to be found as I had brought my inheritance to Libya and should Bashir predecease me I would be marginalised under sharia inheritance law. At the time this subject was not top of our thoughts only that of owning the longed for new house.

We began excitedly planning the renovations. Bashir's dream had always been to have a bar since he liked the idea of standing behind the counter and serving his guests drinks, recreating the English pub atmosphere in our home. Though I loved the idea, and his enthusiasm for it, I expressed my nervous reservations wondering what Libyans would think, especially the family. As ever Bashir stood his ground, the bar was built and many happy evenings where spent with Publican Bashir serving his guests. A common quip among expatriates was that there was more alcohol being consumed in supposedly dry Libya than back in the UK. So long as the production and consumption of alcohol wasn't flaunted, by 1996 police and intelligence officers pretty much turned a blind eye. They were much more concerned with the Islamic Fundamentalists and obviously the drinkers were not a part of that group.

Bashir had made quite an art of the process of wine making, as well as his use of the jargon associated with it. His chardonnay was gaining a reputation within the expatriate community. He had a substantial brew cupboard in which were three large, glass Italian wine making bottles for fermenting the wine. At times the bubbling away was rather too loud in my English classes. The white was made from Swedish freeze – dried wine kits, which were bought in the UK and then carried into Libya under the guise of herbal medicine for my allergies. We also made red wine and I was surprised at the ease of the process. Come September, expatriates would stream out to the special grape growing farms where we would buy carloads of the fruit. The grapes would be placed into a baby bath and wearing jelly shoes I would begin the trampling after which the pulp and the juice would be deposited into a milk churn and left to ferment for about a week, then be decanted into bottles. It was rare to drink something much older than three months; it was a very strong Rioja and seemed at the time to be delicious. Without a doubt it wouldn't have been quite as delicious in London, but we were as ever inventive and the making was all part of the fun.

For a new house to have auspicious beginnings, the purchase of a date palm was considered imperative, as there are several edicts on the benefits of date palms in one's garden in the Holy Koran. We had planted trees everywhere we had lived and now this was to be the one for our final home. The palm was planted and grew to a great height, annually producing kilos and kilos of golden dates. All of the concrete in the garden was broken and flowerbeds were constructed, followed by years of visiting garden centres to source new plants and trees. My father had said that when one reaches 50 one chooses either of the two Gs, God or Gardening? I like to think I chose a bit of both, although the latter became a passion. Our final home was beginning to flourish, or rather so we thought.

I knew that if I wished to progress with my EFL teaching, I had to become better qualified. There was not much to do in Libya apart from sleep and work, work and sleep over and over again, so this monotonous existence prompted me to take a distance/residential EFL Licentiate Diploma course. This involved writing modules, working in an EFL school, taking face – to – face oral and written exams and finally delivering an observed lesson. For me this was quite a demand especially as the Internet had yet to become available and I had not studied for many years. In Libya I had zero access to books and it was long before Skype the only option were expensive phone calls with my tutor. For eighteen months Bashir saw little of me as I was required to teach 15 hours in an EFL school on top of the work that I was doing at the British school, my private lessons and writing the modules. The course had been brilliantly written and I was to learn and adopt many strategies that improved my own best teaching practices. The final stretch was to spend six weeks in

London working at a school and preparing for my observed lesson and written exams. This meant leaving Bashir as he was unable to have leave for that extended time. As ever my friends Penny and Steve came to the rescue, and I was to spend the six weeks working and studying for the final exam with them in London.

I was desperate to pass knowing that this diploma would open the door to many new and exciting opportunities. On my return to Libya I felt that the exams had gone well. Through the post came the result for the first part I received a distinction and I was thrilled, when the second part arrived with a similar result I was ecstatic and then became greedy no longer just wanting a pass but rather hoping for a final distinction. All those endless hours of working in isolation, Bashir's patience cooking meals, cleaning, sitting alone, driving me backwards and forwards to my school resulted in the final distinction. I was a tortoise, slow and steady, but I had reached the winning post with the help of my husband and so many friends, who helped with the logistical difficulties as well as supporting me in overcoming my self – doubt.

My teaching career has been a series of assignments leading from one to the next, each time on a slightly higher rung up the ladder. I also had the luck of being a big fish in a small pond in Libya. I have never reached great heights but each task has been absolutely fascinating and through my teaching, the best perk has always been the exceptional friends and colleagues I have met. When teaching at the language school I met an American lady Khadijah Gummah, who was teaching English at the university. She and I had little in common socially, but in terms of our interest in Education we had plenty to talk about and through this chance meeting Khadijah and I decided to work on some research papers together.

Libyan political events seemed to always have had a knock on effect on my teaching both positively and sometimes negatively. With the handing over of Megrahi and Fhima to the Scottish court in the Netherlands in 1999, secret talks began with the British Government to normalise relations between the two countries. An opportunity arose for the research project when in 2000 the British Council opened a Tripoli office headed up by Tony Jones. There could not have been a better ambassador to take on this difficult task of balancing the wishes of the British government whilst at the same time walking a fine line with the Libyans, especially as the teaching of English in the schools had only just been reinstated.

Libya was sending many students abroad for further studies. I believe the intention in this process was twofold; it was given as a reward to those complying with Gaddafi but also as a way of removing young Libyan men off the street corners since unemployment was estimated to be at 30%, and street corner talk could lead to an uprising. A requirement for entry into UK universities was a band score in the International English Language Test (IELTS). Up until this time it was necessary for Libyan candidates to travel to Malta or Tunisia to take the exam. The British Council realising the large numbers of candidates involved decided to open up a centre in Libya. Through networking I was to learn they needed examiners and I put my name forward, was accepted, went on the training course and took the qualifying exam successfully. Being an examiner was to be my meal ticket for many years as it meant wherever I travelled I could transfer my examiner status to another country and begin working immediately. I was able to do this in the Philippines, Jordan and then back in Libya, resuming work usually within one week after arrival.

Khadijah and I were interested in the administration of the IELTS exam, particularly in investigating Libyan preferences for types of examiners. We wanted to discover whether Libyans preferred a male or female examiner, and additionally whether they wanted a local examiner or a native English speaker. She introduced me to Teri, another American who was very adept on the computer and compiled all our statistics plus constructed graphs to show the results clearly. We were a brilliant team. We ran 150 interviews and our findings were fascinating. The majority of respondents were both male and female Libyans with a few expatriates and all preferred a native speaker examiner, I believe because they felt that they were incorruptible. On the gender choice, most surprisingly 85% preferred a female examiner. This, we believed through discussions, was that they probably considered women as more nurturing and motherly. We were to rerun this research when I went to the Philippines with the British Council and IDP and here we found that the Filipinos were unconcerned whether they had a male or female examiner, but still there was a preference for a native speaker examiner. From this small beginning doing research I was invited to give a number of one day seminars on the subject of gender in testing both in Libya and the Philippines. Before leaving Libya, Khadijah and I also researched and wrote an article for IATEFL entitled '*it's not just watcha Say... it is who ya say it to, where, when, how and just who else's listenin'* (IATEFL Issues June – July 2001). We were thrilled when this was published. The tortoise was moving a little faster as the years passed and my reputation became known.

Once the qualification was out of the way I began to build my client base of private students all of whom were expatriates. Mornings I taught wives, afternoons were given up to support teaching children. My last slot of the day I worked with diplomats, especially on speech writing the latter I found absorbing as I learned of the mind – set of other diplomats' cultures and policies. These were exhausting, long working hours but had the benefit that we were not restricted to living on Bashir's meagre salary. We were able to take exotic holidays, short trips and have the lifestyle of which we had long dreamed.

Bashir never took a second job, as did many Libyans. His only venture into the world of commerce was his shirt fiasco. Whilst still living in India he purchased at US$1 a shirt, one thousand highly coloured, cotton shirts and these were put in our shipment back to Libya. What had prompted this business venture was when in Libya during his intelligence investigation he had noticed that this clothing item was being sold for $45 so he believed he had spotted a gap in the market. Unfortunately so too had many others as by the time the shipment arrived in Libya the market was flooded with similar shirts. He managed to sell or give away some of the shirts but we were left with 900 of these now unwanted items. Final result he was always able to wear a different coloured or patterned shirt whenever he went out. This was the beginning and end of his aspiration of ever becoming a diplomat entrepreneur.

Twenty - One
٢١

My decision to become a teacher was by chance and it had turned out well. Teachers, doctors and engineers were all considered socially acceptable jobs for females within the Libyan society. The position of nurses however, was considered subservient and unsuitable for Libyan women. This was surprising given that Safiya Gaddafi's second wife had been a nurse on first meeting her husband. The majority of nurses were recruited from abroad with the main recruitment areas' being India, Philippines and former Eastern Block countries. When five Bulgarian nurses and a Palestinian doctor arrived in Libya to work in a Benghazi hospital they never could have imagined that they would become entangled in a Libyan Israeli conspiracy charge of spying against Libya.

By the 1990s the Libyan health service was limping or rather close to collapse. A two tier medical system existed which comprised of those that had treatment in Libya being the majority or the moneyed and cronies who were able to pay for treatment outside the country. Old and poorly serviced medical equipment and minimal hygiene standards existed in all hospitals. Doctors received lowly paid government salaries and despite years of tenure only minimal increases resulted, never based on merit consequently morale was low. If a doctor were able to study abroad they were unlikely to return. At the beginning of the revolution Mohamed El Bishti had left Libya and became a senior paediatrician specializing in child kidney ailments in the UK. Likewise the head of Neurology at the London Clinic is Libyan, as is a senior cancer specialist at the Royal Marsden Hospital. The list is endless of doctors who have left to work abroad; a tragedy that they were not living and working in Libya but who could blame them there were no inducements to stay.

For those unfamiliar with Libya's geography it is hard to imagine the size of the country with its 1000Km coastline separating its two main cities Tripoli in the West and Benghazi in the East. Due to the various assassination attempts that had emanated from the East Gaddafi ensured that Benghazi was increasingly neglected. By the 1990s in the UK there was total awareness of AIDS blood contamination. In Libya however, poor hygiene standards and a lack of basic equipment meant that little care was paid to preventing the transmission to others of of this deadly virus. Added to this was the complete denial of the existence of AIDS within Libyan society which was to lead to the Bulgarian six nurses' affair only coming to light through a series of leaks.

Slowly the news from the East reached our ears in 1999 when it emerged that well over 400 children had been infected with AIDS at the El Fatah Children's hospital in Benghazi, and that a further 50 had already died. This was a hospital where a large number of Bulgarians had been working, who had been recruited by the state – owned company Expomed. Benghazi was already a tinderbox of dissent and for the government to have admitted that poor conditions had resulted in this medical disaster probably would have led to an eruption of violence. Instead five members of the Bulgarian nursing fraternity and a Palestinian doctor in the hospital were arrested on a warrant in connection with the case of infecting children in Benghazi with AIDS. Initially it was reported as their being Israeli spies in a plot to kill Libyan children. Parents and relatives of the victims protested and demanded death penalties for the six. The Libyan Prime minister Shukri Ghanem insisted that the trial was a judicial matter. The families also demanded compensation from the actions allegedly taken by the convicted medics.

The first trial, the second trial, the retrial and the commutation to a life sentence and finally the terms of the release of these women and man have been well documented. For the first two years of their incarceration we were in Libya and heard rumours and innuendo, but in our hearts we knew or certainly felt that these six were the scapegoats caused by a lack of investment in the hospital. Without a doubt there was negligence, syringes had been reused possibly due to a lack of finance or perhaps ignorance still of AIDS but it had certainly never been deliberate. These six were being held responsible for the failure of the Libyan health system by the authorities.

The Libyan Defence Attorney on the case was Othman al – Bizanti. He is among one of the most highly respected lawyers in the Libyan legal profession. Although not a young man at that time, probably in his 60s he was given the brief by the Bulgarian embassy working alongside a Bulgarian diplomat who has become one of our lifelong friends to defend the medics. We were to see the stress that it took on Rumen and Ekatarina's lives, as the defendants were tortured into confessing, put through various trials and finally had to serve sentences from 1999 up to 2007 when the six were finally released. During this time I never knew Bizanti but he was to defend both Bashir and myself in 2007 on a trumped up blasphemy charge and later has taken on my court case in 2013.

I cannot imagine the absolute terror that these nurses and doctor must have felt being in a situation where they knew they were scapegoats, where they were being tortured to extract confessions, and were subject to a ramshackle legal system that had to pander to Gaddafi's whims and lies. Being imprisoned in Libya without access to any comforts such as adequate washing and toilet facilities, food and relying on the friendship and help of people within their embassy and the Bulgarian community must have been an experience from hell.

When I sat with Bizante in 2014 in Tripoli I asked him if he was going to write a book. He looked at me with his piercing, black eyes, a still imposing physique and in his deep penetrating voice gave me a strong *no*. His reasoning was client confidentiality, but I'm inclined to think that the trial took its toll on him too and he felt it was best laid to rest. I suspect he has no wish to resurrect the horrors of those years and all the politicking and deals that finally went into the release of the six in 2007.

Much has been written of the Bulgarian six but perhaps the forgotten are the 400 infected children. In 2007 The Benghazi International Fund began giving compensation to the families in amounts of US$1 million per affected child. These children are the real victims; they were let down by the Libyan health service and became infected with an incurable condition. Whatever money or treatment these now young adults receive there will always be the ignorance and stigma of this disease within Libyan society. I have no knowledge as to what has happened to them but I fear that no compensation in the world, however large, is adequate for how they will be viewed within their community. My mind grows tired and weary when I think of their situation as yet another instance of the injustice of the Gaddafi regime.

When the revolution happened, as I will write later, people very quickly changed their spots and allegiances. Among the most prominent of those that did just this, was Mustafa Abdul Jalil, who was one of the judges that sentenced the nurses to death. In February 2011, having just resigned as the Minister of Justice he told Al Jazeera that the responsibility for the HIV infection lay totally with Muammar Gaddafi's regime. This man was to become the Head of the Libyan NTC. What unbelievable, bare – faced hypocrisy.

Twenty - Two
٢٢

The transient life of diplomats is normally tempered by a home posting where one no longer has to entertain, go out night after night and not always be on show. For me, Libya was always to be like a posting, except that we now had a permanent, beautiful home although our friends would still come and go. Neither of us had made any firm friends from within the Libyan community. For Bashir, things were obviously different as it was his home country and he had his family and old friends. This was where he wanted to spend part of every year in his retirement; he imagined winters in Libya and summers in London. At the time this also seemed like a good compromise to me as well.

The end of this period in Libya before going on to another posting I think was the happiest I had ever been in the country. This I say from a purely selfish point of view, as my life was easy compared to the majority many of whom were living a meagre, hand – to – mouth existence and others were incarcerated in prisons around the country without due process. We were all afraid to open our mouths about anyone in the regime, Gaddafi or his children.

I was a big fish in a small pond and my teaching business had boomed with a long waiting list of students. I would take a couple of pro bono Libyan students annually and seeing them reach their goals was always my biggest reward. Financially, as a result of my work, certainly not poor Bashir's miserly salary from the Foreign Ministry, we were able to live comfortably and to enjoy wonderful holidays. Those long distant days of worrying how we were going to pay the telephone bill and at times losing sleep over how to make our food budget last until the end of the month were in the past. Now there was an element of permanence and security in our lives in so far as we had a house that was legally ours with its garden that gave us great pleasure. Being on a posting was very different, knowing that we would only be stationed somewhere for four years and then have to move on.

Our friends came from all over the world many of whom were diplomats and others working for international companies. Thanks to the Internet, I am able to keep in touch with and occasionally meet many of them. There are not many countries in the world where I would be unable to find a friend or contact we had made over the years. As for the Libyan climate I had grown used to the hot summers, mild winters, living a mile back from the sea where there was little humidity and during those hot months always a light, nightly, sea breeze. I loved sitting on our terrace in the summer under a desert star filled night sky with the fragrance of the jasmine and a glass of our homemade chilled chardonnay.

I have mentioned before that birthdays were a special event for us and as neither of us had been to Italy we decided one year to visit Rome and the island of Elba to celebrate Bashir's birthday. Rome was just an hour's flight from Tripoli and from there we took a train down to Pisa where we saw the iconic tower. An early morning ferry took us out to the island of Elba. I am sure that when Bonaparte first glimpsed the island his heart must have sunk but for us it was perfect in its relative isolation, wonderful beaches and delicious Italian food and wine.

The Elba birthday holiday was September 2001. One morning not long after arriving we had relaxed and swum at the pool when we noticed people turning on their radios and talking loudly in horrified chatter. Even our poor Italian was enough to understand the tragedy that had occurred in New York on 9/11. This was a new style of terrorism that we realised would stigmatise Muslims. I am sure that the horror of that day will stay in most peoples' minds forever. It was noticeable how the thawing of relations with the West had changed the Gaddafi rhetoric of the past. Perhaps for the first time he empathised with the Americans by condemning the September eleven attacks on the USA by Al Qaeda as well as expressing sympathy for the victims. Additionally he called for Libyan involvement in the War on Terror against militant Islamism. Gaddafi probably saw that the interests of his regime and its bizarre ideologies were best served by sidling up to the United States at this very difficult time. Later on seeing the demise of Saddam Hussein after the second Gulf War in 2003, he renounced Libya's possession of weapons of mass destruction quite obviously fearing that he could be next. 2004 saw the rapprochement move one stage further with the visit of Tony Blair to the man in the tent.

In all the years of waiting and hoping for Gaddafi's regime to end, it was appalling to see him welcomed into the fold as a long lost friend by Blair. It was obvious that the lure once again, of the Libyan oil was the catalyst. This seemed so unjust that Gaddafi a man who had committed such horrendous crimes during his time in power should now be entertained and fawned over by Heads of State, Kings and Queens in the world's capitals. It seemed as if he and his cronies were exempt from their crimes and in fact that these crimes had actually *paid*. All Libyans were only too well aware of the corruption of this Libyan Nero figure and his thugs.

Gaddafi wanted to control every aspect of Libyan life and this he did through patron/client relations with tribal communities, rewarding with positions and money while repressing others. Those from Sirte, Sebbah and Bani Walid were the main beneficiaries of this largesse. Gaddafi's strategy was to give to one and destroy another, then build them back up again. This was how he maintained power with cohesive groups never being allowed to flourish. King Gaddafi never stopped shaking his bag full of rats.

The economic sanctions imposed by the West on Libya created tremendous hardships on the Libyan people as the majority were on fixed public sector salaries, which were insufficient to provide a reasonable standard of living. Considering Libya's vast oil wealth, employees nevertheless had to make substantial social security contributions plus pay income tax. At various times there were additional tax deductions for specific demands, for example in the 1980s a monthly *Kalashnikov* contribution of LD30 during the Chad War. This made us all want to spit when we opened our salary envelopes at the end of the month. Nothing was ever voted by the Peoples Committees just a rubber stamp agreement. It was simply King Gaddafi's decisions at his whim at any particular time. Many were forced to seek second, even third jobs to earn enough to support their families. Sanctions crippled Libya's economy leading to inflation estimated at times to be at 25% with unemployment at 30%. It is believed that Libya lost $40 billion from oil revenues due to the sanctions. As a result of privatization, the gap widened between small groups of rich families connected to the political structure and the growing sea of dispossessed people.

The opening up of the economy and promises of a better life as a result of the suspension of sanctions in 1998 for ordinary Libyans has never materialized. Today's online discussion forums and Twitter are awash with apologists for the Gaddafi regime arguing that the Libyan people were given housing, wedding allowances, free medical treatment and education. Nothing could be further from the truth. I was recently at a lecture in London where a man stood and argued the case for the regime, citing all of these myths as examples of just how fair and reasonable Gaddafi had been; I nearly exploded. On another occasion a woman argued that her husband, a British architect had been in Libya building 17 new universities and how Gaddafi was a socialist caring and using the Libyan money wisely. I refrained from comment just thinking inside did the country really need that number of additional educational institutions for a population of just six million people? Gaddafi turned a blind eye to the opportunists who exploited the political situation and made millions. However, if any of these opportunists stepped out of line they well knew the consequences. Meanwhile the majority were being paid a pitiful monthly average salary of US$150 that is if they were lucky enough to have a job. This period saw the awarding of lucrative contracts to upgrade Libya's infrastructure whilst at the same time lining Gaddafi's own coffers and those of his family. Between 2001 and 2005, US$35 billion worth of contracts were signed and these are only those that are known. No contract was signed without the green light of someone in the Gaddafi clan.

Gaddafi was growing increasingly eccentric. His youthful good looks had long disappeared to be replaced by failed plastic surgery and hair transplants and a bizarre selection of clothes. Rabia Ben Barka was the leader's clothes designer and it would be interesting to discover if she were to write her memoirs, whether both she and Gaddafi were aware of the humour that was expressed in her designs. Perhaps she was only responding to Gaddafi's odd demands. These ranged from the bizarre Michael Jackson look, to pictures of dead people pinned on his military jacket, to the huge map of Africa on his breast. He wanted to stand out and he always drew attention with his female bodyguards and unorthodox clothes; in this he succeeded but more as a laughing stock rather than as the great leader he believed himself to be. For the Libyans he was an embarrassment and a source of shame, for his career diplomats such as

Bashir the refrain was commonly 'I just hope he does not visit on my watch.' There were obvious mental health consequences for the life that he lived; his daily consumption of upper and downer drugs, never sleeping in any one place for more than a few hours due to his fear of assassination, coupled with his mistrust of all but a few. Every appearance and speech saw him becoming increasingly more erratic. He craved adoration and it was withheld by the Libyans. This need to bolster his ego was fed by generous visits to Africa where people would come out in the streets to sing his praises. His children now adults were also playing an increasingly important role within the country and it was becoming obvious that they were the only ones he trusted. Each of his sons had their own elite military brigade. So there were armies within armies and foreign ministries within foreign ministries controlled by one or other of the sons or Gaddafi himself. This was a worrying trend for the Libyans having thought that sooner or later they would be rid of Gaddafi by natural causes at worst, but now it seemed as if he was preparing the young princes as his successors. Libya was to have a Gaddafi dynasty.

When considering the utter instability that is Libya today, people speculate that perhaps the western intervention in the Libyan revolution was a mistake, and it would have been better if Gaddafi were still in power. I tend to argue that revolutions take time and cite the examples of Romania, Russia and even France. Change takes time and Libya is no exception. Gaddafi knew that he satisfied a need as a scapegoat for the West but he was less recognised as the guardian to prevent the spread of Islamic extremism. Perhaps also forgotten was the 50 million Euros paid by the EU in October 2010 to stop African migrants passing into Europe. From his death until today there have been initiatives to stem the flow of illegal migrants fleeing from Africa into Europe but the consequences have come home to roost on the shores of the Mediterranean with a vengeance and tragedy. In all too many ways as time went on he served the West's purpose while the Libyan people were left out to dry.

The Gaddafi children were to have an increasing high profile role in the country and it is necessary to know a little of how they were to fit in the picture in the lead up to the revolution. My neighbour Mohammed from Gaddafi's first wife, Fathia was never considered one of the main clan primarily as he was believed not to have been involved in the violent killings and torture connected with his brothers. I believe that he kept a low profile whilst at the same time focussed on accumulating his wealth. He was rumoured to be very thrifty. Once when the gates were changed on his house, one of his guards asked for the old ones. Rather than give them to his employee, he opted to sell them to him. Similarly, when he was head of the Telecommunications Company he had many new iPhones on his desk and again a guard asked if he could have one. Mohammed's response was to tell him to go to a shop and buy one since those on the desk were for the boss. Personally, we never had contact with him apart from the wave of a hand from his car and likewise us to him. That was good enough for us not wanting anything from him and thankfully he wanted nothing from us. One of my colleagues taught his children English she was neither paid nor given any help in situations where it was asked for. The rumour that he was mean and wanted to accumulate wealth was probably true. Throughout my Libyan teaching career I always made a point of avoiding teaching any of the Gaddafi cronies or ministers despite being asked on numerous occasions. Bashir wanted no connection with the Gaddafi gang trying to create the biggest gulf as possible between he and they without it being apparent.

Gaddafi's second wife Safiya's children were to see nothing wrong in demanding ownership of franchises, shipping companies, food and drinks factories, in fact every business deal needed to have Gaddafi or one of his children involved. They were absolutely ruthless and were unquestionably loyal to their father right to the end, although there were slight waivers. They knew where their bread was buttered and one wonders if and how they would have survived in life as ordinary citizens.

The first occasion we came across Saif's antics was when he was studying in Vienna for an MBA. Initially OMV, the Austrian oil company, which has oil fields in Libya and as such is reliant to a certain extent on Libyan oil, were delighted on learning Saif was to be studying in Vienna. What they had not counted on was Saif bringing two of his white tigers to Vienna and seeing no reason why he could not walk the streets of Vienna with these beasts on a leash. On learning that this was not to be permitted he threatened the Austrian government with a breaking off of diplomatic ties and the withdrawal of landing rights for Austrian Airlines in Libya. We were friends with Axel, the Manager of Austrian Airlines at the time and certainly he never imagined how he would become embroiled in a diplomatic standoff over two wild animals. We saw him losing quite a bit of hair having to deal with the antics of this infantile playboy wanting his own way and unused to not having it. Finally a deal was negotiated that the tigers would be kept in the Vienna zoo with Saif stating that he was delighted with the outcome as he could visit them whenever he wished.

One of Bashir's colleagues, who was posted to Vienna told of how Saif fancied himself a great painter and held an exhibition to which everyone had to attend with embassy personnel being expected to extol the virtues of the paintings and pressurised into purchasing them to ensure rows of red dots.

At this time Saif also developed a strange relationship with the Austrian fascist Jorg Haider, both sharing a dislike of the then Austrian government. Given that Haider's known homosexuality was forbidden under sharia law, it was a bizarre relationship and was frowned on by the conservative elements in Libya. Saif used this friendship to bring pressure on the government to have his residence visa reinstated. The two were reputed to have done several lucrative business deals together. Just like his father, Saif knew how to make money talk. Bashir thanked his God a million times that he was not working in the Austrian embassy, as he would have found it more than difficult, if not impossible, to pander to this young man.

Saif's founding and involvement with the Gaddafi International Charity and Development Foundation was used as one of the channels to facilitate the lifting of sanctions and as a means to change Libya's image as a pariah state. Before our arrival in Manila we were aware through the media of the kidnapping of 21 hostages including ten tourists in May 2000 by Abu Sayaf guerrillas who occupied a Malaysian dive resort. Subsequently the hostages were taken to an Abu Sayyaf base in Jolo Sulu in southern Philippines. Abu Sayyaf made several kidnap demands including the payment of a ransom. With the involvement of Saif under the auspices of his charity, most of the hostages were released in August and September due to a believed payment of US $25 million, which had the caveat that the money was to be used for development aid in the Mindanao area. When we arrived in the Philippines a book was being widely distributed on the subject of the release of the hostages and the Libyan involvement. Obviously the book was immediately banned in Libya and copies were not taken into the embassy. One juicy story revealed in the book was that Saif's emissary had taken a suitcase full of dollars to the Dusit Hotel,

Manila and arranged for a prostitute to come to his room. She found the bed covered in US$ bills and was expected to perform her duties on top of the ransom money; probably true. Bashir heard from colleagues who had been in the embassy at the time that when the cash money arrived by private jet the suitcases containing the dollars were taken to the embassy overnight. Apparently, unscrupulous Libyan personnel were reported to have visited the embassy under cover of darkness and the $25 million cash was reduced to $20 million when it was handed over. I have little doubt as to the authenticity of this story. Stories such as these as ever raised the continually loud exhortation of why foreigners and not the Libyans were always the beneficiaries of the Libyan black gold. The flagrant waste of the country's riches by the cronies and the sons further inflamed the Libyans.

By 2009, Saif had acquired properties in London, Paris and Nice owned a large part of Montenegro, a Lear jet, a yacht and probably much much more secreted away in offshore bank accounts coupled with an unbelievably lavish lifestyle. Saif had learnt from his father and he too pulled people into his spider's corrupt web. This was the case with having his MA and PHd written by others but passed off as being his research and accepted by the London School of Economics. The million dollar donation which was given to the University was to figure in the resignation of staff when the background to the false writing was exposed. For the majority of Libyans with access to the Internet nothing was secret any longer and the international press liked to expose Saif's excesses it made good copy. Enough was enough, anger was reaching boiling point.

Al Saadi Gaddafi was one year younger than Saif and certainly was not the brightest of the clan being well – known for having extremely violent tendencies. His passion was soccer. He leveraged his family's Italian business connections and in 2003 managed to put himself on the books of Perugia football club and became a major shareholder in Juventus. His career was brief as he failed a drug test and thereafter headed Libya's football Federation. Gaddafi ensured that each of his sons controlled an area of security and Saadi's role was as the head of the country's Special Forces. His background was always murky especially when he was involved in a particular nasty murder of a footballer in his club's locker room. Libyans knew him for clashes with the police in Europe, taking drugs and throwing extravagant parties.

Mutassim wished to see himself as the heir apparent and there was strong rivalry between himself and Saif, and at times they hardly talked to each other. We always hoped that the children would kill each other rather like a Shakespearean tragedy. Mutassim held the rank of Colonel and was appointed as National Security Advisor. We always laughed at his choice of clothes, long, dark, shoulder length hair and fashionable designer stubble as if he were off to a nightclub rather than a meeting with US Secretary of State Hilary Clinton. He began an affair with Talitha van Zon, a Dutch model who had once been a Playboy centrefold, holidaying with her in St. Barts in the Caribbean. On the internet at one New Year's Eve party we were to see Beyoncé singing for Mutassim at a reputed cost of $2 million dollars for four songs. He bragged that he spent US$2 million a month, probably an underestimate. Bashir's brother Ibrahim, as Head of Foreign Currency at Central Bank, said that the Gaddafis believed it was their personal bank and so could call on funds as and when they liked, which was an extremely frequent occurrence.

Hannibal's only interest in power seems to have been that he had access to funds and that his famous name avoided prosecution in European capitals. His exploits were to lead to a diplomatic stand off between Switzerland and Libya when his violent temper led to both he and his Lebanese, former model wife being arrested for allegedly beating their maids, resulting in serious injuries. The Gaddafi family insisted that they held diplomatic passports but refused to acknowledge that one only has diplomatic immunity in the country to which one is accredited and obviously this was not the case for the two of them in Switzerland. They were eventually bailed out to the tune of nearly half a million dollars. This prompted Libya to cut off oil supplies to Switzerland, boycott Swiss goods and place a ban on Libyans visiting Switzerland as well as an airline ban. One Christmas Hannibal and his wife were staying in a suite at Claridges hotel, London and the police were called due to the sounds of fighting coming from their suite. He and his wife were taken to a police station and the Ambassador was called to arrange bail, accommodate them at his residence and get them out of the country quickly. This was another instance of Bashir thanking his lucky stars that he was not in the London embassy. The Gaddafi family seemed to think that the way they behaved in Libya was acceptable when travelling abroad and that they were above the law. December 2015 found Hannibal hiding in Syria and subsequently being abducted out of the country and handed over to the Lebanese authorities. He is complaining of having been tortured and calling the Lebanese authorities 'hywaan – animals'. When the family was in power they used and turned a blind eye to all torture and atrocities but once as now the boot is on the other foot they are the ones who are shouting the loudest of Human Rights violations.

Khamis was educated in a military academy in Russia. From that early age when Bashir encountered him at the 20th celebration, he had his Khamis Brigade which would comprise in the future of some of the best trained, well – equipped and loyal soldiers in the regime. Without a doubt it was his military training and men who were able to hold at bay the revolutionaries in Western Libya for such an extended period during the revolution in 2011.

Ayesha, Gaddafi's only daughter was a lawyer. When attending the Libyan courts we noticed that probably 85% of all the lawyers were female; why was this? Although it seems admirable it was as a result of her attendance at the Faculty of Law, Fatah University. Gaddafi issued a dictate that no male law students were to be given entrance to the law faculty until Ayesha had completed her law degree. In 2006 she married her father's cousin and my friends in the foreign diplomatic corps who attended the wedding commented on the excessive diamonds and Dior dresses worn by the Gaddafi women. Her husband's family used their connection with Ayesha to sequester properties at their whim and gain lucrative trade deals. Like her brother Saif, Ayesha ran a charity in support of disadvantaged women. Just before the start of the revolution she was successful in changing the law so that children of a Libyan mother married to a foreigner became entitled to Libyan citizenship, schooling and free medical treatment. We too had visited her office and handed over a request asking her to look at the rights of foreign wives married to Libyans who were unentitled to own property. The response was that she was unable to help. Perhaps as she had recently been appointed a UN ambassador such an international high profile role was more her cup of tea than marginalised foreign wives. There was little if no adoration for her from the Libyan masses. She was considered shrewder and smarter than her brothers. What infuriated the Libyans was her flaunting of wealth and arrogation of Libyan property it could no longer be hidden, as her father and mother had been able to do prior to the days of the Internet.

There were, however, instances when Gaddafi obviously felt that his children, despite their age, needed reigning in. One such instance was the relaxation beach in Gargaresh where the Committee had built a harbour for the Leader's boats and a beach house. This was a pattern to be followed by Revolutionary Committees throughout the country to acknowledge the greatness of the Leader. Gaddafi, on discovering that his sons were using it for drinking and entertaining prostitutes had it knocked down. Likewise when we returned from Manila, we were delighted to find that the former steward on Gaddafi's plane had built a restaurant and sports club on Regatta beach and was building a spa beneath the building. We paid the membership fee and were looking forward to using the facilities. Unfortunately, one evening Safiya arrived with the wife of Saddam Hussein to find her sons eating, drinking and entertaining prostitutes, much to her embarrassment. Her anger was shown by the restaurant being closed, never to reopen, the spa building stopped plus we were never refunded our membership fees. The sons were probably unaffected as they had recently built their palaces on the hill above the sea on Regatta beach. All they needed to do was to find cooks for their kitchens.

After the revolution when photos and videos were displayed of the Gaddafi palaces and beach houses in Libya and around the world, the interior designs always resembled that of five star hotels. Both their parents came from humble backgrounds and became the super nouveau riche with gaudy, bling taste. Family life as such was probably unknown to them.

I have included here many details of the *Gaddafi Royal Family*, as they became known in the mutterings of the Libyan population. Without the Internet we probably never would have known of many of their exploits and blatant greed. I am sure that this was to be one of the triggers for the revolution.

However, corruption and greed was not restricted to just the royal family but equally to their cronies. I remember so well a visit to our home by a young attaché working for Bashir in the UN Agencies section. He saw bragging about how much money he was making through his various uncles who were all powerful friends of Gaddafi as nothing wrong. Bashir cautioned Hatem that although there had been times when he too could have taken bribes, he had never done so and consequently he slept at night and never feared any knock on the door. Hatem's response was bribe taking was normal and this was the only way he could make money especially as his uncles might not be in power in the future. These uncles are no longer in power and were a pretty distasteful lot. I do not know if they were killed in the revolution or they escaped into exile, taking their bounty. Hatem has squirrelled his bribes into property and gold and the source of his wealth is unlikely to be found out. What will he teach his children? How will he explain his money? Does he sleep at night? Sadly I rather think that he sleeps well in the current climate of lawless Libya. He is no different to hundreds of thousands of young Libyans who grew up under Gaddafi and see corruption as being part of the normal way of life.

The timeline of what I have written on the Gaddafi children took place partly when we were living in Libya though some of the greater excesses were when we were in Manila. Oh Glorious Manila. When Bashir originally heard the news that we were going to the Philippines, he was furious. All of his postings had been hardship and he felt now was the time when he should have been rewarded by one of the more prestigious postings. In fact he knew in his heart that no one was sent to London unless they were part of the inner clan and obviously Bashir had never signed up to the Revolutionary Committees and was therefore unlikely to be picked for one of those prime embassies. As always we should have believed in our fate, as it was to prove to be one of our favourite postings. We packed our things this time leaving nothing of value, found a Polish diplomat to rent our house and we were on our way to Manila.

Twenty - Three

Bashir's name means *the bringer of good news*. We had been together for 22 years when we were about to leave for the Philippines. There had been the rough periods but whether good or bad, life had never at any point been dull and the joy of being together and going on another adventure still held the same thrill.

This was the first time that I felt a slight tinge of sadness at leaving Libya. It was true that the country had opened up, but we always questioned for whom. We had built a gorgeous home which by Libyan standards was small but then we were both quite small people in stature, so we had no need of a huge place. We had exactly what we needed. The garden was our ultimate pleasure, winter or summer it gave us freedom that the outside world of Gaddafi prohibited. Every visit to London I had bought freesias, varieties of daffodil bulbs, dahlias and seeds. Everywhere in the garden Bashir had created umbrellas of fragrant, pungent smelling honeysuckle and jasmine. In the road we had planted jacaranda and flame trees, giving us privacy and in the spring showers of light lilac and scarlet blossoms would cover the trees; the Avenue of the Flowers looked splendid unmatched anywhere else in the area. A special find was a tree that in the autumn had large white flowers in the morning that turned to an exotic shade of pink in the evening. On investigation I discovered that the original tree had been brought into the country in the 1920s by an Italian sea captain who travelled to Asia but had fallen in love with Tripoli and brought his botanical finds back to his house in Tajoura. Our house was always surrounded by colour and perfume.

During this period many, firm friendships were established with people who lived all over the world. We were given leaving party after leaving party but it was time to move on and Bashir was impatient to reach Manila and rekindle his diplomatic work. Best of all, as Libyan diplomats we were no longer to be associated with that bad odour of previous years. In fact people wanted to finally know about Libya being as there was now so much potential for lucrative contracts. The scent for making money was strong.

Our plane took off from Tripoli and our possessions were on their way, shipped at our own expense as usual. In that respect nothing had changed in terms of allowances for Libyan diplomats; there were only stipends for returning home shipments. For me, I always wanted to make a home so my pictures and personal keepsakes moved with us wherever we went and this time there were also teaching materials. Bashir knew better than to discuss as to what could or couldn't be taken after the Indian fiasco of losing so many of our treasures.

We were delighted to learn that the Ambassador was a career diplomat, though was known to be a bit of *a climber*. Perhaps a better term might be that he was an opportunist, but nonetheless at least he was not a revolutionary green flag waving committee member surrounding himself with those that wanted to hear his support of the theory. The best surprise of all was that our old friend Habib and his wife from Seychelles were to be in the embassy for one further year. Bashir was by this time a Counsellor Minister, he was in effect number three in the embassy. It is good policy in the diplomatic life to never cross anyone, be they in your embassy or another as there is a strong likelihood of meeting up again. In fact in Manila, the children of diplomats we had known when we had been young diplomats ourselves, were now the young diplomats in various embassies. It was fun reuniting.

Our arrival in Manila followed a rather similar pattern to that of Delhi. Kind Habib had booked us a hotel room in Burgos, a notorious red light area. I think this decision was more because rooms were cheap rather than for any other reason. The criterion for most Libyans was if it was cheap it was good. It was dirty and noisy and we arrived at midnight; business was booming in the building and at that time of night there was no possibility to change hotels. Ever resourceful, we went out and bought some cleaning materials from a nearby 24 – hour shop to clean the bathroom, as well as some bug spray, and a bit of food. Thankfully there were no bedbugs but there was the scuttling of cockroaches and the continuous noise of drunken tomfoolery from outside all night, so a new hotel had to be found.

Rents and hotels are expensive in the Philippines, so a compromise had to be made on our choice of hotel and home. We knew nothing of the country therefore had to rely entirely on the advice of Bashir's colleagues whose criteria was as ever different to ours as theirs was to save and ours was to live in a comfortable place where we could entertain for Bashir's diplomatic level. During the first year we rented a flat but as both Bashir and I had grown up in houses we liked to have our feet on the ground. Additionally, in the Philippines there is the permanent fear of earthquakes and when these happen the building begins to rock and the lights swing, which is quite alarming although at least by now we knew what was happening.

Bashir settled into his embassy life and I began to make my contacts to become an examiner for the British Council and IDP in the Philippines. Good fortune was on my side as they were desperate for examiners and so within one week of arriving I was working five days a week. The demand in the Philippines was huge due to the volume of nurses and doctors wishing to go and work in the UK, Australia, Canada and USA and the IELTS exam was a requirement for acceptance. I was later to create workshops on familiarization courses for the exam so within a very short space of time business was booming. I was also doing the research on the exam and thanks to the Internet it was easy to work with my colleagues in Tripoli. How different life was as a diplomat in terms of communication now, from that of Sierra Leone in 1980.

However, I was not in the Philippines just to work. I wanted to discover the country, culture and people. Strangely I had no contacts in the Philippines apart from the Judge who had rented our house when he had been the Labour Attaché in Libya. When we discovered that his main area of interest in reigniting our friendship was to make amorous advances on my female friends that was one old friendship that was quickly dropped. As ever my source of information was to be the 'Lonely Planet' and the local newspapers.

On spotting an announcement for a one – year course at the Ayala Museum on the history of the Philippines for expatriates I immediately signed up. Here was a unique opportunity as the museum had dioramas showing the history from prehistoric times to the present day and we were to learn how to become volunteer docents. I have always been a firm believer in working in a team and under the more than able leadership of Mary we were to put together a course that was replicated certainly until after I left the country. We were not only native English speakers but also there were participants from Japan, France, Germany, Switzerland to name but a few of the nationalities on the course. Weekly Monday meetings saw two course members give a presentation on the diorama of the day and inviting a guest speaker who was knowledgeable on the subject. Once a month there was a tour, which for our group included meetings with former President Mrs Acquino and Mrs Marcos, a visit to the presidential palace, Corrigador Island and to old Manila so my travels continued and I learned in depth about the Philippines. The course participants were definitely my kind of people and I developed firm friendships. The following year I wrote a two day course on speaking and writing presentation skills to help those non – native speakers when it came to giving their talks and writing their hand – outs. It was a time consuming exercise but was so well received that I was asked to replicate the course annually until I left the Philippines.

The course had also publicised my name in terms of being an English teacher. Soon, I had a full teaching schedule of private students, the majority of whom were Japanese. This was a country that I had never visited but whose art and culture I have long admired. Dotted around my flat I have keepsakes given to me by these students as thanks for helping them learn English. They invoke strong memories of my students' kind faces and their so admirable work ethic.

As always Bashir had bought a car and we were looking to have our own driver. Cars in an embassy are a constant source of dispute amongst Libyan diplomats' wives, so by having our own car I was never involved in their arguments. In fact it seemed that for Libyan wives their major preoccupation was shopping which has always rated at the bottom of my list of things to do, so we had little if any contact. We did however need to find a driver whom we could rely on and we hoped would stay with us for the duration of our four – year posting. It was proving difficult despite putting out feelers and an advertisement in one of the newspapers. Fate, chance or luck was to solve this problem.

We had received an invitation to a Filipino birthday ball celebration; for those that have wealth in the Philippines, they have much. Big extravagant parties at posh venues would come to be part of our diplomatic life and this birthday celebration was one such occasion. We were seated at the top table and my quite elderly neighbour I was to discover had also been married to a diplomat. Chatting I learned her husband had been the Philippines Ambassador in Canada at which point her face seemed strangely familiar. On further discussing various postings all was revealed it was Mrs Mendoza, the mother of Peachy, Amar Hanesh's girlfriend from Nairobi. This was truly a chance encounter and a dinner arrangement was made for some days later along with Peachy whom I could hardly wait to meet again especially to hear the end of her love story with Amar; great gossip and completion of another circle. Over that meal we were to learn that Amar had asked Peachy to marry him and wished to escape with her to South America. He argued that Bashir and I had done it, there being no reason why they shouldn't do the same. To her family he revealed his bank statement, which showed he had accumulated US$140,000, acquired from a combination of various deals as well as a loan from Colonel Ali quite a considerable sum in 1983. It is interesting to note that by comparison, Bashir arrived in London with $20,000. Peachy's family strongly dissuaded her from marrying him aside from the risks there was also the dimension of their different religions. Amar returned to Libya and married his arranged bride and went into private business. He has hidden under the shadow of respectability whilst being one of the profiteers of the Gaddafi regime. The current lack of law enforcement, transparency and justice is the perfect feeding ground for those such as Amar. Peachy had a narrow escape; this man was a snake. The Mendoza family were obviously interested to find out how we had survived the difficulties of our romance, which they had seen grow in Kenya and now of all strange coincidences we were reunited again in the Philippines. Peachy admitted that she had had a narrow escape being far too young and naïve in Nairobi to know the true twists, turns and poisonous bite of the Hanesh snake.

Mrs Mendoza offered her help, which we eagerly accepted, in our quest to find a good driver. Jericho one of her two drivers was suggested and an interview was arranged the following day. Just the name Jericho conjures up wonders, and this man was and is truly a wonder. Bashir promised that when it came time for us to leave Manila that every effort would be made to find him a job in the embassy or with another diplomat, but there could be no promises other than an understanding that we would do our best.

Jericho stayed with us for the full four years through all of our good and bad times. His reward for such loyalty initially was a job as a Libyan embassy driver but since he has been promoted as the embassy Liaison officer. Having a good salary over the years has enabled him to put his son through university, and his two daughters have nearly completed their university education. When I think of the Philippines, he is the first person I think of as he was my daily companion. I hope that I have been able to repay him a little after everything that he gave us.

With my passion for reading I found it strange that Jericho would wish to sit in the car waiting for me doing nothing or sleeping. On enquiring why he did not read, his response was that he could ill afford books. A bestseller at that time was Dan Brown's '*The Da Vinci Code*'. As I knew this to be a straightforward, compulsive, page turner I thought it might whet his appetite for further titles and it was bought as a trial. The bait worked and not only has he become an avid reader but so too have his children, encouraged by their father. Thanks to cheap book parcel post from the UK I am able to send Jericho titles. This introduction has now gone one step further as the local Libyan embassy staff members have a book group thanks to Jericho's encouragement; my father I am sure must be beaming.

Jericho is my Filipino hero along with Eden who was to come into our life later during our stay. Like so many from that country Jericho, Eden and their spouses have sacrificed so much for their children in order that they can have a better life. This we were to see continually during our stay in the country and likewise from Filipinos working in Libya. Their goal for their children was not to become a professional footballer or a soap star and earn millions but rather wanting them to qualify to work in professions where they would be able to help their people. The Filipino smile, despite crippling adversity together with their spirit of tolerance and endeavour to work together should be a beacon of inspiration to youth throughout the rest of the world. There are routes to achieving success, as there are different opinions on what is success, but on numerous occasions there were instances when I was truly humbled on seeing the Filipino work ethic and sacrifice for others.

Twenty - Four
٢٤

Manila was quickly proving to be an ideal posting. Despite Bashir's initial reservations and anger at where we were being sent, it wasn't long before he realised the opportunities that we were being given. Living by the sea was a real plus. We had always found sitting on the sea shore watching the waves and the colours at different times of day or season restful. This was especially true in Libya during troubled times whether the Mediterranean was rough or calm it never disappointed and was always therapeutic. Here in Manila we were able to do the same. The climate had proven easy, as unlike Thailand, there was little of the oppressive humidity found in many tropical countries. We had both found interesting work and amiable work colleagues. The beauty of Bashir working in one field and me in another meant we had a wide circle of friends from completely different walks of life and soon we were turning down invitations. Socially, Manila life was hectic, interesting and stimulating. The first year and a half were probably pretty typical of a diplomat's life.

Not long after our arrival I was invited to a diplomatic afternoon tea party for new wives. It was the time of year when changes took place therefore a good opportunity to meet some of the other new faces. For some unknown reason the Israeli Ambassador had also been invited. Filipinos love taking photographs and so the inevitable group photo was called for. I had learnt over the years to avoid being in photographs that could potentially compromise Bashir and this certainly was one occasion. A quick unnoticed slip to the bathroom would have been a good way to escape but I was caught by the hostess who pushed me into the picture, where worst scenario, I found myself next to the Israeli ambassador. This was definitely going from bad to worse and with a forced smile I moved down to the other end of the group citing my height. I know that I was being hypersensitive but I had just arrived and did not want to jeopardise any posting. As the clicking started I was certainly the least relaxed in the picture. Thankfully it appeared in only one magazine and was unseen by embassy staff, so no intelligence investigation.

One of the hotels where we often used to eat was the Five Star Penninsula. Bashir was a generous tipper and probably as a result was always warmly welcomed by the doormen as we alighted from our metallic blue CD car. Our first Manila New Year was to be with friends at the hotel. We arrived for lunch and after the meal as was our usual pattern went to our room for an afternoon siesta. While I was sleeping Bashir awoke, wanted a cigarette and wearing extremely brief boxer shorts and his hotel slippers went out onto the fire escape but what he had failed to notice was that the door had closed and locked behind him. Yes, he was stranded on the tenth floor with no phone, the only solution being to descend to the main road, walk round to the central entrance followed by the greatest indignity of walking through the lobby in just his brief underwear and hotel slippers. The worst moment he retold was when the doormen saluted and said 'good evening Mr. Ambassador' without even a snigger or questions showing on their faces as to Bashir's almost naked attire. Wherever he went, whatever he was wearing or even how little he still looked wonderful and held his head high. If it had been me in that situation I would have snuck into the hotel and probably would not have recounted the tale; much to the mirth of our friends. Bashir became a legend at the Pen according to Jericho our driver who heard the gossip later from the doormen.

Thankfully, among the few things that I managed to retrieve from Libya were our photographs. In front of my bedside lamp is a photo of Bashir smiling with his twinkling eyes encouraging me daily. The few letters and cards we wrote to each other plus my mother's last letter remain in Libya. These are among my material losses.

As we had experienced in India, when working in developing countries one is able to afford to do things that one would be unable to do in one's own country. Birthdays as ever remained important and two parties were celebrated for Bashir. An Arabian night became a much talked – about event and was replicated by many especially the Filipinos who love glamour. The profit for the Palestinian catering and music groups was that they received continuous bookings from being showcased at our party. For us we had not only had fun but also introduced our guests to a lighter side of the Arab world its music, dance and food.

As we had in Nairobi, we found our way to the racecourse in Manila where they had evening racing. We loved the atmosphere although we had no idea on the form of the horses, jockeys or trainers. It was just a great time out with the locals encouraging on their horses in the warmth of a Manila evening. For a birthday party we rented the huge VIP box, the charge for which was minimal brought in our own caterers and the punters were invited it was almost Derby day but in Manila. Bashir's happy, happy birthdays can never be erased from my memory they remain as nights of happiness and serve their purpose of never forgotten times gone by.

Two people especially opened my eyes to Filipino art and music. An unlikely encounter at a ladies dance group was where I met Tessie Luz, the wife of Arturo who is probably the most well – known contemporary Filipino artist. Was it fate, luck or chance? In my London flat I have a small glass etching of a man playing a magical pipe created by Arturo. Daily, it reminds me of Tessie's invitations to concerts, art exhibitions, talks and introducing me to people associated with the arts. She became my guide and mentor through her knowledge and her tireless work in promoting and encouraging Filipino artistic and cultural talent.

Martin Lopez a music impresario became my second guide. The most memorable opportunity Martin offered was the chance to accompany a guitar quartet tour to Panay and Negros. We visited the cities of Iloilo where he had his ancestral home then onto Dumaguete and Vallehermoso, where his family owned banana and pineapple plantations. Martin's goal for the tour was to bring classical music in an engaging way to children in the islands. Their faces listening to the music followed by enthusiastic loud clapping and stamping at the end of the performance was the sign of the success of the venture. Concerts were held in football fields, schools and church halls and a shopping mall where the children were assembled to listen and learn about classical music through guitars. It was the most uplifting experience to see these youngsters' love of music being developed. There had also been the added bonus of venturing further afield into some of the 7,000 Philippine islands with Martin as my knowledgeable guide.

We managed to travel throughout the country for holidays but perhaps one of the other most memorable trips aside from the guitar quartet was swimming with the whale sharks. They are not nearly as frightening as their name suggests although their size is truly daunting. They are slow – moving filter feeding sharks, known to grow up to 12.65 metres and weigh approximately 21.5 metric tons. They have massive mouths which act as filter feeders for the plankton on which they live. The area around Legaspi is one of their feeding grounds at certain times of year. On disembarking from the plane in search of these creatures our first view was of the Mayon volcano a spectacular sight but there was yet much more to come.

For this adventure we headed out with our fellow travellers, the Gibson family. The hotel was basic and Bashir was having difficulty finding a signal on his mobile. This was a serious problem since he was Charge d'Affaires at the time and sadly he had to leave and return to Manila on the first flight out the next morning. As expected, of course, nothing had happened in his absence at the embassy and nothing did on his return but it was necessary for him to be in situ nonetheless just in case. Many times during all of our postings when we were about to board a plane or ferry we would spot one of the embassy administrators standing on the runway beckoning Bashir back for an emergency. It was all part of his job though this obviously was one of the downsides of working in a small embassy.

On the first night before Bashir's departure we learned that the kitchen was closed. The staff informed us that they had run out of food, to the groans of the Gibson boys with their black hole stomachs. Ever resourceful, Bashir and Carolyn invaded the kitchen, found vegetables and eggs and a few other items plus spices and herbs. They began organising the staff and cooked a feast. We knew we would never starve with the Carolyn Bashir combination neither of whom would ever accept no for an answer.

The next morning Bashir left. It was truly a shame as he was not to experience a swim with these giants of the sea. As we walked to the boat my luminous pink flippers were a source of much hilarity but they were in fact to prove to be a lifesaver on the swim. We chugged out a mile offshore in a small locally made skiff and waited while a Filipino sat on the top of the mast scouting the sea to spot one of the giants. As soon as one was sighted, the boat took off at high speed and then aligned itself in the path of the oncoming fish. As the shark came alongside we were given the order, 'jump' and there we were next to this mammoth fish. It was truly awesome swimming within almost touching distance of its colossal gaping mouth although I have to say mingled with a more than slight feeling of trepidation. Since I am a weak swimmer quickly the shark, family Gibson along with the boat had disappeared in the distance, chasing to keep abreast with the fish. I was left waving my pink flippers in the hope that sooner rather than later they would return and find me. The water was warm, the sky was a brilliant blue and I felt at peace in the tranquillity though a few times the thought that the pink flippers might not be spotted did cause moments of anxiety until I saw the skiff returning. It was truly a unique experience to have observed at such close quarters these incredible animals. At the time of our adventure this sight was not widely known and ours was the only boat out at sea that day. Subsequently I have seen photos of swarms of unregulated boats taking swimmers to view these fish, causing the sharks to be injured at times by the propellers of the boats and frightened by the volume of people. Tourism has given jobs and employment to the locals but at the expense of the safe sanctuary of the sharks. This industry has to find a way to remain in harmony with the environment so both can live safely alongside each other.

The Philippines gave us the opportunity to travel widely in the region and we managed trips to Indonesia, Cambodia, Vietnam and New Zealand. Every place that we visited gave us an insight into how others in the world were living. Cambodia was truly shattering as we saw poverty there that we had not seen elsewhere in all of our travels even in Africa. It was truly heart breaking, especially as there was little that we could do to help. I hope that when recounting our personal anecdotes to friends, colleagues and acquaintances that we have been able to highlight some of the injustices that we have seen.

For Bashir, he was ever on the search for projects that could perhaps be replicated for the benefit of Libya. A Swiss company that had developed cement pyramids, which were placed at strategic points in the sea to help regenerate coral reefs, immediately reminded him of his damaged Gargaresh beach where perhaps a similar project could be implemented. Desalination plants were always of interest as the water from Gaddafi's Libyan Great Man – Made River project would not last indefinitely, despite its massive cost. I have no doubt for Bashir there was always an element of despair at seeing how other countries were able to develop and innovate yet Libya remained under the control of Gaddafi. Furthermore now also added into the mix were the Gaddafi children with no care for the Libyan environment or the welfare of its people.

Bashir had never worked on the Asia desk on a home posting so there was plenty of reading to be done to catch up on the political situation within the country. There was of course the strong link between the Philippines and Gaddafi. Any group that was revolutionary, anti – western, seeking independence, had a Muslim affiliation and needed military support, Gaddafi would willingly be their champion. Mindanao became one area of his focus. Between 1903 and the 1970s the southern area of Mindanao became designated for development under a 'Homestead Programme'. This was a way for Christian settlers to move into untitled Muslim and tribal residential land resulting in the Muslims feeling that they were being robbed of their living area and its opportunities.

As a result of these land grabs 1968 saw the founding of the Moro or Mindanao National Liberation Front (MNLF). Its founder Nur Misuari and his freedom fighters began a protracted armed struggle to regain independence of the region. When Bashir met him he was an old man who had fought, been imprisoned and re – imprisoned, yet still had the fervour of his cause after so many years. He remains a controversial figure even today, although he was always to be one of the predominant links between Libya and the movement. Between 1969 – 1975 there was intense, continuous fighting that resulted in the deaths of both thousands of government and MNLF soldiers. Under pressure from Libya, the Organisation of Islamic countries (OIC) imposed an oil embargo. The Philippine Government was affected disastrously by this embargo and were pressurised to initiate a move to convince Nur Misuari to sit down to peace talks. President Marcos sent his first lady, Imelda to Tripoli to request the assistance of Gaddafi to broker a ceasefire. Cynical people smile wryly about this meeting, as the night before the agreement was reached there were no signatures on the table. Early the next morning it was discovered by officials that Imelda and Gaddafi had both signed and Gaddafi aptly named it the *Tripoli Agreement* between the MNLF – GRPH. President Marcos had an adept envoy in Imelda. It was later witnessed and recognised by the OIC. The agreement called for a ceasefire and autonomy with the proviso that Mindanao would remain part of the Philippines. Further agreements were reached on each occasion with Libya as a broker in 1989 through President Corazon Aquino and in 1996 under President

Ramos whereby a final peace agreement was signed allowing the region a legislative assembly, executive council, regional security forces and an economic and financial system.

Mindanao became one of the main areas of Bashir's work with one assignment to travel on an Organisation of Islamic Countries (OIC) delegation down to the region on a fact – finding mission to report to the Annual OIC conference. The OIC is the second largest inter – governmental organisation after the United Nations and has membership of 57 states spread over 4 continents. During Bashir's time in Manila the Philippine Government lobbied for observer status of the OIC but was denied repeatedly; the most recent being in January 2015. The mission to Tawi Tawi, Sulu Jolo, Zamboanga and Cotabato had an element of danger. Splinter groups had formed in the south over the years but perhaps the most fearful was the Abu Sayyaf Group (ASG) led initially by Khadaffy Janjalani. Abu Sayyaf is intolerant of other religions and calls for a continuous jihad to pursue a pure Islamic state in the Mindanao region and believes in the 'killing of enemies' and 'depravation of enemies' wealth.' The OIC delegation was going to be travelling extremely close to Abu Sayyaf strongholds. It was an important delegation made up of representatives from Malaysia, Indonesia and Saudi Arabia with Bashir representing Libya they were an obvious target so security had to be tight.

As ever Bashir was good at keeping me in the dark until after the event. On his return I saw the photographs of their convoy. Each car was designated to the country of the delegate so Bashir travelled on his own at least not flying his country's flag which could have been a red rag to a bull in the area. Bashir's companions were heavily armed soldiers pointing their guns out of every car window and having front and rear bodyguard vehicles. At one point Bashir said that they found themselves within only 20 feet from an Abu Sayyaf group hidden in the dense undergrowth watching silently. Their convey drove off at top speed with Bashir praying that he would not be captured and held as a hostage in the jungle of Mindanao by that group.

For him the tragedy was seeing why projects with funding from the OIC had never materialised. During this visit the delegation was asked to attend a road opening celebration and yet the road was only 40 feet long. The rest had never been completed as somewhere along the way the money from the project had vanished which was a reoccurring theme for so many of the projects. In Tawi Tawi, Bashir was truly horrified at the poverty and the contrast between the Philippines of the north and that of the south. There was a total lack of sanitation, drinking water and electricity, all the basic necessities of life. Roly, a friend who Bashir used to sit and chat with at length, told me how shattered Bashir had felt seeing the poverty and inequality in the region first hand. Throughout the visit everywhere they went, as is the Philippine way of hospitality, lunches and dinners with sumptuous displays of food for honoured guests were fed to the OIC guests. Towards the end of the visit they were taken to Sulu Jolo for one such lunch. The table was creaking with food and yet they had just seen people in abject poverty. Sometimes emotions take over from diplomatic protocol and Roly continued that Bashir felt he could no longer stand all the excess food and left the table telling his hosts he was taking his food out to his driver and guards and that the people waiting outside should be invited in to enjoy the buffet feast as well as the VIP guests. Bashir succeeded in everyone being well fed that day, not just the fat cats. He was diplomatically unorthodox but many times this proved successful but at other times with raised eyebrows. He fought long and hard to have his amendments on the final report document to the OIC General Conference reflect the true facts of the visit. Sadly he was not the messenger at the assembly, and it was watered down.

From that visit he worked with other Non – Governmental Organisations (NGOs) on interfaith dialogue, especially with colleagues from the British Council. Bashir was a great believer in diplomatic rather than military solutions, and I feel sure he would be greatly saddened to see what is occurring in his own country today. I have serious doubts if he would have wanted or been able to work with his own people in today's atmosphere. I have expressed my opinions and those of Bashir many times and I feel sure there are many who are in total disagreement with the views expressed. However, I hope that I am not only a good talker/ writer but also a good listener and my current assessment is that we all talk too much and listen too infrequently. Recently I attended a reception for Nelson Mandala day and a woman sitting next to me said we forget that we have one mouth and two ears, an obvious thought. Mandela was truly a man who listened and whose name is held in awe worldwide today. Gaddafi rarely listened, only talked endlessly his people have learnt too well to follow his example.

I had several encounters with Mrs Marcos, notable worldwide as an eccentric icon for her shoe collection. Due to the connection between her and Gaddafi, she frequently came to Libyan national days and dinners and also lived in the same building as our Ambassador. I was always truly amazed and surprised at how forgiving the Filipino people were after everything that this woman and her husband had done to the country. In my opinion the Marcos family plundered the country of its wealth and yet her children are in public office today with both living opulent lifestyles. Money seems to talk. On Sundays she would sometimes eat at one of our favourite Italian restaurants and arrive with a posy of maids, one to my amusement carrying her handbag, together with drivers and bodyguards. There would always be photo taking of her by Filipinos at every opportunity and on national day receptions this was no exception. On one such occasion I was standing next to Imelda and mentioned how I hated having my photo taken with her, she looked shocked, to which I quickly explained that this was due to our difference in height she being an extremely tall woman and I short. Perhaps the most memorable conversation we had was when she regaled me with stories of all the amazing men she had met in her life. President Marcos used her on many occasions to broker deals as he had done in Libya. I was curious to discover who was the man other than her husband whom she most admired her reply of 'Richard Nixon' was astonishing. She qualitied her choice by praising him as a peacemaker in the dealings he had with China, which paved the way she felt for a more peaceful world. He certainly would not have been my choice.

As diplomats we are exposed and have an opportunity for access to places and people not within the normal sphere of living. In our second year Bashir became Charge d'Affaires when the Ambassador was away, as Habib had returned to Libya. On one occasion in his capacity as CdA we were invited to Malcanang Palace to celebrate Philippine Independence Day. Until today I have always found it rather surreal being in the CD1 Mercedes with the Green Libyan flag flying. On this occasion traffic was moved out of the way by motorcycle outriders with the car shooting through the road blocks up to Malcanang. On my bucket list I wish I could replicate the car and outriders but down Park Lane, London obviously this one is unachievable but a fun one for my list. My meeting with President Gloria Arroyo was converse to that with Imelda Marcos as

I was finally to find someone who was shorter in stature than me and we were able to meet and talk eye to eye.

The first years of our stay had been comfortable and uneventful but as ever we wanted our feet on the ground and we found and moved to a house with a tiny garden in San Lorenzo one of the Makati villages. It was here that Bashir developed his passion for orchids. Our garden was always full of these flowers and he continually tried to find new ways of producing bigger and better blooms. From a Hotel, Banqueting Manager he learned how she managed to have such wonderful orchid blooms in her office. For those wishing to have continuous flowering plants the explanation was that she boiled up cheap, white rice, giving the water to the orchids and then ate the rice. This was to become a routine in our house until we left and the orchids bloomed prolifically. On our departure Jericho became the guardian of all of the plants in his house and I am sure they are in more than able hands, being fed their weekly dose of rice water.

Manila really was proving to be an ideal posting. We were assured that our house was being well looked after under the stewardship of brother Lamin. He was paid for his work and whenever he asked for loans his ever – generous brother Bashir forked out. His true character was only to be revealed much later in my story. For now, it seemed that finally we had hit a period of good luck, prosperity and peace.

Twenty - Five

٢٤

Gloria Arroyo had been the President when we arrived but inevitably there were alleged cronyism and corruption charges as there had been with all previous presidents. However, diplomatically there seemed to be relative peace in the northern part of the country although there were always the inevitable whisperings of rebellion. I have come to realise that we were obviously not the pair to live anywhere without there being revolutions or coups in our lives and Philippines was to prove to be no exception. Perhaps Bashir's name was not always the bringer of good news.

On the 27th July 2003 I had been examining at the Intercontinental Hotel with my exam room overlooking the Ayala shopping centre and Oakwood. A pleasurable lunch and chit chat had been taken during the break and I along with all the examiners returned to our rooms to begin the afternoon session. It was then that I noticed that the Ayala mall was surrounded by army trucks, small tanks and armed soldiers. From experience I knew this was not a good omen. Thankfully everyone by this time had mobile phones and I called Bashir to try and discover the cause. Suddenly, life was not as peaceful as we had believed. An armed mutiny of 321 soldiers who called themselves the 'Bagong Katipuneros' wanted to show the Filipino people the alleged corruption of the Arroyo administration. They also stated that they had seen signs suggesting that the President was going to declare martial law. The soldiers had entered the premises of the Ayala Center in several separate groups, disarmed the security guards and taken over Oakwood. They planted claymore mines around the building and in the vicinity and snipers were posted on the Oakwood roof deck which I could see from my examining room window. This would be the first time that I was to see snipers but not the last. Bashir as usual was 'cool' and I learned that he had gone by a back route to the embassy in Dasmarinas and had seen heavily armed men in full battle gear marching through the village towards the Ayala centre. His sound advice was to stay in the safety of the Intercontinental. Everyone, it seemed, had been given similar advice, stay put until things became clearer. I cannot remember exactly what I did that afternoon whether we went on examining, but I rather suspect not. I feel sure that in all probability I settled down to read a book which I always carried in my bag, my best companion in times of trouble. When looking out of the window it was like watching a movie but this was not reality TV.

Later in the afternoon the rebels went on air and read a statement presenting their grievances against the Arroyo government. It was obviously going to be a standoff but my problem was how to get from the hotel to home. Fortunately I lived in a village within walking distance from the Ayala centre but Bashir was most reluctant for me to hot foot it home feeling that the situation was too fragile. With diplomatic plates on our car and trusty Jericho at the wheel somehow Bashir managed to find a way into the rear of the Intercontinental hotel. What a relief to see our car and to be driven to the comfort and safety of home and a stiff drink. This was the end of my adventure, which had just been from a hotel window but not for Bashir and Jericho.

On the Saturday evening President Arroyo gave a 5pm deadline on the Sunday for the rebels to give up their positions peacefully and return to their barracks. Although the following day was a Sunday Bashir had asked Jericho to work as he knew that he would probably have to report to the embassy. The Ambassador was out of the country but no one else apart from Bashir was prepared to attempt the drive. Yes we lived closest to the embassy but it did seem that perhaps Bashir had a greater commitment to duty than his colleagues especially those of the Intelligence officer and Military attaché. Both of those officers should have been prepared to at least have accompanied Bashir as had Iyat and Gilban in Nairobi. Nevertheless they stayed safely closeted in their apartments and houses unwilling to move. The career diplomat showed his metal the political appointees their true wimpish characters.

I as always was unhappy about Bashir leaving but had forgotten that he had the ever – resourceful Jericho with him who knew all the back ways into Dasmarinas village, both in and out. Despite meeting various roadblocks and questioning due to it being a diplomatic car, Bashir was able to send a report and return home unscathed where I welcomed the two of them with greatly relieved open arms. Of course we had filled up baths with water, had all the necessary food supplies, batteries etc., in case things progressed negatively we were truly the consummate professional diplomats by this stage.

Shortly before the 5pm deadline the President announced an extension to 7pm and it was during that time an agreement was forged between the two groups. At 10pm it was announced that the occupation of Oakwood was over. It had been a bloodless mutiny or coup that had ended unsuccessfully for the rebels who had failed to rally any real support from the public. I think that the Filipinos had had enough of coups and counter coups and just wanted to get on with their lives and have a better economic future. We had been through two attempted coups now and never thought that there would be more to come which would be much more protracted than those of Nairobi and Manila.

I had no doubt by this stage that the stresses of working under the Gaddafi regime had taken a heavy toll on Bashir's health. People deal with stress in many different ways and sadly Bashir's was to be an extremely heavy smoker. His breathing was becoming laboured but he was reluctant to travel to London for a check – up, believing that there were good doctors in the Philippines. The cardiologist advised him that he needed to have a heart bypass operation. I was absolutely terrified and felt that we should seek a second opinion, but Bashir was as ever stoical saying he had faith in the doctor and the operation was scheduled to proceed. Hindsight is not a good thing as when later he saw a doctor in London the consultant was horrified at what he had undergone as it was obvious from an x – ray that all he had needed was a stint; a simple operation. Unscrupulous doctors may see dollar signs when it comes to embassies paying their bills and probably this was the case or perhaps it was just an old fashioned way of doing things. I like to think the latter.

Bashir went into the hospital the night before the operation and we said our last missives to each other then and there, as he did not want me being over emotional the next morning. I am sure he was right. However, when I arrived home that evening our landline phone was ringing. This was unusual, as we generally used only mobiles but I picked up the phone and a male voice growled that he was watching my house and knew that I was alone and would be visiting me in the night. Obviously, to have called Bashir at that time would have upset him just a few hours before major surgery and there was nothing in reality that he could have done from his hospital bed. Thankfully, Jericho had not left to go home and assured me that he would stay the night. As always he came to my rescue, as he was to do on so many occasions for both of us. Fortunately the voice proved to be only that. I learned from the hospital the next day that prank callers would search hospital records and then call the houses of the patients to discover if anyone was there perhaps as a cruel prank or in order to carry out a burglary. Before driving down to the hospital the next morning I telephoned the ambassador and asked him to put a guard on our house. He told me I was over – reacting but I feel sure if it had been a Libyan wife calling something would have been done. He was proved to be right but it did not give me any peace of mind at the time. I drove down to the Alabang hospital and waited for Bashir to come out of surgery. Every waiting second seemed endless.

Two and a half hours later he was wheeled out and taken to the ICU unit. All had gone well but his lungs were in a poor state and they had left a drain tube in just in case of complications. Much later in the afternoon I was to find him heavily drugged, with tubes and machines everywhere on his body, which was alarming. Bashir was never one to complain and this time he could only sign that he was fine. This was probably one of the most distressing conditions when I was to see him in a hospital but there were more to come.

In the middle of the night he had a relapse being barely able to breath and begged the nurses to call his surgeon but for some reason they delayed acting on his request. Finally in the early hours, the doctor arrived. The following ten days were spent in ICU as a spot on his lung had ruptured and was bleeding. They were hoping with various medications that the bleeding could be stopped. Calves liver meat Bashir loved but hated broccoli and it was these two food items that the doctor thought might perhaps hasten the healing process. Lunch and dinner cooked by the trusty Eden would be brought down to the hospital and finally the bleeding stopped. He never ate broccoli again but admitted that it had been a lifesaver. Twelve days later he was home, very much weakened and it took months for him to be back to relative health. In truth he was never to return to his former self. The one thing that never returned was the smoking going cold turkey the night before the operation that was a blessing.

During our stay in Manila we were to experience many earth tremors, which were unnerving but one truly strong night – time earthquake hit 6.5 on the Richter scale shortly after Bashir's return home from the operation. For those who have never seen or felt an earthquake it must be hard to imagine. Everything moves and sways and what I was to see for the first time that night was the road heaving up and down as if a giant monster was moving under the tarmac. That slow motion scene moved endlessly before my eyes during that earthquake experience. The tragedy for the Filipino people when these quite regular typhoon and earthquake disasters occur is that the people have so little before and they are left with absolutely nothing after the quake or storm.

My house help Eden had worked long and hard building a house in the Tacloban area and when typhoon Haiyan struck both she and her family were in Manila, but her mother was living in the house that Eden had saved for and built over the years. The house was completely destroyed and her elderly mother held onto a piece of wood in the sea for hours. There is no insurance compensation for what these people have lost; they just have to start all over again. It is heart breaking to see and to be pretty helpless in what one can do to assist. Since my charity experience in India I had been reluctant to be involved in physical help again for fear of being reported by the Libyan intelligence. I felt that the best I could do was to help Eden and Jericho and their children and give financially which we did when there and since leaving. It has been the most wonderful reward to observe what they have achieved subsequently.

The Philippines had proved to be one of the easiest places that Bashir was to work although probably not one of the most interesting. When I leave a country it is not the place or the lifestyle that I am leaving behind, but rather the people and friends and so it was in Manila. More than anything else the Philippines had highlighted yet again that I had so much whilst others had so little. I had thought going back to Tripoli was going to be like returning to the lifestyle, work and friends that I had known prior to 2002 but it was to prove to be oh so different. It was to be my biggest endurance test ever in my life with Bashir.

Twenty - Six

The far off memories have been easy to write about now they are long gone and have no effect on my life. The remembering is now nearer and it is becoming harder. Up until 2006 the majority of events in our life together had affected me indirectly but in the following years the danger, hurt and pain would be unleashed directly on both of us. I realise that I have put or tried to put these times into selective memory loss but I know that they have to be reawakened in order to complete my book; it is becoming harder. It is true as time passes memory fades but I suppose recollection improves.

Unlike India, in the Philippines we had been far removed from Libya both in proximity and in the main, politically. Neither of us went back during the four year posting, always preferring to take advantage of visiting countries in the area which we knew we would never be able to travel to from Libya. I visited London on a couple of occasions, as I liked to keep in touch with my family and friends and to soak up the cosmopolitan, city atmosphere. Poor Bashir was beginning to realise that the only contact he would have with his family was when they telephoned asking for money. No phone calls were received when he had his heart operation. Either they were uncaring or unloving or both, despite protestations of love when begging.

Bashir's brother Ismael had eleven children. On many occasions Bashir remarked 'you have your football team surely it is time to stop' adding that financially there had to be a limit on the number but always receiving from Ismael the reply that God would provide. When Ismael's first son telephoned asking for $5,000 for his wedding celebration, he was met with a firm *no* given that if we had been in Libya this would have been ten months local salary for Bashir. It was quite extraordinary what the family expected us to pay for despite knowing that our Libyan wedding had been small and we disapproved of large extravagant weddings, especially when the groom in question was unemployed. It was as if this money was easily come by, as there never seemed to be any acknowledgement that we had actually worked long and hard for the dollars. A gift was sent but in all probability not well received as it was much smaller than the large amount asked for and no thanks were received. Lamin, Bashir's youngest brother clearly saw Bashir as his tap. Before leaving for Sierra Leone Bashir's father had made him promise to always look after his younger brother. He had always kept this promise despite my frustrated protestations. We were and always would be the first to support worthy causes especially for those we felt wanted and wished to help themselves and could be aided with financial support from us. Shkuka family on the other hand, seemed to believe in free hand outs. This was I believe, part of the *black oil curse* as they like many of the unemployed youth saw that the Gaddafi siblings seemed to be entitled to everything whilst they received nothing and this was causing rising discontent. I write this here for a better understanding of the Shkuka family background in what would occur with 9/36.

Our return to Libya was less traumatic than it had been from India, but our house was never to be as we had left it in 2002; that was when it was at its full glory, cared for and loved. A number of things had obviously changed as we drove down into our street. On that day there were intelligence/security guards posted at either end of the street and also surly looking officers sitting outside our house in the shade of our trees. It seemed we had become infested with security and across the road a high – rise palace was being built. This, we learned was to be the new residence of Mohamed Gaddafi, the first son of the leader. When we had left, he had a residence in another part of Tripoli but now he wanted to live near his mother and had bought all the houses across the road in order to create this new home for himself and his family. The building was still under construction at this time and Mohamed was living in his original house at the end of the street.

I believe Mohamed never thought of the welfare of his guards. They were required to stand or sit on plastic chairs whether it was cold, raining, swelteringly hot or ghibili (dusty). The only shelter they could find were our trees, unlike the guards of others who were given a guardhouse for shelter from the elements. For me to have to confront a Gaddafi guard whenever I left my house was a problem that had to be solved, as they were arrogant, lewd characters believing I could not understand the vulgar comments they were making about me. I could. Yes, the character of the street had changed. It was now Gaddafi Street. When we left for Manila it was known as *the avenue of the flowers* by the taxi drivers we used, due to the trees and flowers we had planted on the pavement outside our house. Nothing ever stays the same, one can only hope and look forward.

What alarmed us the most was the house that fronted onto the manwa area had now risen in height to a further three storeys. The outside wall onto the street had been broken down, a gate had been put across and the shared space was now used for parking plus an outdoors party area for the middle house. Apparently the property had been bought in our absence, despite it being under law No.4, and the new owners had taken advantage of our absence. Although building permission laws existed, these were easy to override with *whom do you know* and now they had their new residence. This resulted in our kitchen and bathroom windows being open to their comings and goings and a noisy children's playground. Libyans stay up late, as still the majority of women do not work and the children generally do not have a bedtime. It rather depends what is on the TV or the guests who are in the house. A final painful twist of the knife in the wound was the state of our garden. We had been most specific when writing the lease that the garden was to be well cared for but nearly every plant had gone and the bougainvillea was towering into the trees and hanging everywhere. It was yet another gardening disaster. We were later to discover that every bulb had been removed from the garden and presumably taken back to Poland. It was a sorry state of affairs. There are always ups and downs in diplomatic life, but I was beginning to find the constant rebuilding of one's life extremely hard work. Although there was an appearance that the laws were kept, Libya was in fact, lawless. We were about to find out that laws could be used against people, and being on the wrong side could result in a 15 – year prison sentence.

Things had changed dramatically in our four – year absence. Some major, new roads had been built and it was far easier to move from west to east Tripoli on these highways; this was a plus. However, no attempt had been made to improve the minor roads, which were made up of innumerable potholes, causing flooding in the winter. Infrastructure projects were never a Gaddafi priority unless there was a buck to be made for him personally or his cronies. Perhaps the most astounding noticeable change was the building of houses and office blocks everywhere one looked. These were not small building projects but rather huge duplex houses and offices. One did question from where the money was coming and who was building them? It transpired that people were doing deals with the banks to acquire loans and thereafter renting the houses to foreigners who were flocking into Libya to take advantage of the new oil and gas deals and construction projects; it was boom time in Libya as had never been seen previously. The Gargaresh shopping area, which was known as Tripoli's Knightsbridge was changed immeasurably with new shops being built and the old ones refurbished. Those days of austerity were obviously over. In 2006 if one had money you could find anything and everything you wanted. Mercedes car dealerships, electronics, Marks and Spencer, Debenhams, British Home Stores, luxury brand stores and large food supermarkets selling most of the products which previously we had carried from London as little treats. Wonderful green grocer shops abounded, with the freshest fruit and vegetables brought in season from the farms daily. Behind the scenes, the illicit booze sellers were making a killing. Libya was never dry in the alcohol sense of the word.

The everyday appearance of the people had also changed noticeably. Libyans like to be well dressed; they are a very cosmetic nation and tend to measure people on the cut of their clothes. Both Libyan men and women seem to love the activity of shopping for things to wear as a hobby or something to do on holiday. When I arrived in 1984 it was normal to see men wearing Libyan traditional dress both at weekends and to work. By now this was a rarity during the weekday and it was only to the mosque on Friday that one noticed the national dress, mainly worn by elderly men while the youngsters were clothed in western attire. The picture for women was much more radical since leaving in 2002. It was now rare to see a woman without a headscarf and many were wearing this plus the Islamic long coat, having replaced the *farajea* (white outer garment worn to cover face and body unique to Libya) worn previously. This was perhaps because it was impractical, especially when driving. For those who wished to cover their faces many had taken to wearing the niqabs and black abayas of Saudi Arabia; something never seen previously in Libya. I am unsure what was the cause of these changes? When I look at the group photos of Bashir with his university class in Malta in 1970 none of the female students are covered or wearing scarves and some in fact are wearing mini

215

– skirts. Knowing some of the women in these photos, I now found them heavily covered, a couple even wearing gloves to hide their hands.

A further massive change, and one seen globally, was communications. Perhaps if Gaddafi had realised quite how this would contribute to his downfall, he wouldn't have permitted the opening up of the communications area. There were two mobile companies and charges for internal calls were inexpensive, although one did have to go through a relatively invasive security check in order to obtain a sim card. It was also the norm to have a satellite dish and the innovative Libyans knew well how to tune into popular international TV channels for free. People were learning what was happening everywhere in the world and I began to find that Libyans were often better versed in world politics than those whom I would meet in ordinary everyday life in the UK. They wanted to know and they wanted to find out what they were missing out on and why. Gaddafi and his children could continue as they wished but now the media and the Libyans had them under a spotlight. Of this I think they were either unaware (unlikely) or rather felt they were untouchable.

Although this was not a change I think that it is worth commenting on to establish the conservative religious nature of Libyans. I do believe there was an element of peer pressure with everything stopping for prayers five times a day. At whatever point I might be in a lesson it was books down and all would leave to go to the office prayer room. Anyone who looked as if they might not pray would always be asked 'aren't you coming?' The mosques would be full to overflowing for Friday prayers although perhaps some mosques were fuller than others as a means of networking. Perhaps not well understood in the West is the long standing and always deeply held conservative religious nature of this country. The controls that had been in place when we had left were not as restrictive although all Immans continued to be appointed by Gaddafi. The Islamic Call Society was a hugely rich organisation, which had offices in many countries of the world for the promotion of the Muslim religion. Their office in Manila was run by one of Gaddafi's cronies' who was regularly in conflict with the Ambassador as to what he could or could not do in the country. After we left the Ambassador would be recalled to Libya for an investigation and put under house arrest it was a power struggle between the two.

Gaddafi was enjoying the adoration and prestige that only Africa gave him and announced that he wished to expand his embassies in the region and to reopen old and establish new offices. Africa had always been the backwater for diplomats and was considered dangerous in terms of health and safety. The Diplomatic Institute was now well restablished and there was a law that stated that a diplomat needed to have both a degree and to have graduated from the one – year post – graduate course at the Institute. Gaddafi was aware of a growing discontent due to unemployment and low salaries. He still had his hatred of the old school diplomats and had been seconding his revolutionary followers from other ministries into the Foreign Ministry. This Africa opportunity was good bait to get people out of the country and ensure that his powerbase was secure and happy. It was announced that there would be neither a requirement to remain in Libya for the stipulated four year home posting period and one would be able to jump to the top of the list for an African posting. Nor would there be the necessity to complete the Diplomatic Institute. We thought long and hard as to whether to leave immediately and have a further four years out of the country on a good salary rather than remaining in Libya. We knew Africa and could deal with the difficulties but we had problems with our house that had to be solved and so opted to remain in Libya. Those that went in large numbers were posted across the continent although they were to find it was not as they expected and in the embassies squabbling soon caused many HR problems. The main area of contention was the career diplomats versus the political appointees and the large numbers, in some cases 20, assigned to an embassy where in reality it needed only three or four employees. Our decision was made a home posting for four years and Bashir slotted straight into the International Organisations Department and once again became the Head of Agencies.

I am something of a tortoise as far as my teaching is concerned and through the examining in Manila and various research projects, I knew that my CV was now looking pretty good for an EFL teaching job. I was thrilled to discover that Bell Cambridge was now operating in Tripoli and applied and began working for them on their General Electricity Company of Libya project. This was a first for Bell as their only female employee in the country and also for GECOL. It was very fortuitous as finally I was to be paid an expatriate salary, and best of all have Malcolm as my boss. I have been lucky as three out of the four expatriate bosses with whom I have worked have become both firm friends and people I would regard as mentors. As well I was able to transfer my examining back to

Libya. Yet again I returned to working a six day week, but it enabled us to afford a comfortable life style. Libya had become expensive for the locals and there was rising inflation.

One of the best results from the Bell job was that daily I took a taxi home by standing on the road waving down a car. It was not preferable but that was how I travelled around Tripoli, never having learnt how to drive. On one such night a taxi stopped, and the driver was Khalifah. He became my Jericho. We established an arrangement whereby he picked me up from the office every evening and I spoke to him in Arabic. It was my daily Arabic speaking class and as a result my Arabic skills improved somewhat, Bashir and I having always spoken English to each other. Khalifah also drove us in the evening to parties as Bashir never drove when he had been drinking and Khalifah was tolerant of the fact. He stayed with us until he found a permanent job eighteen months later and at that time the remarkable Yusuf took over. He too was fiercely loyal working right up to my last visit in 2014 when I returned to Libya alone. On that last trip I managed to find him a permanent job with a telecommunications company. I do not know where either Khalifah or Yusif are today but I just pray that they are well and safe. They always looked after my safety and gave me another view of Libyan life. These are the true Libyans who are the backbone of the country, peaceful, hardworking, honest and deeply religious.

The foreign oil companies of course were the goal of all teachers, in particular working for part of the BASF group whose teachers were on rotation, paid a dream salary, given the most comfortable working conditions plus good living accommodation and a car. All teachers coveted the chance to work for this company. For some reason or other they decided that all teaching was to be transferred down in the desert with one remaining slot for the Tripoli office, I applied and was appointed. However, I was paid the half that of the other male teachers and received no car, no accommodation or any other perks. Despite being better qualified than my colleagues, by virtue of having a Libyan husband I was still being stigmatised but felt a change was necessary nonetheless. I was sorry to leave my GECOL colleagues as they had become friends during the year but it was time to move on to new pastures. Furthermore, Cambridge University English Exams needed an inspector for Libya and I applied and was again, appointed. Perhaps you will feel inclined to skip over the pages about my teaching career but I believe they demonstrate how the country was changing under the more open Gaddafi policy but at the same time how corruption and nepotism was the name of the game. The learning of English was back in fashion in a colossal way.

At Wintershall during my first year I was instructed to write a course for graduates to help them improve their English skills. The majority of the participants at the end of the course would be offered a job with the company. It was a small group of eight students, seven of whom were hard working, qualified and deserved a reward for all of their efforts. The eighth was the son of the CEO of one of the large oil refining companies. He arrived on the first day signed and left and was not seen again until the last day when he returned and asked to see the attendance register and began putting ticks next to his name for attendance for the whole course. Telling him that this was impossible he looked shocked and asked if I was aware of his name with the throwaway line that nobody worked for Wintershall unless they were able to help the company. This was a young man who was probably no more than 20 whose place on the course had gone unfilled yet he now wished to rock up, tick the attendance as complete in order that his CV would look impressive. There are so many young Libyans who have the ability but are never given a chance due to their not having a connection. Merit was not the word for getting jobs or opportunities in Libya it was always *who you knew*.

The following year in my free time I formulated a one – month scholarship programme to prepare participants for working in the oil industry. A friend designed a poster advertising the scholarship course criteria which was sent to the Scottish HR Manager for his approval. This man had no interest in serving the Libyan community and was only interested in participating in the pre – existing cronyism within the organisation, for his personal benefit. Nonetheless, eventually I received the green light but with the proviso that it was only for seven participants as the remaining place had to be kept for Shukri Ghanem, the head of the National Oil Corporation to allocate a candidate. This was, apparently, standard practice. I was upset that still one place was probably not going to be given on merit but resigned myself to the fact that seven was better than none. The Head of the Training Department, a Libyan opportunist climber advised he was approaching the Head of the Engineering Department at the university to suggest names, thus further undermining

219

my goal. There was not going to be an open application procedure and I binned the poster. I was irate that no matter what one tried to do to help the less fortunate Libyans it would be muddied by bureaucracy and corruption. Agreement was finally reached that there would be pre – tests from 25 chosen candidates and an interview. It does not take a genius to guess who one of the candidates was arriving for an interview, yes the no show son from the previous year. I could hardly believe my eyes and he was every bit as useless on that day as he had been the previous year. I stood my ground and he was not selected. Those that were, I knew would truly benefit from the course and I have to say I was delighted that there was one female engineer. At the conclusion of the course all the participants gained jobs of their choices; I felt it a job well done. However, I had discovered the full extent of nepotism and cronyism that existed in the oil industry. It seemed nothing had changed since the days of King Idris a new royal family now dished out the choicest jobs or awarded the lucrative oil contracts for bungs. I detested the system and felt that my face did not fit at Wintershall; I was looking for another move.

Gaddafi was anxious to see the youth standing on street corners in groups removed and so MA and Doctorate degree scholarships abroad were being offered in abundance, although of course the usual crony contact was necessary. Increasingly companies too were requiring exam certificates from a verified external examining body so my work with Cambridge University English exams increased. There were centres down in the desert areas where women were not permitted and which required a desert pass not easy to obtain. The oil companies were advised that if they wished to continue exams they had to accept my presence and so I was able to make some remarkable desert trips. They were a chance in a lifetime. On the first visit to an oil field the Training Manager and I flew down in the company plane on a Thursday, carried out the inspection on the Friday and Saturday and flew back on the Sunday. I had always believed that if I had been given the chance then I could have easily worked in the desert with the perk of a high salary and working on rotation one month on and one month off. The desert summer heat is intense, I have been in 45C on occasional days in Tripoli but here it was 45C – 50C day and night; it was unbearable. I had to put a wet handkerchief over my mouth in order not to breathe in hot air. One walked as quickly as one could from one's room to the place of work, dining room or communal games room; after three days I was happy to return to the fresh air of Tripoli.

There is no denying that despite the summer heat, the beauty of the desert, the golden sand dunes set against the blue of the sky and at times the green of the odd oasis dotted with palm trees is unparalleled. On this particular visit I was taken to Ojala which had been one of the once important commercial stations for caravans in the 3rd Hijri century between the Green Mountain and this oasis. Ojala until today is renowned for its dates, which I brought back to Tripoli for Bashir and his colleagues and the fruit was well received. The ancient mosque of Ojala is one of the most important ancient Muslim buildings going back to the 6thHijri century hence it is a deeply conservative area. The locals had created a model village based around old Libyan traditions for tourists. One imagines they were hopeful that sooner or later the country would be opened up but at that time the only visitors that passed were the odd oil workers. Business was not booming and neither were sales of their dates. Security has to be a major concern in protecting the oil camps and it is understandable the difficulty in obtaining desert passes to visit these areas. In this first camp the company had uncovered a Muslim Brotherhood group, all of whom were arrested and imprisoned and accordingly there was no mobile telephone signal out of the camp one had to use a landline, presumably monitored by the security services. Although perhaps the company would rather have employed youth from other parts of Libya, they felt there was an obligation to employ locals but it was from here that the extremist group had come. An indication of how this group had not in truth been stamped out was when at the end of the visit the HR Manager wanted a photo of all the candidates with their teachers. This immediately caused controversy with a couple of the students refusing to have their photos taken as it was 'haram' (forbidden) and when the HR manager included me in the picture a further ten left the group picture refusing to be in a photo with a woman. On this visit many times I encountered men who preferred not to shake hands with me because of my gender.

On a further inspection visit I flew down on a Croatian plane, which was leased by the oil company with a Croatian cabin crew of extremely pretty and sociable females. We immediately teamed up and after my final morning inspection the camp boss organised four Land Rovers to take us out into the desert dunes. These huge mountains of sand were beyond magnificent. I could imagine or wish myself to be Gertrude Bell out in the desert all that I was lacking was the china tea service for afternoon refreshments. Everyone in our party being much younger and fitter left me for a long climb up the dunes. I sat and enjoyed the desert peace and the beginnings of the sunset. It was a truly spectacular experience and gave me an understanding of why people become so enamoured with the desert. Every desert inspection was different but I came to know a part of Libya that was unknown to Bashir and when the revolution came I well understood the plight and difficulty of expatriates trying to be repatriated from those distant, desert locations under fire.

A further highly visible change on arriving back in the country was the seeming abundance of English language schools. This was precipitated by the huge demand of all ages to acquire good English language skills. Also it has to be remembered that there had been no foreign language teaching in the schools since the USA bombing in 1986. I wondered at and was concerned by the number of schools named Cambridge University school of English, or Oxford University Language School and questioned what they were teaching, who was teaching and what they were charging? On investigation it transpired that teaching English had become big business, and additionally a way of money laundering. If you were a native English speaker, whether or not you had ever trained as a teacher, you would be employed to teach the Libyans English at vast expense. At the end of the course certificates would be dished out from the school stating this person passed an 'Advanced English course' without it having any bearing on what the criteria was for advanced. I was concerned as I felt it to be an exploitation of education. On talking to colleagues and friends we discovered that the British Council were keen on introducing an inspection scheme for Libyan English language schools similar to that in the UK and were intending to run a week course on training inspectors.

This I knew would be an extremely positive development as the British Council had implemented similar schemes in Morocco and Italy and here in Libya the country could benefit from those precedents. The BC Head of Schools Inspectors was sent out to Libya to train a group of six teachers to become inspectors and I was to be one of them. How happy we were that the project would now proceed yet how naïve the Council and I along with others were. It ought to have been obvious that many schools would not wish this scheme to be launched. They had lucrative businesses using ill – educated native speakers who were being paid at nominal rates but happy to have jobs out of the house away from their Libyan husbands and restrictive lifestyles. They were teaching Libyans who held the belief that they and their children were patrons of the best possible English schools, acquiring skills from seasoned professionals. One of the larger language schools formed a lobbying group against the programme and the British Council capitulated and decided to withdraw.

I felt truly devastated by this turn of events as did others who had been involved in the BC scheme and a decision was reached to form a local Libyan association with the initiative for there to be an inspection approved criteria for membership. The British Council gave assistance in this endeavour and a launch was prepared with an attractive logo, presentation to both the business community and to language schools. The BC Chief Inspector of Schools, Hilary Parnall was invited back to Libya to give support to the scheme. A one – day launch in Tripoli with the following day a repeat set of presentations in Benghazi was organised. All was set when I received an unwelcome phone call advising that two of the Libyan members of the committee had received visits from the Foreign Intelligence Security demanding they had to immediately drop the scheme or their schools would be closed down and they would suffer severe consequences by continuing with the project. Both women were genuinely intimidated by these visits and succumbed to the threats by dropping out of the following day's presentations and the scheme not wishing to risk further visits from the intelligence and the consequent penalties that might occur. Hilary was already in Tripoli so there was no chance of preventing her from leaving the UK. Interestingly I had received no such warnings or visits. I believe this could have been either as I did not have a school to which the Intelligence could threaten closure or I was British whereas the other ladies were Libyans. However, I too was concerned but nevertheless wanted to continue although Bashir felt it would be better to drop out as well. Having put in weekends of effort and hours of planning I still had a hope that somehow the scheme could be retrieved. What all of us did question was who wanted this project terminated and was able to enlist the help of the foreign intelligence to force the project to close. We speculated but never discovered who sent the intelligence although we did have a pretty good idea.

The presentations in Tripoli to the business community and schools were cancelled on the day with obviously no explanation being given. We travelled to Benghazi to give workshops but again we gave no explanation for the cancellation of the inspection project. We were all pretty shattered and nervous by the intervention of the intelligence as this indicated that big fish were involved. The failure of this scheme along with a further scheme that the Ministry of Education was hoping to introduce for Government Secondary schools inspections in collaboration with an Oxford company also never came to fruition. The education contracts being awarded for government and company training schemes were extremely lucrative and as a result schools, personnel at the ministries and companies were all involved in the money making. Essentially, the actual education and the quality of it was just a sideshow to the bribes being paid for education contracts and licenses. I had become involved in Education initially as a way of having a job whereby I could travel and work with my diplomat husband. It had turned out to be much more over the years with my becoming a firm believer in all levels of education and training as the way to the successful development of a country, from primary through to vocational training. A well – educated population is a healthy population.

Twenty - Seven

I come to what is one of the hardest parts of this story to write as it was one of the most terrifying periods of our time together and was to last for two years as a constant fear. We had already had to move from one house due to the neighbours and now once more our living space had been invaded illegally. Bashir still had his old fashioned belief in the rule of law and as such began legal proceedings to have the *manwa* land restored to being an unoccupied space for all three families facing onto the area. Our land titles were in order and clearly showed the legality of our claim. The neighbourly way of discussion had failed and consequently Bashir began a court case on what was to be a long and laborious task.

The Libyan legal system for such a case has one judge and one hand writing court recorder there are few if any exchanges between the judge and the plaintiff rather just the handing in of papers and then another court date being set at least a further month later if one is lucky. The court sits for ten months of the year, therefore it will probably take at least two or three years for any case to reach a judgement. Bashir managed to find an old contact in charge of court time and our case was heard regularly at two weekly intervals. Contacts were needed once again to achieve anything. Our neighbours of course, had believed that the case would ramble on for years and we would give up. Thus, in their eyes, this was not what was meant to happen as now there might even be a conclusion in our favour within a year. For those who have read Charles Dickens's novel 'Bleak House' this is how the Libyan court system meanders.

These people had gained the house under Law No. 4 and were firm Gaddafi supporters and their daughters were frequently seen with Mohamed Gaddafi's security in the street, especially on football match nights. Perhaps we should have known better and just moved a further time but we had put so much into this house and naively believed that our rights would win in a court of law despite the stress. When it seemed as if we were only a couple of months off winning the case and that Bashir's time and patience was going to be rewarded it all came crashing down in a torrent of water.

It was summer 2007, one year on, and our windows were open and I was about to leave the bathroom when an endless flood of water came into the room from outside. The neighbour's children had a hose and were pointing it into our house and drenching me in our own bathroom. I was soaked from head to toe looking like someone from the film 'The Exorcist'. I think, understandably, I used some pretty rich English swear words as did Bashir on seeing what had occurred but I emphasise again in English. This torture was not enough as they then commenced hurling rocks and bricks pounding down onto our roof. There was nothing that we could do we were two and they were seven. We sat in the living room looking at each other speechless while the seemingly endless hail continued. We could hardly believe this nightmare turn of events but we well understood why. This was followed by a silence only broken by the ring of our front door bell. From our security camera we could see the police pacing outside demanding to talk to Bashir. We had both been drinking our home – made chardonnay therefore it would have been extremely unwise to have opened the front gate. If they had suspected us of being intoxicated, possibly this was what the neighbours were hoping for, then we would have been shipped straight off to prison. Finally the police left leaving a paper stating that we had both to appear at the police station the next morning on a *blasphemy* charge. The neighbours had been sharp, probably using the Gaddafi security in order for the police to come to our house quickly with charges. For an ordinary citizen to call for police assistance, even if you were being murdered would have been impossible. How clever these neighbours had been, they had manipulated a situation and then reported that we had sworn against *Allah* which if proven would result under Libyan law in a mandatory sentence of 15 years in prison. This was absolutely terrifying. I shake even as I write this today and I think at that time it was the end of my ever believing that I had any sort of home in Libya.

Before leaving for the police station the next morning Bashir drilled me that under no circumstances was I to sign or say anything unless he was present. I am sure that neither of us fully realised at this time quite the seriousness of the charges. On arriving at the police station we were separated. Sitting outside the room in which I was placed I saw our neighbour and his wife smiling and laughing with the officials; it certainly needed only a very few brains to recognise that our situation was not looking healthy. They had us, hook, line and sinker. A female policewoman marched into the interrogation room, shoved a pen in my hand, and ordered me to sign a two – sided paper in Arabic. On refusing and demanding to see Bashir I was met with the words 'No just sign the paper' which were repeated again and again and again. When asking for a translator I then realised how futile that request would be as probably they could not be trusted either. I had no idea what to do but resolutely kept on refusing to talk or sign. I felt like I was in some horrible spy movie with officers slamming the desk and shaking fists in my face. I suppose 'Spooks' had actually been a good education to copy being a favourite TV watch at that time. The police turned from being angy to furious but they were always met with a firm 'No'. By the time I had been there I suspect for over three hours I think they wanted to go home as it was nearing lunchtime and Bashir was brought to my rescue. Obviously, the paper had been a complete series of fabrications and mistruths. A true statement was prepared which I signed and we were allowed to leave being given a court date and bail. This was now a criminal charge and could affect Bashir's work. It was imperative to have a not guilty verdict otherwise we would both have criminal records. Friends came to our rescue in the form of Rumen and Ekatarina from the Bulgarian embassy. They had more than enough experience of Libyan courts and introduced us to Bizante who agreed to take on our blasphemy trial.

As I have said previously Bizante has a real presence and is well known due to his age and experience as one of Libya's most senior criminal lawyers. He was to be our rock throughout the proceedings. The court was presided over by a single female judge in a tiny, dirty, dusty room no bigger than 10ft x 10ft with a court writer both of them sharing an old, wooden desk sitting on rickety chairs. Never having been in a court in my life before then here I was standing in front of this Libyan judge hardly understanding any of the short conversations that occurred; I was intimidated. Bashir held my shaking hand giving it the occasional encouraging squeeze. Bless him it did the trick and gave me confidence. What we had forgotten was that Gaddafi had empowered women and our neighbour's wife was one such very pro – Gaddafi supporter. She knew how to play the femme fatale with tears and all of her female antics were used in the court. However, what she had not counted on was the masterful Bizante. He could deal with the devil and his wife and on occasions when he questioned her and her witnesses he slaughtered them for their all too apparent lies. Bizante was imperious and we won the case but we had overlooked the fact that our neighbour's wife was a nasty, vengeful woman. Although we believed the matter was finished she appealed the decision and once more there would be the saga of the Appeal Court with yet more weeks and months in court. Of course the best lawyers do not come cheaply and our legal fees were mounting, but jobs were on the line and we had to succeed.

The Appeal Court was in front of three female judges one of whom I felt was hostile but the chief judge seemed to be more sympathetic and at times lost patience with our viper of a neighbour. It was a hideous, horrendous time and I am having great difficulty in writing about those months. People have told me that it would be cathartic writing my story. I have looked up the definition: 'providing psychological relief through the open expression of strong emotions causing catharsis.' I hope this will be true when I have finished writing but at the moment it is just reopening a wound, which I had believed had healed or at least was buried so deeply that it was impossible to be resurrected.

Nearly every other week we had to return to that miserable courtroom. I felt like the foreigner standing in front of the judges as I never saw any other European women in the courthouse. I was an alien with my blonde hair and western clothes. Our pit bull of a neighbour continued to play her strategic games by non – court appearances resulting in session after session being rescheduled. She wanted to prolong the agony and we were especially concerned as to whether or not any of the judges had been bribed or there might be some family or tribal connection, which again would persuade them against deciding in our favour. The court had a large prisoner cage to one side but thankfully we were not imprisoned there, probably we just looked too pathetic in our business suits. The judges sat on a dais with piles of handwritten files, which they leafed through for each case. Sitting with us on dirty wooden benches were other defendants. The whole court was covered in dust and sand; the law seemed to be about as broken as the building. If convicted it was, as I have written, a 15 – year automatic prison sentence and it was incredible to believe that a neighbour's land dispute could have reached such a level of a fabricated crime. It was our very own Salem witch trial. Bizante was to show the background to the case as being a land dispute and how my Arabic language was inadequate to have used the name of the prophet when swearing. His carefully planned strategy led the pit bull and her gang of hounds including one of Mohamed Gaddafi's security officers into trap after trap, exposing their lies. Eventually this case also was thrown out. We had been lucky as it could well have turned out otherwise and at times we had been truly despondent, Bizante always telling us to believe in God's justice. I think too that the judges, on seeing Bizante and knowing his reputation for honesty and integrity was pivotal to our freedom. This was the first and I hoped would be the last time that I would ever have to be in a Libyan court feeling that my destiny was in others hands despite not having broken the law. It had made for an indescribable two years. My life has never been how I have imagined and the land dispute was not to be my final time in a Libyan court. On the next occasion I would be alone without the honest Bizante at my side, or my beloved husband holding my hand.

In August 2008 Bashir had a bad recurrence of the malaria that he had contracted in Sierra Leone. He was seriously sick and we rushed to an A & E hospital where they misjudged the strength of an injection, which was to send him into the most horrendous catatonic state; his entire body was jumping off the bed. It was truly alarming. The Libyan hospital diagnosis was that he had Parkinson's disease. When we were finally able to air – evacuate him to London the diagnosis was obviously not Parkinson's; it had been due to the overdose of the injection. On returning to Libya Bashir was in a much weakened state, wholly dependent on new medications to help his heart and now diagnosed with emphysema. He resigned as Head of Section and became just an ordinary employee in the International Organisations Department with no special responsibility. I believe his spirit to help had been broken. Even the Libyan medical system had let him down.

I had a feeling of failure in everything connected with Libya; the land disputes, the court cases, the failure of the inspection scheme and the resultant intimidation, my inability to set up a free and fair scholarship scheme at Wintershall and Bashir having to have gone through those years on the black list. We had both worked hard and wanted to see good things for the country and the youth but it seemed as if whatever we touched or were involved in brought us grief. In September 2010 I resigned from Wintershall in disgust and went back to work for Bell Cambridge. It was the right move, I was back working with UK expatriate teachers and I had a reasonable boss. My one thought was desperation to leave Libya this was something new. Enough was enough even my house was no longer my castle. No where in Libya felt like home and the majority of our friends had retired or been posted elsewhere. Throughout all of these trials I had my Everest Bashir. Whatever I wanted to do he supported and told me to believe in myself and be confident. Despite all the perceived hardships or problems that I moaned about, I knew in fact I was truly lucky to have such a loving husband who never failed to carry me through all these traumas.

Finally there was some recognition of the work that Bashir had done over the years when he came home in December 2010 with the announcement that we were to be posted to Jordan. We had been back in Libya for the required four years so had been hoping, but one can always live in hope in Libya and nothing happens. This seemed a strange posting as Bashir had never worked on the Arab desk but apparently the Foreign Minister, Mousa Kosa knowing of Bashir's poor health had seen Jordan as having good medical facilities. Even Mousa had no power over European postings as these went to the Gaddafi cronies. Frankly anywhere out of Libya at this stage was good news and we started the process of trying to find someone to rent our house. I wanted to sell up and buy in London but for Bashir this was giving up everything he had fought for and he loved his country so we searched for a tenant.

This would be the final posting being the one whereby we would save for our pension as obviously the Libyan pension would be insufficient to live off in London. By renting our house, both of us working for four years we were calculating that we would have a nest egg on which to live in the future. Plus we had an investment in the land Bashir had inherited from his father.

I write here on Libyan law in terms of land ownership. I had Arab Libyan citizenship but despite having tried since arriving in Libya in 1984 for Libyan citizenship, the formalities had, just like everything else, dragged on. Finally the paper with my name and that of six other foreign wives was sitting with the Prime Minister waiting for signature to grant us the longed for Libyan citizenship in September 2010. The importance personally of the citizenship being that only Libyans could own property and therefore our house was solely in Bashir's name. Under sharia inheritance law should Bashir predecease me I would only be entitled to a 9/36th share of the house the majority being divided between his siblings due to the fact that we were childless. This law has no regard as to what Bashir's wishes might be and sadly he knew that his family would not be honourable. This was the reason for my wish to sell the house but understandably Bashir felt we would become rootless. Also our agreement had been and remained that we would spend 50% of our time in Libya and 50% in London on retirement

There always seemed to be a false pretence in the Shkuka family that everyone liked one another. I had come to the realisation by this time that either Brother or Uncle Bashir and I were viewed as being good cash cows not having any children. A large parcel of land in Gargaresh had been inherited by the Shkuka siblings from their father Mohamed and had been divided into six pieces with Bashir's sister inheriting a smaller piece than her brothers (sharia inheritance gender discrimination). This land was to become one of the main issues of dispute between myself and the family after Bashir's death. Before leaving for Manila, Lamin the youngest brother had asked his siblings if he could use the land as collateral against a bank loan the family had agreed. By 2009 the bank wished to call in the loan as not one repayment had been made by Lamin which would have resulted in the whole family losing their shares in the land. Lamin asked Bashir to pay off the loan in exchange for his inherited share probably to appease his other siblings. As Gargaresh land values were soaring Bashir was eager to secure this potentially excellent land investment. However, the only way he could finance the deal was to use my London inheritance money. I was more than reluctant to agree refusing on many occasions not having any trust in Libyan investments. Since we had always shared everything I finally agreed and transferred the money from London to the bank in Libya. Yet again the land could not be in my name due to the nationality problem and Lamin created a myriad of excuses over a period of two years for not transferring his share into Bashir's name. I no longer trusted this brother as he had been given endless loans over the years, none of which had ever been repaid. I became totally frustrated and it

231

was one of the few occasions when Bashir and I were in dispute. He still had a belief in his brother but how misguided this would prove to be. As I have said many times loans in Shkuka family were viewed as gifts. You may think as the reader that I am bitter and jaded with regard to Bashir's family. Over the many years that we had been together I had always tried to be mindful of their needs and to treat them respectfully. When asked for help in terms of my teaching or contacts these had always been given readily. Today my bitterness has changed to pity for a family so obsessed with money over family loyalty.

Bashir was always eager to seize opportunities to help his family and was particularly fond of his nephew the fourth son of his brother Ismael. Unemployment was at 30% in the country and Mohamed, rather than sitting at home complaining about his predicament had taken a menial job working as a receptionist in a print company while working on improving his English. At one of our dinner parties a guest mentioned that he was looking for an honest, reliable assistant. Bashir seized the opportunity and mentioned Mohamed and an interview was arranged for the following week. Mohamed succeeded in being appointed and was almost immediately sent to London on a training course and subsequently to Switzerland on both occasions proving himself to be a charming, capable, employee with potential. Bashir's brother Ismael never called or thanked Bashir for his intervention without which they never would have heard of the job. Mohamed after the revolution was sent to the United States where he continues to work. He too turned his back on his uncle who had given him a chance in life and a career. Today without Bashir's interference probably he would be jobless and without money living in war torn Libya. I should like to think that he was weak in the face of family peer pressure rather than forgetting the help of his uncle.

Twenty - Eight
٢٨

Due to his health problems, Bashir's role in the Foreign Ministry became minimal. We obviously heard rumours and innuendo. Since the 9/11 terrorist attacks Gaddafi sought to gain favour by supporting the USA in its so called War on Terror. He agreed to share intelligence information with the CIA on al – Qaeda and other radical Islamist groups, and endorsed the US rendition policy. The latter we were to learn through the foreign media and more so currently today with the various court cases being brought by the Libyan victims of the rendition policy. All we saw was that business was booming for some, and for the majority nothing had changed.

It was impossible not to know that Gaddafi, members of his family and his circle of cronies enriched themselves through deals with foreign companies seeking to do business in Libya. We had tried to do various deals over the years but no sooner was an idea partly initiated than mysteriously we would be advised that the contract had gone elsewhere. We were never to know why or how or where although it was obvious to everyone. In 2009, Gaddafi reportedly demanded that fifteen executives of international energy companies pay Libya the sum it had paid in compensation to the victims of Pan Am flight 103 as a condition of their continuing to operate in the country. Although not all companies complied with this demand, several US – based companies allegedly acquiesced. Every deal was accompanied by a rumour on a Gaddafi deal. Libyan culture was rife with corruption, kickbacks, strong – arm tactics and political patronage. When American and European international oil companies, telecommunications firms and contractors moved into the Libyan market, they discovered that Colonel Gaddafi or his loyalists often sought to extract millions of dollars in *signing bonuses* and *consultancy contracts* or insisted that the strongman's sons had a piece of the action through shotgun partnerships.

I have always had a strong admiration for the Libyan youth as despite all the hurdles and corruption they never gave up and still had a belief that they too could make the dream come true. I have so many faces in mind when I think of the students in my English classes endeavouring to improve themselves to build a better future. Their goal was the longed for wife, family, and home that they were hoping to have when they had made enough to pay for the demanded wedding dowry. The reality was that the liberal economic policies adopted by Gaddafi led to the emergence of a commercial class which was intent on maximising its gains to the exclusion of ordinary Libyan citizens. Popular disenchantment with this trend of development, the government's inability to provide jobs, and repressive state policies in dealing with dissidents and curbing civil liberties generated further public dismay. The seeds of an anti – regime rebellion were well planted and fertilized by an utterly incredible cornering of any opportunity in the country by a privileged few.

My last visit to Benghazi was in September 2010 where I was to carry out an exam inspection at the largest English language school in the city. On driving into central Benghazi from the airport the first thing one noticed was a distinct lack of any large posters of the great leader Gaddafi. If one thought that the streets of Tripoli were in disrepair then those of Benghazi had in many places turned into dirt, mud tracks. When looking at the shops they were full of rather cheap, synthetic items mainly from China unlike the flashy Italian, French and British clothes and goods of those in Tripoli shop windows. In the language centre I noticed a teacher who was wearing a pair of worn out shoes with holes. Here was a woman with a degree and a British teaching qualification but her Benghazi salary was the half of that of an equivalent post in Tripoli although neither salary was sufficient for everyday living. These people were genuinely feeling Gaddafi's wrath for their lack of adoration for their leader. His response; no investment for Benghazi and enjoy your suffering until you tell me you love me.

Once when talking to an oil exploration engineer he considered that Gaddafi always felt that perhaps the East would rise up against him. Consequently when it came to the issuing of oil concessions the majority of these were only being awarded in Eastern Libya. Likewise all the major oil fields from where oil was being exported were in the Eastern region save for the Ghadames basin in the West and some offshore fields. Gaddafi was saving the known deposits of the West should the worst come to the worst. I write this here purely as speculation but it certainly does have a suspicion of truth if one looks at the facts.

For the diplomats, the shame and indignity of having Gaddafi as their de facto leader was great. He had become the laughing stock of the international media with his antics. The revelations of his Bunga Bunga parties with Berlusconi the Prime Minister of Italy had created a new word for the lexicographers. Even worse for the poor diplomats in the Rome embassy was when in 2009 Gaddafi was scheduled to attend a forum on Food Poverty and demanded that 500 'beautiful Italian girls' were to be supplied for a gala. There were even stipulations that they should be 5ft 7ins. between 18 and 35 and should not wear mini – skirts or plunging necklines although high heels were acceptable. It was rumoured that the ambassador had been given two hours notice to organize the event. The girls were bussed to the Ambassador's residence where they had to wait an hour without any food or drink and then were given an hour lecture by Gaddafi on the Koran. On leaving the women were given a signed version of his Green Book on democracy and political philosophy. Of course, the press revelled in the event and filled the news stations with photos and statements from the ladies. All of this further highlighted just how eccentric the leader was becoming or had become and how the Libyan wealth was being wasted on Italian hostesses. This obviously did not sit well with the conservative Muslim clerics.

Perhaps the biggest embarrassment in 2009 was when Gaddafi finally saw his dream come true of attending the United Nations General Assembly in New York. He was no longer out in the cold and he would have the world stage as a platform. The arrangements for his trip were complex and it must have been a nightmare for those in the embassy with his known fear of lifts; in Manhattan every building has lifts. However, it was to be his speech or rather his rant that was to hit the headlines. UN Heads of States speakers are supposed to limit themselves to 15 minutes and in normal circumstances the person is given a polite warning if going over the limit although speakers in the committees are just cut off. As usual Gaddafi broke with protocol bringing his own interpreters, including his ever faithful Zlctni for the English translation. Apparently Gaddafi said that he would be speaking a special dialect that the UN translators would not understand but in fact he spoke standard Arabic. When in full flow he rambled on a range of subjects from Israel becoming Israelatine, the Taliban, swine flu, the US invasion of Granada and a suggestion that the Security Council should be renamed the 'Terror Council'. After 75 minutes of incoherent ranting, Zletni was heard to cry out in Arabic into a live microphone 'I just can't take it any more'. He had to be replaced by the UN's Arabic Section Chief who translated the last 20 minutes. At the end of this incoherent ramble, the chamber was half empty. Nobody could endure any more of his babble, save of course for the poor Libyan diplomats. However, Gaddafi had achieved his long wished for goal of talking at the UN. I hoped on that day that the late Dr Ali Treki, who was the newly installed President of the General Assembly and was sitting on the dais, felt at least a moment of discomfort. What a crime that Treki should have been appointed to this position but then the Libyan black oil paid for so many crimes and positions. Even today El Badri, the former head of the Libyan National Oil Corporation, is still the OPEC Secretary General. These men are survivors and movers and never sweat.

Was it the drugs, the lifestyle of never sleeping, the constant moving from fear of assassination or the belief that he was a man with a vision or just the megalomaniac coming to the end of his days? Bashir felt blessed that he wasn't in New York having to walk through the corridors of the UN on that day to what were inevitably going to be the sneers and laughter coming from other delegates. It was not a proud moment to be Libyan. One would have had to simply walk as quickly as possible hoping to be unrecognized, while at the same time having to keep one's lips firmly sealed. When was this excruciating horror – show going to end? The problem was further exacerbated with his sons' antics and their absolute belief in their right to succession. Not forgetting that all of them had their elite well – armed battalions with which to control the nation. They believed it was only they who were capable of leading the poor Libyans who in their eyes needed their charity and guidance. At that time no one in Libya was yet able to foresee an end to what was becoming the Gaddafi dynasty.

Twenty - Nine
٢٩

At the end of 2010 we watched in horror at the absolute despair of the Tunisian Mohammed Bouazaz who had doused himself in paint thinner and set himself on fire in front of the local municipal offices in Sidi Bouzid. He felt there was nothing in life to look forward to, was unable to look after his family and the authorities had taken away even his precious scales; his means of livelihood. No one suspected that the incident of the snuffing out of Mohamed's light would ignite a fire across the whole of the Arab world. We watched on our television screen, never in a million years suspecting that we in Libya would be next in a series of dominoes to fall; it seemed an impossible New Year wish.

Christmas and the New Year 2010 saw us in Libya as we were scheduled to leave for Jordan at the beginning of March. I had resigned my job with Bell with a leaving date at the end of February and a tenant had been found to rent our house. The order for the destruction of the manwa had been put on hold, as it was valid for five years. We realized that if we took the demolition path, the pit bull and her family would make life impossible for any tenants who might be living in our house during our absence. From the distance of Jordan such matters would be impossible to deal with therefore it was better to let sleeping dogs lie which they were doing for the time being. There was only an uneasy truce but it seemed as if things were proceeding well for our exit. I could hardly wait. My spirit was battered and I needed to have an interlude out of the country for my optimism and enthusiasm to be restored.

The Libyan revolution produced an earthquake of fear throughout the country. Everyone deals with fear differently but certainly it also produces the brave, both the heroes and their unsung counterparts. At the start there was one common enemy, Gaddafi and his cronies. At the end, there still appeared to be only one enemy but 42 years of hatred has not resulted in the euphoria that was so longed for in those early days. I also have absolutely no doubt whatsoever if it had not been for the media, Gaddafi or one of his sons would in all likelihood still be in power today. We had seen on the international news channels what had happened in Tunisia and Egypt but they, unlike Libya, did not have their two major cities separated by 1000km and a people who had suffered differently under the Gaddafi regime. I believe the Libyans reached a tipping point and on seeing others in the Arab world standing up for their rights and harbouring a desperate longing for democracy, it gave them courage which had previously lain dormant. *If they can do it, we can too.* Gaddafi no longer controlled the airwaves and before their eyes the people could see the Arab Spring in minute – by – minute detail in both Tunisia and Egypt. This too, was *their* time.

Why did I not leave at the beginning of the revolution, as had everyone I knew as well as the vast majority of foreign wives married to Libyans? Perhaps if we had had children then I am sure that I would have been one of the first fighting to be on the outgoing planes but we didn't. We just had each other. We had been through so much together and I knew only too well the difficulties of a distance relationship relying on phones or emails in war situations. To be in opposite parts of the world, Bashir suffering from ill health and I sitting in London with no awareness as to how long I could be there, speculating on events and relying on the media for news just never seemed like an option. In fact in my mind the question never even arose. Bashir asked if I wanted to leave as it became obvious in those first few days how intense things were going to become, but I had no doubts. I was not leaving. In retrospect it was absolutely the right decision. When we became husband and wife I had married the man but also I had married his job and his country and therefore I had to accept the consequences, good or bad. Of course in 1983 I never could have imagined the situation that was to unfold in February 2011. There was no bravado on my part; I was where I wanted to be.

Some years have now passed since that eventful week and my mind is blurry on the exact details of the events that took place. This time, perhaps more than any other I wish I had kept a diary. I knew this was a far more dangerous period than ever before and therefore potentially it would have been suicidal to have started writing, especially given my neighbour with his security and vengeful and unhinged father Gaddafi. We were to be under the 24 – hour scrutiny of three different sets of security and intelligence. The Gaddafi family no longer trusted *anyone*. *The thief was watching the thief watching the thief.*

The first that we heard of protests was from our former driver Khalifa who had paid a deposit on government housing, only to learn that his along with others' units had been earmarked for chosen revolutionaries. Similar protests were taking place in Bayda, Derna and Benghazi where protesters clashed with police and attacked government offices. These people's hard earned dinars were going into the pockets of the property developers. Khalifa along with his wife and two children had been living with his parents and now it seemed as if his long working hours in order to have his own home was being stolen in front of his eyes. He came to Bashir asking for help but Bashir knew no one. The only suggestion he could make was to appoint a lawyer but the truth of this was that it would be costly and still probably come to a negative result. The reality of a lack of housing was well understood by the regime and the government responded to the housing unrest with a 20 billion Euro investment fund to provide housing and development. Good for the contractors, huge profitable kick – backs for those awarding the contracts but only a long term fix for those waiting to be housed, *if* it was to be believed. Three years on when I was in Libya I learned that Khalifa was still living with his parents and had never seen his deposit refunded.

The beginning of February saw Jamal al – Hajji, a Benghazi writer, political commentator and accountant calling for an internet demonstration to be held in support of greater freedoms in Libya. He was inspired, he said, by the Tunisian and Egyptian revolutions. On the 1st February he was arrested and on the 3rd February was given a trumped up charge of having injured someone with his car. People were beginning to be outspoken and Benghazi was to be the cradle of the Libyan uprising. On the evening of the 15th February between 500 and 600 demonstrators protested in front of the Benghazi police headquarters over the arrest of human rights lawyer, Fathi Terbil. Even without arms people knew how to show dissent with petrol bombs, rocks and stones, which they hurled at the security services and were met in kind with tear gas, water cannons and rubber bullets. Between the 17th and 19th February there were continuous protests in the city with the security forces opening fire on the protestors. As the numbers of dead rose from each protest march so too did the numbers of protestors. Gaddafi flew in mercenaries from southern Africa in order to restore order but this action only further inflamed the unrest. For us as everyone in western Libya the form of communication became text message, mobile photos, emails and rumour. As the west saw what was happening in the east it was to be replicated in Zawiya, Zintan, Misrata and Tripoli where protesters called for an end to the Gaddafi government.

We lived five streets in from the two western main roads into central Tripoli. On one side was the Gurgi and on the other the Gargaresh road. We had spent the weekend quietly, alone slowly packing our things into boxes and contemplating the new adventures we would encounter on arrival in Jordan; a mostly unvisited part of the world for us. It was around seven on that Saturday evening that we heard chanting, banging and shouting coming from the Gargaresh road flank of our house. We rushed to our outside wall crouching and looking out onto the street and saw Mohamed's security walking up and down the road, now carrying guns normally stored in the guard house. It was obvious that something was happening that had necessitated this action. We had heard that Libyans in exile had called for a *Day of Rage* and we assumed that perhaps this was the Libyan youth following the precedents set by Benghazi and the other Arab countries. Land – line phones were dead as were the local radio and TV stations. This was obviously serious. All mobile phone lines were busy with everyone wanting to know what was happening. It was not until the following morning that I could see with my own eyes out of the Bell company car window that the People's Congress Hall had been burnt, not to the ground but severely damaged. On driving further we noticed that the television station had likewise been torched. Before leaving Gargaresh we had seen the police station was a burnt out shell as was what had formerly been the Eifel Tower restaurant which had been taken over by the local revolutionary committee. It had been a night of bedlam and it was hard to believe the draconian state of Libya. On driving on to the office we noticed other burnt out government buildings and most surprising of all one of the intelligence offices had been torched and burnt to the ground. In our usually chatter – filled car, there was a rather deathly silence.

Few students turned up for lessons and in fact no one was really in the mood to teach or be taught. I have talked of fear many times in this book and on that day one of the ways that fear was overcome was with humour, although some sat silently pale. I had been given the nickname by one of my colleagues 'The Fidget' and it was perfectly perceptive. I could not just sit there and listen to what was being read out from the Internet and instead embarked on preparing a speaking project. The others were involved in discussion as to what was going to happen, how were they going to be evacuated? They were all expatriate teachers who wanted to leave but there were colleagues in Benghazi and it needed the green light from Bell Cambridge. I completely understood their anxiety and need to leave it was not going to be their fight after all they had only come to Libya for the money, not to lose their lives. I have to say that I would advise anyone contemplating working in a developing country to have an *escape clause* written into their employment contract. I was to see and hear in the next four days employees who were left to their own devices to survive in the chaos. Bell was to prove honourable in the extreme. Lessons were cancelled until further notice and the teachers went back to their staff house in Janzour and I left for my house in Gargaresh.

It could be seen on arriving at my street that at both ends there were small armoured vehicles with mounted guns. The company car was prohibited from dropping me off outside the house. Having waved a forced cheerful goodbye to my colleagues I walked rapidly down the street past heavily armed guards with snipers on all the roofs of the Gaddafi houses. The reality of what was about to come was slowly sinking in and it was not pleasant. I learned from Bashir at lunch that the previous night the Gargaresh youth had marched along the road until they reached the People's Congress Hall where they had been met with tanks and heavily armed soldiers with weapons raised. The protest was meant to be peaceful but someone gave the order to fire and Bashir's brother, nephews and friends recounted how suddenly they were diving for safety from a hail of bullets being shot indiscriminately into the crowd of protesters. This was when the march broke up and the burning and ransacking of the buildings took place. What the protesters had failed to realize was that they were being filmed for future identification purposes. Those who had taken part were forced into hiding as the intelligence and police raided houses searching for the demonstraters. Those caught were imprisoned, some never to be seen again and others not released until the end of the revolution. The reality of the situation was dawning.

The Libyans had been roused and presumably felt they had nothing to lose. I heard from young friends and colleagues 'live or die, we do not care. This is our chance' A further demonstration was planned to take place in Green Square on the Tuesday. Bashir was alarmed at the possible outcome as everyone knew of the march and it was obvious that Gaddafi would never allow it to take place. I have absolutely no hesitation in writing that if Bashir had been in better health and perhaps twenty years younger he would not have had any second thoughts in joining the Green Square demonstrators. Despite the initial dithering, he decided to join the march. He had been waiting years for this moment like so many. From a purely selfish point of view for his safety I had strong and serious misgivings but in my heart knew there was no stopping him. That fateful night as Bashir walked down our garden path to the garage he heard Mohamed's security being given orders to leave immediately for Green Square and be well – armed with orders of *shoot to kill*. It was not going to be peaceful rather a looming blood bath. Bashir telephoned everyone he knew warning them of what he had just heard and advising not to go but was met with blank refusals. Later he learned from his brother how it had been impossible to leave Gargaresh as there were snipers on every street corner and rooftop. No one from Gargaresh it seemed was able to reach Green Square. For those that succeeded in arriving at the demonstration it was indeed a massacre. It is estimated that between six to seven hundred victims were shot. This was the beginning of the Tripoli uprising and soon after the International Federation for Human Rights concluded on the 24th February that Gaddafi was implementing a scorched earth strategy.

Although it was February the weather in Tripoli is always mild and for the next four months my garden would be my walking area, my fidget space. My library was to be my only companion other than Bashir. Over the years I had built up a large collection of books believing that when it came to my retirement I would have limited finances and so on reading a book and liking it I had stored it on the shelves to be reread at a later date. With teaching suspended indefinitely ironically I selected 'War and Peace' quite a tome which I could get my teeth into and would take me an extended period of time to read. As I was to discover, this was probably not the best choice under the circumstances and later choices of second read books would be more wisely chosen. 'May Contain Nuts' even on a reread continued to make me laugh and that was something much needed. The house was cleaned from top to toe but after that there was nothing else to do but watch the international news programmes, hope, pray, read and wait.

The fight to leave the country during that first week was horrendous, a living nightmare. Those with no air tickets or finances rushed to the Tunisian border, which on the 20th February saw between 70,000 – 75,000 people fleeing the country; on the Monday alone 14,000 passed through Tunisian immigration. At the airport it was pandemonium; a war zone with people fighting to get onto planes or even just reach the airport. The Bell teachers were lucky they were tall, strong men and were able to keep their heads above the crowds but even they later said that it was an intolerable fight. Bell managed to evacuate all the teachers via various routes to London by the Thursday. The teachers later recounted how they saw the police hitting and kicking men, women and children in an effort to try and form queues; it was a hopeless task. Bribes were being given by one and all to reach the top of a queue to board a plane. By the end of the week the last plane out had left and for those remaining who wanted to leave their only means of exit had to be by sea. The HMS York was on its way to Benghazi to rescue the stranded British nationals in the east. They recounted that once they were on the ship it was something of an adventure but it had been terrifying trying to discover if, when and how to reach the port. I have to say that I felt thankful and proud of how the Foreign Office organized the departure of so many British citizens out of the country. The British were lucky; those from developing countries were left stranded to fend for themselves and they were the ones with few if any finances. We who stayed formed a close link in order to keep each other up to date on where necessities could be bought and the danger hot spots. The reality was nobody, not Gaddafi, not the Libyans nor the world leaders had any suspicion as to what was coming next.

Thirty

The two of us had seen how Gaddafi had operated in 1986 and likewise Saddam in the Iraq war. Bashir was concerned that I could be held as a human shield, especially as the Gaddafi guards were swarming around our street. For this reason I did not leave the house for four months. The security would allow no one into our street so the only person I talked to face to face during that time was Bashir. We were well prepared with water, canned and dried food while also keeping the car full of petrol. Our departure date had been set but this was now on hold. No diplomats were leaving especially with Libyan ambassadors defecting; the embassies were in turmoil. In my opinion, given that many of the ambassadorial defectors had joined the revolutionary committees in order to hold prestigious, powerful positions, they were not making a bold stand but rather changing their spots; rapidly sensing the way the tide was turning. Also they were in no danger from doing so unlike those of us living in Libya. The Ambassador in Jordan was from Benghazi was from Benghazi had been a gung – ho Gaddafi supporter, even calling one of his sons' after the Colonel. He had been active in revolutionary housing projects in his area and was reputed to have made a large personal fortune as a result. Everywhere in the embassy were pictures of him and the leader; clearly this man was a Gaddafi chancer. It was obvious even before we reached Jordan that the relationship between he and Bashir would be awkward at best.

I think that we, like the majority of Libyans, only knew what was happening through the international media. It certainly wasn't through the local newspapers which nobody read although they were given away daily for free. Writing on *all* the political events that took place during the revolution would need another book and I can only record how specific events had an impact on our lives.

The interviews by ABC, BBC and the Sunday Times correspondents at the beginning of March are insightful as to Gaddafi's mind – set at that time. I had not realized until their interviews quite how weak his English was; his statements such as *'They love me, they love me. All of my people'*. These snippets would be made into rap songs and repeated in the streets the next day. The Libyans were getting inventive in their displays of musical opposition, as were their imaginative cartoons and graffiti. One of the most memorable of which parodied Gaddafi's speech *'zenga,zenga, dar, dar, beit beit'* claiming he would hunt down the stray dogs/traitors *inch by inch, street by street and house by house*. This particular rap was written by an Israeli but widely played throughout both Libya and the Middle east and became a rallying cry. These lightened up the intensity of everyday living in a war zone. The American ambassador to the UN stated that Gaddafi was 'delusional and disconnected from reality'. It hardly needed a genius to make such a statement but help was needed fast. It was looking as if the people of Benghazi were going to be slaughtered as the Gaddafi army neared the city.

I have mentioned the revolution producing unsung heroes and one such person has to be Ibrahim Dabbashi. He had joined the Foreign Ministry at the same time as Bashir and they had worked alongside each other in the International Organisations Department. At the start of the revolution Ibrahim was Libya's Deputy Permanent Representative to the United Nations in New York. The Permanent Representative was Abdel Rahman Shalgham who had previously been the Foreign Minister and was one of Gaddafi's old comrades from the south. The mission was reportedly divided between those who supported the leader and those against him, primarily the career diplomats against Gaddafi's political appointees.

When it became apparent that the people of Benghazi were going to be annihilated if there was no western intervention, Ibrahim and other members of the mission called on Gaddafi to resign and stated that crimes against humanity had been and were about to be committed in Libya by the regime. He called on the United Nations to enforce a *no fly zone*. We knew through colleagues in New York that Shalgham had been in hiding since the Friday and that his whereabouts were unknown. He was obviously a close confidant of Gaddafi. However, it did not take long for this former minister to recognise the writing on the wall as he thought from the safety of New York. By the Monday he made a high profile defection speech and became another of the chameleons. This compared to Dabbashi who through his intervention at the UN probably saved the lives of thousands in Benghazi. When asked if he feared reprisals from Gaddafi he said *whatever the risk, it will not be the risk that the Libyan people are facing*. His statement was bold and brave having family in Sabratha and knowing only too well that one of Gaddafi's menacing policies was to attack families in retaliation for standing against him.

After the revolution in November 2011, everyone at the Foreign Ministry was expectant and hopeful as it had been reported that Ibrahim was to be appointed as Libya's Foreign Minister by the National Transitional Council. The Ministry needed a minister who was well versed in international diplomacy, knew the failings of the Libyan system, to be a reformer and was well known and highly respected by its diplomats. Bashir viewed the appointment of Ashour Bin Khayal as Foreign Minister as being yet another indication that the revolution had been hijacked; it was a missed opportunity. The diaspora were ruling the roost for the time being. Ibrahim has remained in New York where he is Libya's Permanent Representative. A diplomat is the mouth piece for one's country carrying out orders from the Minister and rarely if ever voicing the diplomat's own point of view except perhaps in private. As Bashir was to learn the role of a Libyan diplomat is always a fine balancing act. Today Ibrahim Debbashi has become a victim being sacked from his position at the UN; the in – fighting and power struggles continue. I no longer have an insight into the goings on in the Mission in New York but I feel sorry that such a capable diplomat who saved Benghazi through his knowledge and expertise of procedures at the United Nations should end his career in this way. Perhaps he will be reinstated or be appointed Foreign Minister one lives in hope for appropriate people to be in positions of power in the future.

On the 17th March, the Security Council approved a No – Fly Zone over Libya, authorizing 'All necessary measures' to protect civilians by a vote of 10 in favour with 5 abstentions. It was important to see the abstentions of China, Russia, India, Germany and Brazil as it gave Gaddafi a perceived credibility against those of the ever evil West. It is widely believed that if this resolution had not been passed, the war would not have been won. Today there are and seem to be many questions as to whether or not it was the right decision. It is easy to sit in comfortable homes in the West and say it was wrong, however, if you had been Libyan to the vast majority there was never any question as to its validity. Ibrahim is my and was Bashir's unsung hero by taking the stand that he did and enabling the resolution to go through the Security Council.

We never saw the aircraft but we heard their thundering roar and I used to stand on my terrace beckoning them to come waving my hands much to the worry of Bashir in case I were spotted by the snipers on the opposite roof. It was my small gesture of rebellion and I am quite sure that no pilot saw me but I felt better doing it. I wanted to put a big sign on the roof as my father's Libyan acquaintance had done during the Second World War, but I knew that would be a move too far.

What started to be a worry personally was that Bashir's medicine was beginning to run out. The inhaler for his breathing was unavailable in Libya; we had brought it from London. We knew there were smuggling networks but everyone was cagey and his medicine would hardly be a priority. We were fortunate that our landline telephone had not been cut (probably due to living opposite Mohamed) and we continued to have a mobile link with the outside world although there was now no longer an internet link. Obviously, one had to be extremely careful as to what one said as presumably calls were being monitored through trigger words. Thankfully, yet again, a friend came to the rescue. Christine's husband, then based in Paris was meeting in Tunisia with his Libyan fixer and it was arranged that he would bring the medicine to Tripoli. It was a major relief on receiving the green light call resulting in Bashir meeting the fixer and receiving the medicine; all very cloak and dagger along a dark alleyway. We were safe for a further few months, we had been lucky; there were others who had to do without and were seriously suffering. It was back to the old days of everyone helping each other rather than the brazen selfishness of the previous period. Where I lived, due to having the Gaddafi family opposite and Hweldi Al – Hamedi around the corner, the Colonel's strong men surrounded us and it was difficult other than through the foreign media to have an accurate understanding of the direction of the war. It was the areas further out from us in Zawyia to the West and Misrata to the East where we knew there was the fiercest fighting, dreadful casualities and suffering.

A further event that was to confirm our decision that I should remain housebound was the distribution of cars, money and weapons to hired followers of the regime to drive around Tripoli and attack anyone showing dissent. Suddenly from no where our neighbours' were all driving flashy, new cars it was not difficult to see where their loyalties lay. We also learned of nightly feasts at the Bab Al Aziziyah Barracks where drugs, alcohol and Viagra were all freely distributed to young men. The latter was of deep concern as it was believed that the motive was to encourage rapes in rebel held or disputed areas. For those that followed the Libyan revolution, they will remember Eman al – Obeidi bursting into Tripoli's Rixos Hotel six weeks after the Libyan uprising screaming in front of foreign journalists staying at the hotel, showing scars on her body and pleading for help 'Look at what Gaddafi's men did to me.' She became the Libyan who personified female courage by breaking all the social taboos by speaking openly about a horrific sex crime. Eventually moving to Qatar and from there to the United States where she was given political asylum in Denver. She received an assistance cheque every month but with no counselling help she struggled to get by and cope with her new life. Today she has faced serious drug charges and subsequently has received a prison sentence of six years. For her like many the Arab Spring has turned into the Arab Winter. The transition of having one's life controlled by a dictator to one of absolute freedom and having to care for oneself has proven too much. I hesitate to put forward this point of view but it is an alternative thought to be put into the mix. Perhaps the answer for all of these countries in transition is to have a benevolent dictator; rather than what seems to be the case in Libya at the moment with more and more opportunists pushing their particular brand of democracy.

We sat, waited, watched, walked around the garden, read and prayed, but there was nothing we could do. It was the young and able to fight whom we had to rely on. Daily we heard of funerals held in secret in order to prevent Gaddafi's security coming to their houses and arresting the siblings of the deceased. We knew of incredible acts of bravery by nurses, doctors and of youngsters treating the war wounded by setting up smuggling rings and hospitals in their homes. The next problem that *everyone* was to experience was a lack of money. Government salaries were not being paid, the foreign companies had left but for Gaddafi, ever one to spot a chance he offered every Libyan family LD1000 for supporting his efforts against the revolutionaries. For many this will seem like a pathetic hand out to win over the masses, but for the Libyans (bearing in mind that the average salary was LD150 a month) this was a substantial donation to rapidly depleting funds. At the same time salaries were raised and Bashir's salary went from LD500 overnight to LD1000. Apparently Gaddafi was heard to say 'LD10 is enough for them.' He was so far removed from the lives of ordinary Libyans but this time his advisers won the day, as they knew the reality. It was all too late; NATO planes were overhead and throughout the country there was armed resistance. Libya is a paper money economy so thankfully all of my earnings from my private students were stashed away in a brief case under the bed. We had enough to last for a while, but the majority were forced to queue at the banks. Riots broke out, as there was always insufficient cash for everyone to receive this hand out. Things were beginning to unravel very quickly.

Gaddafi's sons gave a number of interviews to foreign journalists. It was the Saif finger pointing that incensed the Libyans and such words by him as 'Listen, nobody is leaving this country, we live here and will die here' 'This is our country, the Libyans are our people,' adding, 'First of all, we don't have money outside. We are a very modest family and everybody knows that.' When Saadi Gaddafi was interviewed by Christiane Ammanpour he said, 'only the travel issue bothers me' 'I gotta go to Safari' and showing him in the Tripoli zoo with his personal tigers and lions. When she asked him whether it was justified for the Libyan people to want more, his answer was 'everybody always wants more. There is no limit'. It was quite apparent the whole family were so far removed from ordinary Libyan life surrounded like their father by their sycophantic followers that they knew nothing of Libyan street life. If they had been asked if they knew the price of a loaf of bread or a litre of milk I am sure the Gaddafi siblings would have had absolutely no idea. Every time they spoke they further dug their graves. Few believed what they said they only aroused increased animosity.

Bashir continued to go to the office but petrol lines were starting to increase as the various desert oil fields came under heavy fire and moved to and fro from control of the brave Libyan fighters to the still loyal Gaddafi supporters. I had seen none of the effects of the NATO bombing, not having left the house, but Bashir remarked on their incredible accuracy. Beside the Foreign Ministry was a Green Book Centre and in their forecourt were two palm trees. Bashir arrived from work one day relating that a bomb had gone straight between the two trees down to a bunker that had been hidden below. Apparently in all buildings and camps about to be targetted they were given a five – minute NATO telephone warning to leave, so stories of deaths from the bombings were largely unfounded. Our house certainly did rock with the ceiling lights swinging and windows and doors rattling. The night skies always alight with tracer flares and the huge roar of unseen planes followed some moments later by the crash and tremors of bombs dropping. By this time I was pretty hardened after all that we had been through over the years although it was profoundly different this time. We both held back our fears just trying to get through as best we could. We had to live for the day. We had always had a personal unspoken rule of never leaving for work without kissing each other goodbye; it was our little ritual but those kisses became more intense whenever Bashir left the house, as one never knew where and when a bomb could drop. We soon came to realise that NATO was targeting the bombing incredibly specifically and for this the Libyans have to be thankful that the science of warfare proved to be so accurate.

I was astounded therefore when In May Bashir came home with the news that we were to leave for Jordan ASAP. This was a dilemma; if we said NO then it showed that we were against the regime and if we agreed we were going to an embassy where the Ambassador had defected along with two other members of his staff which indicated we were pro Gaddafi. Bashir decided that we should leave as he felt that he could be of greater use to the revolution away in an embassy that was proving to be quite strategic rather than by just sitting in the house doing nothing. At least perhaps he could obtain information on money laundering and mercenary recruitment, which could be passed onto people who could use the information. Finally, after all of those years as a diplomat he was also going to become a spy. He started to make contacts that he could use when he would be in Jordan.

We had collected keepsakes from our travels everywhere in the world and I had items from my childhood, my parents' and grandparents' homes, which I wanted to ensure, were all safely stored away before we left. Obviously we would be unable to find a tenant for the house as all the expatriate workers had left but I was worried that an empty house was an open invitation for looters. In all this turmoil we needed to find a shipping company that still had packing boxes. After numerous calls we eventually found one with just 120 boxes. Our plan was for our things to be divided into two loads, those with Gargaresh written on them, and those with

Amman. The latter we hoped could be shipped onto us at a later date when there was an end to Gaddafi but in the meantime were to be stored in a warehouse that Bashir owned on the Shkuka inherited land. Bashir collected and put the unmade up boxes into our car making several trips with them to our house ready for packing. They were heavy to offload but such was his determination that the task was accomplished successfully. By this time I had become quite adept at packing and completed 95% of the job. There remained a few last heavy items to be packed and then to transport the boxes to the Gargaresh warehouse. The problem was that nobody was allowed into the street and certainly not a lorry. Bashir spent the next week going backwards and forwards to Mohamed Gaddafi's security and from them onto the Leadership office until finally he was given a twenty minutes maximum window for one empty lorry in and then loaded out. We smuggled two packers into the house and finally we were ready for the lorry. Down it came into the street the packers jumped off the lorry, raced into our house and began carrying out the 120 boxes. This being managed in 18 minutes then drove out onto Gargaresh main road to the warehouse. It was a real achievement. I finally felt relaxed in the thought that whatever happened in the future in our street, my books and a few precious items were safe; or so I thought.

My American friend Teri, who is married to a Libyan, phoned on the Friday to relate how rumours were spreading throughout the country both true and false. She had been in a large room of Libyan women where one of the them related in *a know it all voice* that Mohamed Gaddafi was preparing to leave the country as a large lorry loaded with boxes had been seen leaving his street, headed down Gargaresh road. This was obviously our shipment and it brought a smile to my face and also a little pleasure as rumours such as that were not good news for the Gaddafi regime, as it would fuel rumours that they were leaving the sinking ship. I have read since on Wikileaks of cables between the Saudi government and Mohamed in which it reveals that he was requesting asylum for five members of his family, presumably himself, his wife, two sons and his mother during this period. Mohamed was the only one of Gaddafi's children at the end of the revolution who was not wanted by Interpol, who had not died or fled and subsequently been captured by Libyan rebels. He now lives in exile in Oman.

That Friday we drank a special glass of our chardonnay thinking that soon we were to be out of the bombing and possibly Bashir would be able to make at least a very minor contribution to the war from Jordan. Things were never to pan out as we hoped as on the Sunday Bashir received a new memorandum informing that his posting had been postponed. In my usual style I had started giving away items that I had been unable to pack. I no longer had my books those were in storage plus we only had two cups, two knives, two forks, two spoons, two plates and two saucepans in the house. Thankfully the sheets were still on the bed as were the towels in the bathroom. With only the barest of items we began camping for the next two months. I had kept a few books back to take to Jordan which related to the area, *Desert Queen* the extraordinary life of Gertrude Bell and for peace of mind *An End to Suffering, The Buddha in the World*. I also had Elena's book on Libyan jewellery. I rationed myself daily to chapters or half chapters as for me to be without a book would have been a living purgatory.

By May the weather is in the mid to high C20's always one of my favourite times as we could sit out in the garden day or night. It was surreal hearing the unseen war planes and drones but at the same time knowing they were there to help us. During the day the bombing was less intense than at night although it seemed to be getting closer and closer. I was becoming concerned that something might have been hidden in Mohamed Gaddafi's house and NATO would decide that he was a target along with the rest of the Gaddafi family. If his house were hit no matter how accurate it might be, I knew we would feel the blast as well. Bab Al Aziziyah Gaddafi's headquarters is just 5km from our house and we could feel the tremors at night as it was being pounded and hit by NATO bombs. Tripoli, unlike other areas of Libya such as Misrata had remained unscathed. Gaddafi was now swearing that he would take Tripoli down if the Tripolitanians stood against him and there was ever the fear that perhaps he still had stores of chemical weapons and mustard gas that could be unleashed on the city.

The petrol queues grew to streets in length until people were waiting for one, two and at times three days to buy fuel. Along with the queues, tempers were becoming frayed; it seemed as if those who had guns were using them in the queues to have petrol. Thankfully we lived near enough to the shops so that we could walk and Bashir began taking taxis to work rather than using our car. There weren't only petrol shortages; the shelves in the shops were beginning to look bare and obviously with no petrol it was becoming difficult for farmers to bring fruit and vegetables to the Tripoli shops. The capital, which had been relatively unaffected, was now feeling the brutal onslaught of nightly bombings along with fuel, food and medical shortages.

The start of the war had seen significant gains on the part of the rebels shattering the confidence of the Gaddafi supporters. They had been further weakened with the intervention of NATO. By May there appeared to be no apparent end in sight. Neither side seemed strong enough or had the ability to fully neutralise the other. The Colonel's sons had their elite, well armed and trained brigades, especially that of Khamis, guarding the gateway to Tripoli. The coastal towns were receiving the full brunt of the Gaddafi onslaught and we began to speculate how much longer they could hold out. Everyone began to wonder when the citizens of the capital would rise up, and why they seemed to be leaving the revolution to their out – of – town compatriots. Were they in reality Gaddafi supporters? Was the security still too tight in Tripoli to make a move? These were the questions we kept on asking ourselves every night repeatedly. Certainly our neighbours were confident of a regime victory, singing revolutionary songs at the top of their voices from the balconies of their houses, carrying in huge boxes of special food items and electronic goods with green flags flying off every point of their houses. Ours was the only house in the street not flying the green flag but I think the authorities had much more important matters to deal with than two old fogies living alone. The street was closed off anyway.

The closure of the street was a major problem. It meant that the few friends who were still in Libya were unable to visit and my leaving the house without being under the ever – watchful eye of the Gaddafi security and intelligence was impossible. I was fidgeting insanely by this time and longed to stand on Gargaresh beach for just five minutes to smell fresh air and see the sea. As there was no gate on the back wall of our house, despite everything Bashir elected to knock through the wall and hang a gate so we would have an alternative entrance and exit. This would enable free movement, avoiding the beady eyes of Mohamed's thugs. Bashir managed to find a metal worker to make the gate and two Egyptian workers were employed to come and break through the wall to install it. As ever what we had not counted on was the vindictive nature of the pit bull neighbour and her sons. We were the enemy and any construction that we attempted she would try and stop, and added to this we had no green flags adorning our house. I find it hard to understand when bombs were showering down and the country was in utter turmoil that anyone would have had the time or the inclination to be bothered with such activities as those of their neighbours.

Enlisting a couple of Mohamed's guards presumably for intimidation purposes and her sons, they descended on the house confiscated the workmen's tools and ordered us to stop as we were building illegally without a permit. At that point we had broken through the wall so there was a gaping hole straight into our garden, which made us extremely vulnerable. Bashir had been a diplomat for years but with these people there was no discussion. In the hope that the matter could be resolved peacefully he enlisted the help of a family living up the street that was from Gharian, the same area as the neighbour and he asked them to mediate. Finally, through their intervention, the tools were returned and the gate finished. I write this story to show that despite a war, old animosity and tribal allegiance were still the healers and dividers in the midst of revolutionary Libya. I left the house by the back entrance for the first time since February 17th and stood on Gargaresh beach beside the tranquil Mediterranean; I calmed down and went home. It was exactly the medicine that I needed.

At the beginning of May it became apparent that there was beginning to be liaison between the revolutionary units and NATO, the strategy being to wait for an air strike and then go in on the ground. This was proving to be a successful tactic. Furthermore, the fighters from western Libya seemed to be much more competent than those from the east had been, possibly because they had now learnt from their errors. However, the years of division that Gaddafi had created between the tribes still existed, and units were divided by townships and areas; there had to be coordination for success and a victory. The National Transitional Council, based in the east seemed to be composed of a group of crony, business suited, middle aged men who had been living in the West in exile and were now coming back to rule along with those who had changed their spots. We wished to see bright, young Libyans who had suffered so long under Gaddafi in leading positions. These were the well – educated fighters, who along with the returning children of exiles were leading the revolution on the ground. Both of these groups from that generation knew what was needed to rebuild the country but we never saw or heard their voices, neither during nor after the revolution. The fight was beginning to be lost before it had even been won in what was to come in the following years. It needed those with not only vitality and flair but also a grasp of the aspirations of a nation, not just a personal or tribal agenda. There was no charismatic figurehead, only the sober, old men of the NTC.

Perhaps I have gone forward too fast. Since the end of April we had been sitting with our two place plastic dinner service waiting and hoping that the fighting could somehow end quickly. Too many young men were dying daily or suffering horrendous wounds that would severely limit their ability to operate normally within the society in the future. A compromise of some sort had to be reached. The Foreign ministry was ineffectual and unwanted since the power bases of Gaddafi and his sons had long since taken it over. Phones and Internet did not work in the offices and in fact the only work that was being done was the serving and drinking of tea and coffee. In addition there was the increasingly difficult problem of even being able to get to work as the petrol queues increased while stations waited days for new supplies to arrive. Those days of water being more expensive than petrol were a thing of the past and now one had to pay anything from one to three dinars per litre. That is, if you could find it. Bashir rarely went to the office and then only to show his face and hear the rumours and gossip though everyone was looking over their shoulders.

In the meantime Mousa Koussa, the Libyan Foreign Minister and former head of the Intelligence had defected at the end of March initially to England where a few days later the EU lifted sanctions against him. This enabled him to travel and he fled to Qatar where he would be safe from Gaddafi's people and any UK legal challenges. He was nicknamed *Gaddafi's black box* as he has never spilt the beans and probably never will as by so doing would have to acknowledge his own involvement in sending arms to the IRA, the UTA bombing and so many other abominable crimes he was complicit in. A new foreign minister was appointed Abdul Arti al – Obeidi, the former foreign minister who had come to Nairobi and had a strong liking for women and drink. The man however who took over the reins for the day to day running was Khalid Kaim, a real chancer who was utterly despised by the career diplomats. Why he chose at that point in time to throw his lot in with Gaddafi in such a high profile manner would only seem to indicate that those surrounding the family had no doubts of victory. He along with Moussa Ibrahim, a smooth talking spokesman became the face of the regime giving almost daily press conferences. We would spit at the TV screen every time they appeared spouting their lies and fabrications.

We likewise hated the appearance of a delegation from South Africa, Mali, Maritania, Democratic Republic of Congo and Uganda representing an African Union Panel for the resolution of the conflict in Libya. They came at the beginning of April and then again at the end of May. The latter visit was to try and persuade Gaddafi to come to some sort of compromise and even to step down. For Gaddafi it was recognition but for us it was a further example of greedy African Heads of state coming for hand outs, especially when they brought their wives in the delegation. There must still have been a few diamonds swanning around to be given out. Why else would anyone bring their wife to a war zone?

By the end of May any hope that people had of the war being finished quickly was more or less dead, and with the increasing food and petrol shortages the rush to the Tunisian border began, and this time it was the Libyans leaving in their droves, not the expatriate workers. Bashir was therefore staggered when he received a call from Mehdi, his boss at International Organisations Department informing him that there was a memo instructing him to leave immediately for Jordan. Yet again there was the dilemma over whether to go or stay but Bashir by now had his contacts in place and we set about leaving quickly before the decision could be reversed. As we had learnt a decision made one day did not necessarily mean that it would be valid the following day.

The main problem was how to reach Tunisia? There had been intense fighting along the route plus the added difficulty in securing enough petrol to cross the border and finally to find a car to take us. It was the beginning of June, excruciatingly hot and we had seen people waiting at the border for up to one or even two days after they had managed to pass through war torn Zawiyah. It was going to be extremely risky. Lamin offered to drive us along with a friend and we managed to buy what we thought would be enough petrol to get us to Ben Gardane in Tunisia. Four suitcases filled with summer clothes and a few winter jackets and coats were all that we were able to leave with. In fact it seems in hindsight so much compared to the queues of refugees fleeing from conflict zones today with only a single plastic bag or just the clothes they are wearing; their circumstances are truly unimaginable.

We left in the dark, at five in the morning after yet another night of heavy NATO bombing via the newly installed back gate sneaking out like burglars in the night. With Lamin driving our car we travelled through war battered Zawiyah. We saw the burned out and crumbling brick buildings from the continual barrage of fighting, although that morning there seemed to be an unearthly lull. Realising that contacts were going to be needed if we were to be able to get through the border unhindered we were fortunate that our co – pilot was the nephew of the Head of Police in Zawara. He had agreed to accompany us from Libya across the border into Tunisia. As ever contacts were still the name of the game. Despite his best efforts and a police escort, it still took us 14 hours to pass out of Libya into Tunisia. It was extremely nerve racking with tempers erupting in the sweltering heat and the crush of people and cars. Everyone had the same agenda and just one thought; get out of Libya. At the back of our minds was also the possibility that perhaps the Tunisian authorities might close the border at any moment. I think that this stampede was caused by a real fear that Gaddafi was going to use chemical weapons if he was forced to give up Tripoli. It was a similar picture to when Libyans ran to the mountains in 1986, except this time there was nowhere safe in Libya.

Finally we reached Ben Gardane, put our suitcases into a taxi to take us to Djerba, filled up our car with petrol and those of extra containers in the car's boot and waved goodbye to Lamin and his friend who now had to return to Libya. It was a bizarre parting not knowing when, where, how and if we would meet again. The war was a deadly, harsh reality. The following morning on Tunisian news it was announced that 25 diplomats had crossed the border the previous day. We had seen a couple of blacked out Mercedes pass across the border but who they were we had no idea. A diplomatic passport did not necessarily indicate someone working for the foreign ministry; all the ministers and their families seemed to hold the red passport we suspected that these were the ones in that convoy. What it seemed to indicate was that many who held positions of power were deserting the Gaddafi flagship. This was optimistic news

Thirty - One

This was the fourth time that we had left on a posting but it was unlike any of the others. We were unsure exactly how we felt; in a way we had wanted to remain in Libya as the end seemed to be in sight, also we felt guilty for leaving. On the other hand Bashir had been sitting doing nothing for four months and wanted to make a contribution to the war effort and knew that the only way this could be achieved effectively was from outside the territory.

The Sofitel, Djerba was our first night of peace in four months. I am sure that everyone has an 'if I were rich' wish list and one of mine is to have one – thousand thread Egyptian cotton starched sheets on the bed daily. This is a pure indulgence wish but our hotel that night did not disappoint. It was utter bliss to sleep without the room and windows shaking and the incessant buzz of drones and the blast of bombs landing. We had not understood at the time exactly how or what we had been living through; it is only after the event there is the realisation.

From Djerba we flew to Tunis along with a planeload of other Libyan refugees. After four months of not seeing a hairdresser as ever this was my first port of call. A visit to a beauty salon is always great therapy as I have mentioned on a number of occasions when escaping from Libya. On this occasion my hair was like dried out rats' tails strewn with twigs. A miscommunication as a result of my poor French, and even worse Arabic led to the hairdresser giving me a hair – straightening rather than the conditioning treatment I thought I was requesting. Bashir had a completely new – look wife for a new country. It didn't matter and he rather liked the change.

Unlike our arrival at any of the other countries we had been posted to, Bashir's colleague was at the airport and took us to a hotel where we were to stay for two weeks until rented accommodation could be found. That night Bashir met his new colleagues, all of whom were waiting anxiously to find out what was happening in Tripoli. They were all carefully measured in what they were saying and how they were saying it, while gently probing to find out where Bashir positioned himself politically. Due to his long tenure at the Foreign Ministry he knew most of these men and where they stood. Obviously there were the few political appointees to be avoided. What Bashir had not counted on was that Gaddafi's only living sister's son was on the way for a second tour as Charge d'Affaires. This put the embassy into a different position. Rather than operating under a career diplomat, Amman's embassy was now going to be *directly* under a Gaddafi. Bashir was horrified, wishing in less than 12 hours of being in Amman that he hadn't agreed to the move. This man would be coming along with his posy of minders and intelligence thus any hope of being useful and leaking information was probably going to be unlikely. In truth this nephew had a very low profile when living in Libya, but nonetheless he was a Gaddafi and he was coming to take over the embassy. He had apparently been there previously and had given all the employees US$1000 as a gratuity for their loyalty. Bashir was only too thankful that he had only just arrived, as he would have found great difficulty taking that money, much as he had with the LD1000 handed out by Gaddafi the latter was easy not to take as it went unnoticed. These were going to be extremely difficult times.

The following day I remained in the hotel happily reading the thousands of emails that had accumulated in the months of having no access to the internet. On returning to our room all the old fears returned as I heard aircraft screeching across the sky. My immediate thought was that we were in the Middle East and Israel was attacking. From the fat to the fire I was petrified. At least in Libya we were on our own territory. I was to discover later in the day that it was *Jordan Army Day* with a fly past for the King. Even today if an exhaust backfires loudly I jump; my inner traumas are deep from those dark times. When I consider the relative safety that I experienced during the revolution in Libya as compared to those in all the war ravaged countries of today's world, I can't help but scream inside that these people need our help. Their numbers increase daily without any resolutions to their endless, escalating conflicts. The world is producing nations of traumatized, displaced and desperate people. I am still coming to terms with what has happened in my life but realise I am one of the lucky ones who has largely escaped unscathed. I am looking, as I hope others will too, at ways that I can help and perhaps this book will be one path that can highlight the plight of these peoples.

Bashir resorted once again to the old Sierra Leone ploy of being unwell and having to visit doctors, thus being out of the office frequently. Actually it was at this time that his health troubles began to become more apparent. He did have the thought that perhaps now was a good time to defect, but due to the reputation of the Ambassador he had no wish to align himself with that man. It transpired that when he had defected he had cleaned his computer of all files and looted the monies from his safe. He left no trace of his pro – Gaddafi activities prior to the uprising. Additionally he was still using two embassy cars and drivers and living in the palace that had been leased for him by the embassy. He had hardly been inconvenienced by his defection financially and was sitting it out in the safety and comfort of Jordan. Coming from Benghazi it probably made more sense to defect than to remain with the Gaddafi regime as Benghazi was held by the revolutionaries and possibly his relatives might otherwise have been targets. There needs to be a lot of truth before there can be any reconciliation over what people did during the Gaddafi regime. Everyone did what they did at the time and perhaps only those with blood on their hands should be in court today; vendettas are surely not the answer. Diaspora Libyan Jordan was obviously divided into two those with Gaddafi and those against. Before the war it had been a major destination for further studies for students and many still remained in the country, either unable or unwilling to return to Libya.

Fortunately I had three good contacts in the country and yet again my teaching was to be a life – saver. Firstly Bell had recently opened a school with a Jordanian partner and to my joy I found my Tripoli colleague Rupert in charge. Within a week I was once again working alongside the man who had nicknamed me *the fidget;* a wonderful piece of luck, fate or perhaps chance. It was not the perfect set – up but it would keep the wolf from the door until there was some certainty in the embassy regarding salaries. Jordan is surprisingly the most expensive country in the Middle East, so to have a job was a blessing. Of course IELTS examining was a possibility, so my second port of call was at the British Council and within a week I was on their team; a second string to my bow.

I had no personal friendships, only business contacts in Jordan, but during that first week I was to meet Jacqui who was to become the best and dearest friend from our Jordanian adventures. It seems as if one thing leads to another in my life. December 2010 had seen Mike Rundell the Editor of Macmillan dictionaries, an old Cambridge friend visit Libya. It had been thrilling having him in Tripoli as he is one of our few UK friends who saw our house, the city and Leptis before the bombing. He introduced me to his area representative who reciprocated with an introduction to Jacqui who was Macmillan's Jordanian representative. At the time Jacqui was looking for a teacher trainer to give a series of lectures on a new set of EFL books that Macmillan were launching the coming September. She had great faith in me and I prepared a two lecture series along with in – house training for schools. It was a wonderful project and gave me a comprehensive initial insight into the teaching of English in Jordan. The working relationship has blossomed into a lasting friendship.

Bashir saw Gaddafi's nephew only once when he returned to Jordan some six weeks later. He was surrounded, as expected, by a band of intelligence officers when he reintroduced himself to the embassy staff. Bashir shook hands as required and left immediately. Ramadan had now started and our new Libyan Charge d'affaires decided that he wanted to host an Iftar celebration (breaking of the Ramadan fast) for the diplomatic community and Libyans in Jordan. I can only imagine the horror on the faces of Ambassadors receiving these invitations and wondering what the right protocol would be, either to attend or not and what the consequences of either action would be.

This was also Bashir's dilemma to attend or otherwise. He decided once more to engage the *sick ploy* and dipped out of the reception. The next morning he went to work but returned quickly. At the reception the Gaddafi supporters had been ordered to stand on the roof of the embassy with signs and flags, playing revolutionary music supporting the Great Leader. On the street below there had been a counter – demonstration of revolutionaries taunting in response, which soon moved onto rock throwing and Molotov cocktails. Finally the Jordanian diplomatic police and army arrived to establish order. None of the diplomats were able to leave the embassy until the early hours of the morning. The Jordanian government were left with a quandary over how to maintain peace in the area. On deciding the only option was the closure of the embassy until further notice, they cited an inability to control the Libyan warring factions.

All of those on the roof had been photographed by the revolutionaries below, and these images appeared on Facebook pages the next day. The scene that night was to be the picture that has been repeatedly replicated across Libya since the start of the revolution until today. Even from his grave Gaddafi can still divide.

The dilemma of Gaddafi's nephew was resolved two nights later as he took an unmarked car, his suitcases filled with dollars, and disappeared into the night across the border into Syria. Where he is today and what he is doing, like so many of his kind, I have no idea. Repeated internet searches bring up nothing. He had money so he could survive but perhaps when fleeing Jordan he did not have the foresight to realise that Syria was next. He was, however, one problem removed for Bashir.

I had work and salary cheques and we found a comfortable, tiny flat on the internet with a beautiful balcony to enjoy drone and bomb free desert night skies. Peace and tranquillity were not in our minds however, as we nightly watched the dawn of the end of the Gaddafi regime on TV. Daily we were to see the horrific loss of life for so many young, brave Libyans. Bashir was sitting at home, the embassy was closed, and there was no work.

At this point he decided along with a couple of other foreign ministry staff in the embassy that they would make an independent move and try and defect, but not under the umbrella of the ambassador. Bashir thought his colleague Musbah Allafi from his New York days, who was the Ambassador in Australia, would be able to give them some indication as to the route to the NTC in Benghazi. Chancers are chancers and on calling the embassy on three occasions Bashir was told that firstly the Ambassador was busy and would return his call, on the second and third times that he was unavailable. The meaning was clear. Prior to the revolution there had been many unflattering rumours of Musbah's activities in Canberra, probably they had some element of truth. Where there is fat there is fire. A few months later it was also interesting to see a press conference he gave that was almost a verbatim quote from an article that Bashir had written earlier on the status of diplomats being apolitical. Musbah never sweats, when he saw Bashir later in the year he greeted him as a long lost friend; Bashir was frosty. Despite everything that people had gone through, total common unity was still elusive. This would be the ultimate failure of the battle. Unsurprisingly, with the country in complete turmoil and with all contacts failing, Bashir and his colleagues produced a written statement and sent it to the NTC in Benghazi via handheld and various other routes but no reply or instructions were ever received. They were out in the desert alone. Sit, wait and hope yet again. I believe this was because the NTC wanted only to liaise with the Ambassador and not those in the embassy; he was to be their focal point.

The one piece of luck we had before the embassy closed was that we had bought a car and employed Yahya. He was to be the last of our permanent, faithful, drivers whom we could always rely on becoming also a needy companion and I trust today a friend. Yahya spoke no English and I found his Jordanian dialect hard to understand. Bashir was an amazingly accurate judge of character and Yahya followed in the path of the others who had worked for us. He was one of the best; we were fortunate. He was a deeply religious man who exemplified the best of his country. Our phone calls to each other until today on high days and holidays are short due to our language difficulties, but he will always have a special place in my heart. We were to stay in Jordan for a year and it always felt temporary but then in reality everywhere we had lived was temporary. In Amman however, our feelings of transience were far deeper than they had ever been previously.

Thirty - Two

٤٢

I like combinations of numbers, either their repetition or their rhythm. Our birthdays were 9/1 and 13/9, a similar rhythm, repetition of the number 9. The 20th day of Ramadan in 2011 fell on the 20th of August, forming a repetition of numbers with a good rhythm 20/20/8. It was a highly symbolic night as it commemorated the dawn of the Prophet and the beginning of the revelation of the Koran to Mohamed and the centrality of God and knowledge in Islam. '*It is believed, the doors of forgiveness are opened to all who ask, the decree of God is reconsidered and determined for every human soul, and salvation is brought closer for anyone who seeks it. It is a night full of praying, seeking and acting goodly.*' We were all waiting for Tripoli to rise up not really knowing from afar how or when it was going to happen. We knew that all over Tripoli there were cells and they were waiting for the co – ordinated order to rise up. NATO had dropped leaflets over Tripoli telling the Gaddafi troops it was time to put down their arms. When the code came through, stating, '*Let's have soup tonight.*' That was the green light for those who had been waiting; they knew the meaning. That day also, Mustafa Jalil the head of the NTC gave a speech 'The noose is tightening; you have to rise to the event.' There were now two codes and the auspicious night of the 20th August, the 20th day of Ramadan had been selected. We watched and saw the entrance of the brigades from the east and west into Tripoli, and Green Square which has now been renamed Martyrs Square.

On the 21st August we learned from our sofa in Amman the bizarre sequence of events leading to the arrest and later escape of Mohamed Gaddafi. Bashir's nephew, Mohamed Yusief was the only one of his nephews to fight during the war. He had always been a bit of a renegade coming to England to live with his sister and her Libyan husband, reputedly to study but then overstaying his visa and being deported. He had always been a bit of a tough odd ball. Given that he knew our street well, he was able to give information to his brigade as to the best way of entering the street and surprising Mohamed Gaddafi's guards. They used the back entrance of our house, coming over the wall into our garden and then out into the front street facing the guards. It was this surprise element that led to Mohamed's guards being over – come and surrendering. The puzzle is why Mohamed was arrested and then kept in custody in his house overnight by only two guards? He gave a phone interview to Al Jazeera, saying that he had surrendered to the rebels and had been treated well, but then the line went dead and gunfire was heard. Apparently his half – brother Khamis entered the street from the top in an armoured convoy, which overcame the few guards who remained and Mohamed and family escaped, firstly to Algeria and then into exile in Oman. I am just so thankful that we were not in our house that night as it would have been terrifying. When later we returned to Tripoli in the November our garden was littered everywhere with empty gun shrapnel and there was a bullet hole through the glass of our kitchen window, all of which attested to the initial tough fight to capture the first son of Gaddafi.

On the 22nd August the Internet in Tripoli was reconnected. Tripolitanians were back in contact with the outside world and their friends. They had been without the connection for six months. It was a good sign Gaddafi must have left in extreme haste.

I think most are aware of the gruesome picture of the killing of Gaddafi. There are differing opinions as to how he met his end and the justification for how it was executed. I believe that in fact he was lucky; although gruesome his punishment was quick. I certainly wish that it had not happened that way, as it reflected extremely badly on Libya in this *eye for an eye* barbarity. Omran Shaban, the Misrata fighter who discovered Gaddafi in the drain pipe and who had posed in photos with the Colonel's golden gun was captured a year later by Green Resistance fighters from Bani Walid. They tortured him until his release was finally secured by the NTC. It was too late, as he died some days later from his wounds in a French hospital. Libyans during this so – called peace period were mercilessly vengeful and it has proven to be completely (though unsurprisingly) destructive. It is no good wishing otherwise but I do wish there had been a humane and fair judicial ending for the Colonel. Probably my opinion is unlike that of the majority of Libyans. The revolution was over, and Muammar Mohamed Al – Gadaffi was dead and gone, buried in a secret location in the desert.

Thirty - Three

٤٣

It is easy to win a war but far harder to win the elusive peace as has been so evidenced by post – Gaddafi Libya. October 23rd was Liberation Day and held in Keish Square, Benghazi, which had been the cradle of the revolution. We watched the TV in Jordan and felt this was truly going to be the most significant day for New Libya. Not for long was our optimism to remain as we began to hear rumours that one of the female politicians had been ordered to wear a scarf. Therefore, we were partially prepared for the speech of Mustafa Abdel Jalil, Head of the Transitional National Council. He started encouragingly *'This revolution started as peaceful, to demand the minimum, but Gaddafi started killing people with heavy weapons' 'our goal is to build a new Libya.'* so far, so good. At that point he then deviated from his written speech and announced *'We are an Islamic state'* and *'we will get rid of regulations that do not conform to Islamic law.' 'The interest on loans will be wiped out.'* All these bold announcements received thunderous applause from the crowds and he then announced that there would be changes to the marriage laws to make it easier for men to take a second wife. My mouth dropped open. It seemed he was trying to win support from Islamists within the military command whilst at the same time trying to score points with ordinary Libyans fed up with high interest rates on loans. Perhaps this was going to be a new Libya with strict sharia law. We were both stunned but there was more unwelcome news to come especially for the two of us and for those in the embassy.

Obviously the Ambassador had been in contact with the NTC during the revolution and had developed his contacts. On a number of occasions he had been to Benghazi; he was without a doubt a good networker. It was therefore unsurprising when we learned that the Jordanian authorities had agreed to the embassy being reopened under the leadership of the Ambassador. As I have written, he had been a very pro – Gaddafi supporter, yet here he was, back in a position of power and worse still, Bashir's new boss. He was one of the old political appointees, just wearing a new coat which was no longer green.

On the first day of the embassy's reopening the Ambassador was found organizing a huge, lavish, celebratory reception with invitations for the diplomatic community and a few selected Libyans. He shook hands with his diplomats and questioned Bashir on his views; this was a test for Bashir, realising that he would have to work for this chameleon when in fact he despised the man. Barely a few days later he made his eviction move but thankfully Bashir was at a doctor's appointment. We later learned this man's gang of so called Libyan students had stormed the embassy declaring that the diplomats working in the embassy during the revolution were Gaddafi supporters and should be thrown out. The diplomats were given 10 minutes to pack up their personal possessions and leave the embassy. The Ambassador, although present, did not intervene; this was his way of purging the embassy of those who knew his background in Jordan and had worked with him prior to the revolution. The career diplomat who had been Charge d'Affaires during the revolution was given a recall letter from Tripoli. This left Bashir as the most senior career diplomat in Jordan, but without an embassy. Some days later they allowed him into the embassy to clear his office. I was happy when he returned without any confrontation as everyone had been polite and respectful, which was a relief given Bashir's sometimes tinderbox nature.

Throughout his career Bashir had never written articles for the press, but I think that after everything that we had been through and more especially seeing how the Libyan youth were being marginalized, he felt compelled to put pen to paper. What seemed worse was to see these old cronies back in power; it was all so *unjust*. Over the years he had trained many young attaches, all of whom were more than ably qualified to hold responsible positions in embassies but they were overlooked by new political appointees. I insert his article, which was written in Arabic and was published widely in many of the new Libyan Arabic newspapers. It is translated here in English as for his written word Bashir always chose Arabic.

'The Plight of Libyan diplomats'

The job diplomat for many would present a stereotype of someone driving around in a big chauffeur driven car, attending parties and receptions in some exotic location and earning a large salary. Never was this further from the truth as far as Libyan career diplomats are concerned. For political appointees perhaps the above scenario is much closer to the truth along with fat cat bank accounts and golden parachutes.

Gaddafi always had a bee in his bonnet believing his diplomats in the 70s to be from the old elite and against his Green Book theory. This was probably true but these were a group of enterprising Libyans who had chosen not to join the then booming oil industry or the military and instead worked for Libya abroad and at home. Their salary never came near to that earned by the oil company workers and on average was US$150 a month and abroad reflected the cost of living of the various countries. By and large they were liberal in their outlook and reflected a good picture of the Libyan population whilst trying to minimize the Gaddafi propaganda within their sphere of work.

By 1979/80 the Student revolutionary bodies were in full swing and Gaddafi, ever one to introduce his own system of government abolished embassies and replaced them with "Peoples Bureau." There were no longer to be ambassadors but rather Secretaries of the Committees with two or three other people selected as members of the Committee. Of course anyone could become an ambassador, it needed no particular qualification apart from being a member of his Student Revolutionary Committees because 'everyone is a partner not wage worker.' Never was the latter further from the truth. Thus was ushered in the era of the butcher, baker, becoming ambassadors with the resulting bombings and killings with these committee members always being rewarded financially or with grants for their children to study abroad and residing abroad for sometimes up to ten or twelve years. Libya became isolated through Gaddafi's megalomaniac sponsoring of terrorism and a nation of cronyism and corruption became entrenched in the Libyan way of life to many. Obviously those in the foreign ministry generally opted out of joining the revolutionary committees and continued with their normal diplomatic duties in fact with no prospect of climbing the diplomatic scale to the post of ambassador. The path had by this time become highly competitive with 4,000 – 5,000 applications being submitted by those wishing to join the ranks of Libyan diplomats. A job that had by this time become wanted as a means of leaving the country and earning a better salary abroad and as a way of educating ones children in foreign schools as the Libyan education system was now almost defunct. For those original diplomats from the 70s this was the career that they had chosen and were good at and they would as best they could promote another face of Libya other than that of Gaddafi, oil and terrorism.

With Gaddafi being welcomed back into the fold in 2004, the once stagnant economy began to boom and the opportunities for corrupt contracts and embezzling funds became rampant. 'One doesn't work for this company unless one can do something for the company' was the refrain which of course meant that you knew someone in the Gaddafi Royal family who would facilitate whatever problem or signature was needed. Gaddafi still clinging to power knew that he had to control the Libyans like never before and started seconding employees from various ministries into the foreign ministry firstly as a means of controlling any dissident diplomats and secondly to get his people living abroad so as not to spread dissatisfaction at home. The numbers of these Libyans now holding dual British/Libyan, US/Libyan passports is quite staggering. In the 70s there was a requirement that having passed through the selection process that one spent one year at the diplomatic institute and then as an attaché and third secretary working in the various departments of the foreign ministry before being sent abroad to work in an embassy. Despite it being the law that no one could work abroad without a certificate from the Diplomatic Institute this was largely ignored and the foreign ministry became flooded by hordes of ill – educated self – serving personnel whose goal was to just make money anyhow, anyway.

By the time the 17th February 2011 arrived in most Peoples Bureau the post of ambassador was generally a political appointee or political appointee career diplomat who would be a diehard pro Gaddafi loyalist with the majority of career diplomats silently working away to serve the Libyan people abroad and promote a better image of Libya. As these political appointees started to see their Great Leader lose power and a new wave sweep Libya they jumped ship by defecting to the National Transitional Council in very high profile defections covered by the world news media. It was so easy to just change one's spots and no one seemed to question why the abuses against the Libyan people from which they had been suffering for some 42 year should now be acknowledged by these defectors. What perhaps is even more alarming is that these Gaddafi political appointee ambassadors are being reappointed as ambassadors without being asked to answer for the millions that they have stolen over the years, or the harassment of disaffected Libyans living abroad etc. To add insult to injury the long serving career diplomats are now being sent home in disgrace being labelled as Gaddafi supporters as they did not defect. In most instances, unless one came from Benghazi or the east it was virtually impossible to defect as if one did so one's family members would and were arrested and in some cases have disappeared to those mass graves which keep resurfacing around Tripoli. Career diplomats should be apolitical so be it Blair or Cameron, Bush or Obama in power, one serves that particular government. Values that diplomats must adhere to are now being called into question. Many European governments expelled diplomats from Libyan missions but perhaps it should be asked, were these diplomats career diplomats or political appointees? The Financial attaché in an embassy is an employee of the Ministry of Finance as is a school teacher in the Ministry of Education as is a diplomat an employee in the Ministry of Foreign Affairs. Ministers come and go but diplomats should stay, as they know the nuts and bolts of the job. Sadly the old Machiavellian ambassadors are back to stay once again in the New Libya but they do not want their old staff with them, as they know all their dirty tricks, so they are resorting to the ploy of the 80's to use student bodies to throw out career diplomats who were just doing their jobs. The latest example of this can be seen in the Libyan embassy in Jordan where the diehard pro – Gaddafi ambassador from the old regime has expelled all the career diplomats back to Libya in the name of the 17th February Revolution.

As these political appointees are reappointed one does wonder was it all worth it were these lives lost in vain? One would hope that these political appointees would be made to answer for their crimes, along with everyone else who is suspected of wrongdoing. At best they should be asked to return the stolen millions and not be allowed to have positions in the government. New Libya has to show that it is transparent and to adhere to moral ethics in all spheres of life, otherwise the Arab Spring will turn into the Winter of Anarchy. What was a day of rejoicing when Tripoli fell could well turn into a replica of the old regime with just a new flag, new anthem; no Gaddafi but the same old henchmen in positions of power.

The National Transitional Council has an enormous task ahead of them towards a path of national reconciliation but any criticism must be taken as being constructive rather than destructive.

– Bashir Mohamed Shkuka: Counsellor Minister Libyan Foreign Ministry

Quite obviously with the publication of this article in many Libyan newspapers it was unlikely Bashir could work in the embassy in Jordan or at least with the current Ambassador, Bashir had stepped out of line. Apparently the article was extremely well received and widely read in Libya. It was especially, of course, welcomed by his colleagues. He continuously sent messages to Tripoli HR but with always the same answer, 'stay at home and wait you will receive your salary.' Feeling that nothing was going to be achieved by just sitting in Jordan, he wrote to Tripoli asking permission to return and pick up his possessions, which is the usual entitlement when leaving on a new posting, and hoping that this would elicit some sort of action. Instead, a letter arrived from the The Foreign Ministry HR department giving permission for the trip with an order that the embassy should issue two return air tickets for the two of us to fly to Tripoli.

We left for Tripoli on the 19th November, arriving at two o'clock eager to be back and soaking up the atmosphere of post Gaddafi Libya. The airport had been severely bombed and in places was just a shell. The heavily armed Zintan brigades were in charge but everywhere there were the usual friendly, Libyan faces. It was good to be back and we were hoping to receive a clearer picture of what was going to be next for us. It was when we were walking down into a temporary building to await our luggage that suddenly mobiles started ringing with everyone, everywhere talking on their phones. People were shouting, cheering, slapping each other on the back, high fives and jumping up and down. Saif Gaddafi had been captured. He had been discovered in the south near the town of Obari where a number of his father's old comrades originated. From there it was reported that he had been taken by plane to Zintan. The NTC had insisted that any war criminals should be tried in Libya and not extradited to the International Criminal Court, which that June had indicted Saif for war crimes and crimes against humanity. How any trial for this man was going to play out would be the picture given to the world of the new Libyan justice.

Moving forward to 24th July 2015, the Libyan court sentenced Saif to death by firing squad. Claudio Cordone, Director of the Human Rights, Transitional Justice and Rule of Law Division of the UN Support Mission to Libya commented 'the prosecution did not present any witnesses or documents, confining itself entirely to the written evidence of the case

271

file.' Bashir and I knew this Libyan judicial system only too well. Saif is still held prisoner in Zintan and since his capture and transfer to Zintan, he has only made two court appearances, both by video link. When I see him sitting alone in the video link I wonder what must be going through his mind. Perhaps it is relief at what he knows was probably an inevitable verdict, and a hope that a bullet will bring an end to what must be a living purgatory. Possibly he still hopes that his sister or his mother will be able to contrive an escape using the billions of dollars they have at their disposal. Maybe he believes that everyone has a price in Libya and he could eventually be freed. I look at this young man with all of the advantages in life he was given, but with a father who always controlled this largesse. Did he stay loyal to his father because in fact he agreed with the Green Book policies and supported him? Or did he just think right up to the end that his father would survive the uprising? Possibly he was too afraid of him.

My feelings on capital punishment have never waivered since the 4th April, 1962 when I wore a black arm band to school to mark the hanging of James Hanratty. My punishment on that day was a week of detentions. The news of Saif along with former prime ministers and heads of intelligence that have also been condemned to death is not what I would wish to see. The Libyans I have talked to are all saying that they hope the quicker the firing squad take aim and fire the better. They do not realize the simple fact that they are going the same way as Gaddafi. It was they who fought for justice, peace and stability, all precious things that they had never known in the Gaddafi era. Sadly they have come from a 42 – year culture that understands revenge. Libya is my adopted country but I maintain my beliefs and realise my voice is probably incomprehensible to the Libyan way of thinking and also to that of some others reading this book. I wonder too why there has been little if no comment from Western nations. Perhaps the condemned know too much and it might be more convenient if they were executed. Certainly I would imagine this to be the case with certain members of the Blair government and the British Government's co – operation with Libya in its *counter – terrorism measures*. I do find this silence odd and it rather reinforces my fear that in my personal search for Libyan justice I cannot have much hope that my case will be conducted fairly and impartially.

Returning to Libya that afternoon as we drove into Tripoli, everywhere people were hanging out of car windows, waving the new flag, tooting their horns and of course driving like crazy. I felt happy for Bashir as he had been unable to experience the euphoria at the end of the war and this was a small flavour of how it must have been when Gaddafi was captured and the war ended. Yes, Bashir was on that day the bringer of good news. That night we drove out into the streets of Gargaresh to soak up the atmosphere. Immediately I found it alarming as it seemed as though every other person was armed and most were shooting into the air in celebration. What goes up must come down, and in this regard there was little or no consideration for the safety of others. Everywhere we saw pick – up trucks with guns mounted on the back, as had been used in the war, being driven by young men firing into the air along with the others roaming in the streets. Anyone would have thought that the war had not ended. Soon we had seen enough and went back to the safety of our house, fully aware that random bullets do kill. Earlier in the day we had learnt that a stray celebratory bullet to the head had killed the pit bull's daughter. Ironically, it had been fired by Gaddafi supporters, in what was still at that time Green Square. The revolution had been brutal.

We were to stay in Libya for one week and my main task was to pack winter clothes as a cold nip in the air over the Jordanian hills had begun to greet one in the morning winter was on its way. Of course our lovely garden had been totally neglected; I tried to do a bit of weeding and cutting but in truth my heart was not really in the task. We were plagued by indecision, whether to stay in Jordan, come back to Tripoli or be posted elsewhere. The sole decision that Bashir was able to extract from the Foreign Ministry was to return to Amman and wait, with a promise that his salary would be paid and give us time. Bashir fully realized that his case was pretty low down on their list of priorities, therefore after a one week stay we returned to Jordan. It had been good to have made the trip and to have experienced a tiny piece of the new Libyan atmosphere; things appeared pretty positive. As we took off we looked down from the plane onto what had now turned from sandy, brown fields into the vivid, green Tripoli countryside due to early, heavy rains. It was beautiful. Neither of us could have known that this would be the final view Bashir was ever to have of his beloved Libya.

Where we had been living had been perfect in the summer but our Landlady was controlling our central heating and we soon discovered that the flat was going to be freezing during the winter so it was time for yet another move. Through the internet we soon found a flat looking out over the Abdoun hills and we settled down for the winter. I continued my work at Bell and the British Council whilst poor Bashir was bored to death sitting at home, not having worked for close on six months. Usually a patient man, he was totally frustrated at how events had panned out. There was nothing that he could do but wait.

By the end of the year we began to see hoards of Libyans arriving in Jordan and here I am going to include a further article that Bashir wrote in fury at the Libyans who had learnt how to falsely claim foreign currency for bogus medical treatment under Gaddafi and were replicating the crime post revolution. Again the article was published widely in the Arab Libyan press and brought to the attention of the authorities that something had to be done. Below is the English translation. When translating Bashir's Arabic into English it tends to be quite flowery but the point is well made and now in my book I am able to include his feelings from January 2012 through this article. It gives me pleasure as I have included his voice in what was meant to be our book.

SHAME ON YOU who are stealing from the war wounded

The optimism that we as Libyans felt at the end of the Gaddafi rule is being replaced by a return to a regime of ME ME ME. On the 17th February 2011 we were all united with one thought, to overthrow the hated system of corruption, nepotism and cronyism that had become the byword of all business opportunities, jobs, scholarships, political appointees in the embassies abroad etc., etc., etc. It was in fact the cancer of our lives. Nothing could be achieved without one of the Gaddafi Royal Family's nod or signature. Greed was the principle guiding light of our society. A society without any moral backbone and with a people feeling paralysed.

On arriving in Jordan last year it was with a feeling of great pride when Jordanians asked me 'Where do you come from?" and I would reply 'I am Libyan.' I was embraced by one and all for the bravery and heroism of our fighters. Those were the fighters who willingly sacrificed their lives in the pursuit of freedom for us all. To put it into perspective, if we take the number who died, due to the small population of Libya, the numbers do not instantly appear to the outside world to be so large.

However, if we relate the numbers in relation to the population of the United States this would equate to 3 million having died in the conflict; a staggeringly high number. Today as we look at our population, so many wives have lost husbands mothers have lost sons. Are these people to become the victims of our society once again? This is not to mention those who were seriously wounded during the conflict and have lost eyes, hands or legs, or are confined to a wheelchair due to spinal injuries. These are the people whom we should be looking after, not ME who escaped free thanks to their bravery and heroism.

Yet in Jordan today there are 28,000 Libyans who have spent LD260 million on medical treatment when the budget to maintain the Libyan hospitals for 2012 is only LD30 million. The numbers do not seem to add up. As I go round the five star hotels, restaurants, clubs and malls to personally investigate what is going on, all I can see are Libyan men and women going to the spa, Libyan children running around hotel lobbies, Libyans sitting in the coffee shops eating and drinking five star food, the Libyan youth enjoying the Jordanian night life and Libyans in the malls with bags full of designer goods all with no apparent war injuries. What are they doing here? I ask myself. From where did they get the money? Reading the Jordanian press one daily learns of Libyans in the Jordanian prisons as a result of fights, being drunk, taking drugs and stealing to name but a few of their crimes. Is this the new reputation we want for our country? Much has already been written and shown on the television channels about our people coming to Jordan on false medical allowances and of the people working in the Medical Committees taking bribes and commissions from hotels and doctors. These officials have been targeted as the criminals and without a doubt they are; this cannot be denied and they should have to pay for their malpractice. However, surely the people who are taking advantage of this situation should equally be made to feel completely ashamed of the money they are embezzling from the martyrs' sacrifices. These people have left victims behind in Libya who do truly need medical help and yet they are unable to receive treatment because they do not have these corrupt thieves as connections or the financial wherewithal to bribe Libyan officials. Do these chancers not feel one shred of guilt that they are enjoying themselves holidaying in Amman or by the swimming pool at the Dead Sea, in the 5 star hotel spas, having various cosmetic surgeries and minor dental procedures etc. whilst others are suffering? Where are their morals? They are not the clever ones they are the greedy ones who are perpetuating the morals and ethics of the old Gaddafi regime.

Let us not follow the path of northern Mali but rather resolve our differences. Yes it is going to take time to re – educate people that corruption is not the name of the game and this cancer has to be removed from our society. I want to be proud again of being Libyan through knowing that Libyans care about each other more than themselves. Tribal differences should not be the flavour of the day. That Gaddafi is not sitting in Hell mumbling to himself and laughing 'I told you so, by getting rid of me I knew what the result would be; dog eat dog'. We have to think WE not ME; this way we can rebuild our country to act as a flagship of the Arab spring. Be a people who practise the tenets of our religion not just mouthing them five times a day. We need to shame these opportunists or chancers who have taken money from those that do truly need the finance. By so doing we can stop the haemorrhaging of our nation's wealth and give medical help to those that truly need treatment. We can then once more become proud of our achievements and regain our respectability and honour. Rebuild Libya to become the Pearl of the Mediterranean, as historically our nation was once known, thereby ensuring that the sacrifices of so many will not have been in vain.

Bashir Mohamed Shkuka: Counsellor Minister
– Libyan Ministry of Foreign Affairs

Bashir had no authority whatsoever from the Libyan Foreign Ministry to write or have printed either of the articles he wrote in Jordan and in fact it was well beyond his role as a diplomat without being given instructions. His orders remained as ever, to stay at home, wait for instructions his salary would be paid. He felt so incensed at what he was seeing and felt justified, as there seemed no other way of highlighting what was occurring in Jordan. I think too it was a way of relieving the frustration of being inactive. I am glad that it was written, whatever the consequences, as it was a way of letting off steam at the wrongs he was seeing by his fellow countrymen. By including it here it has become a little bit of *our* book rather than just mine. People say that we were joined at the hip; at times we were and at other times we were free spirits. These included articles are when we were completely joined at the hip in our condemnation of these appalling actions.

By the December we had as always made new friends, especially through the British Council and Bashir had reconnected with his former Ambassador from Sierra Leone who had retired to Jordan, having a Jordanian wife. I have a great love of classical music. It was not Bashir's choice and we had long before resolved that if there was something that one of us disliked then the other would go to the event on our own. The Amman Symphony Orchestra was certainly not for Bashir, but I took full advantage of their concerts, going with my new music mentor from the British Council, Gavin and friend Jacqui. The British Council was also very active in bringing live cultural events to Amman. Specifically I remember a Scottish and Jordanian group teamed together with the similarities in their music making for a stimulating evening, especially listening outside under a starry Amman summer night; we enjoyed that one together. Perhaps a much bolder promotion was bringing Ballet Boyz, probably controversial given that Jordan is a Muslim country, but for us expatriates it was a splendid treat. We were able to go to live Arabic music gigs, films and plays that had been banned in Libya, it was a new experience. Jordan was a small cultural hub, with some exciting shows and events that we enjoyed together. I had come to like Arabic music; I believe my ear had become attuned to the different Arabic scale patterns. Yahya was pleased that we both liked to listen to Fairuz in the morning on the way to work. I, like so many Arabs found her voice inspirational.

I did once commit something of a protocol faux pas in Jordan. I had been invited to a chamber music concert at the Dutch Residence. Of course Bashir opted out of that one, so I went alone. On arrival the room was crowded for a drinks reception before the music, and I knew no one. A European woman was standing alone at the far side of the room and I decided perhaps we could start up a conversation. I introduced myself and she gave me her name as Muna which should have been my signal as to who she was, but it was not until we started talking about how long she had been in Jordan and I noticed a bodyguard standing behind her, that I realized that she was Princess Muna al – Hussein; the first, divorced wife of the late King Hussein. I felt a total fool. I suppose it doesn't matter, sometimes when one does not recognize the status of another, one is able to talk to them completely freely rather than being inhibited by their rank or notoriety. As I think of her today, someone who was married to royalty, and my neighbour Fathia married to Gaddafi both divorced from their respective partners, I think of how these women have kept discreet silences on their lives. We are all given a different fate and I am writing about mine.

Jordan, unlike some of the other countries where we had lived was within easy reach of London and friends came and visited doing the routine tourist trek to the Dead Sea and Petra. One realizes Jordan's small size when living there. Probably I, like everyone from my generation had seen the film *Lawrence of Arabia* and of course one of my favourite biographies was that on Gertrude Bell, both of which made this area so relevant. I collected stones from all the places that Lawrence was reputed to have written *The Seven Pillars,* which is probably pretty much everywhere in Jordan or so the guides and guidebooks like to relate. I imagined how it must have been to travel during their age and how rapidly times have altered.

I was lucky enough through my IELTS examining work and my Cambridge Inspections to go to Kuwait, Abu Dhabi and Dubai. My special enjoyment was flying to these locations and looking out over the endless plains and sand dunes. I had experienced the Libyan Desert in summer but Kuwait in August was an incredibly overpowering, unbearable heat. It is not hard to understand why the Arabs from the Middle East escape to Europe in July and August to enjoy our London rain. A wet handkerchief over my mouth whenever going outside was an absolute necessity as there was never any fresh, cool air just burning, scorching air to breathe. Poor Bashir remained alone in Jordan, hoping against hope that he would receive some new instruction from Tripoli. It was at this time that it became noticeable that his breathing was becoming extremely laboured. I had thought that perhaps it was due to the bitterly cold Jordanian winters but even in the spring, our usual long walks were becoming shorter.

At the beginning of August word finally came from Tripoli that they wanted to see Bashir for consultations. He was totally at his wit's end at having sat doing nothing, unable to work in the embassy and just thinking and watching the fault lines develop in Libya. We decided rather than flying directly to Libya that he would have a check – up with his regular doctor in London. An appointment was made with a CT scan arranged before we saw the consultant. That interview was to be the beginning of the end, and how I now come to 9/36.

Thirty - Four

One hears, reads and sees programmes when a doctor gives a poor prognosis but the reality is that one is never ready to hear bad news. I knew those last years had yet again taken a toll on Bashir's health but had thought that it was the stress of the perpetually traumatic events, nothing more sinister. He was my life partner and we would always be there for each other. Those words 'I'm sorry' are devastating but we both knew that quick action at the mere mention of cancer could result in an accurate prognosis and a possible cure. The CT scan had shown that he had a growth on one of his lungs and this was pressing on his oesophagus and an investigative operation was needed urgently. Probably in retrospect we moved too quickly; we had just come off a five hour flight, rushed to our hotel, had a CT scan, seen one specialist and then rushed to another hospital to meet with a further consultant who agreed to do a biopsy the following afternoon.

In short, the exploratory procedure resulted in Bashir being in intensive care with a surgeon looking extremely concerned as he was bleeding severely. The surgeons were unsure of the outcome; only time would tell. I stayed by his bedside and held his hand, willing him to come through. By the morning the danger had passed and two days later we returned to the flat; he was a fighter. It had been absolutely terrifying and we still did not know the best and worst outcomes of the tumour. It meant a week later the same procedure had to be endured. All thoughts of travelling on to Libya were postponed. I truly do not know how Bashir managed to go through the ill health that he suffered with never a complaint, merely quietly commenting that *only God decides the night of your death.'* It was confirmed that he had a malignant tumour and we had to find an oncologist.

I think in many ways Bashir had a charmed life. He always managed to be surrounded by truly inspiring and unique people. Dr. Sanjay Popat at the Royal Marsden Hospital was to become Bashir's oncologist and we could not have been given a better recommendation. To any who have had to deal with cancer the Royal Marsden Hospital has a reputation for excellence and cutting edge research, all of which we were to find to be true and much, much more. Sanjay recommended a course of chemotherapy but the prognosis was bleak. Bashir had stage 4 terminal lung cancer with a life expectancy of between a couple of months and at best one year. I have dreaded writing about this period as it is still so raw and always will be nothing that I write or say can show this period in a positive light. These were going to be the last months that we were going to have together. Unfortunately however, that deeply precious and important time was not dictated by what we wanted to do but rather by the attitude and dictates of Bashir's family. I do not think either of us ever imagined quite the lengths to which they would go to achieve what they believed were their sharia inheritance rights, which led to the title of this book, 9/36. As a result of the combined facts that I was both childless and did not have Libyan citizenship, I was left unable to legally own any of the property that we had built together. Accordingly, after Bashir's death there would be an immediate distribution of his estate our house, the land and our savings, between Bashir's family members. My share would be one quarter.

Bashir still believed in Lamin his youngest brother who I have to admit over the 33 years had been helpful and kind. I am sure however, as I write that he went to the brothers and told them of his brother's terminal illness despite being ordered by Bashir not to breathe a word to anyone in the family. The goal was to sell both our house and the inherited land as quickly as possible. Property prices at that time were booming with many diaspora Libyans returning and looking for land and houses. As had seemed to be his pattern Lamin used delaying tactics saying that he had received an offer but he could do better and so the saga continued. Knowing that time was not on our side I enlisted the help of Christine an expatriate friend who had a Tripoli based relocation and estate agency to try and find a buyer. Her frustration grew with Lamin for the most part not turning up for appointments when she brought a client and the subsequent loss of her time and a potential sale.

I was frantic with worry not knowing what my lot would be in the future, as without access to the funds from our property I would have nowhere to live in London without having to pay a heavy monthly rental. Libya was never going to be an option on my own, I had no UK pension and I was going to have to fight for a Libyan pension. We thought we had planned well always believing that the last posting was going to be our pension pot. Obviously, far more worrying was Bashir's state of health not only he was undergoing chemotherapy but also he was unable to fly, so we were in effect stuck in London. I tried hard to hide my fears as Bashir had more than enough to cope with and always there is the faint light of hope that the treatment could be successful.

For once there seemed to be some gratitude from the Foreign Ministry as they transferred Bashir to London. Finally, in ill health, he was able to reach the role he had always coveted; he was Minister Plenipotentiary at the Libyan Embassy, London. Unfortunately, the Ambassador was unwelcoming. He was a 72 year old, political appointee who had lived in London since the 80s and possibly viewed Bashir as an intruder, being that he was a senior career diplomat. He tried to put obstacles in the way of the appointment but thankfully the Foreign Minister personally intervened, advising the Ambassador on the phone that Bashir was to spend the rest of his days in London working for the embassy.

When Bashir had come to England for the first time in the 60s with best friend Bishti, their first language school was in the Kings Road next to the fire station and that part of London although much changed had always remained one of his favourite areas. Since returning from Manila we had always stayed in SW3 in service apartments and so now yet again we set about looking for somewhere to live. Bashir's salary included a very generous housing allowance and we rented a flat by the Sataachi gallery just behind the Kings road, also within easy access of the Royal Marsden Hospital. I never could have imagined living in SW3; it is hugely expensive but I know that it brought Bashir great happiness. He loved being able to walk out of his front door into the buzz of his favourite London road, take the bus up to enjoy Hyde Park sun, snow or pelting rain. It did not matter he felt peacefully at home.

What was home to us? We had lived in so many places and countries together. Houses, flats, hotels and service apartments all became our home at different points in our lives. Libya was home for Bashir but in reality I do not think that it was ever really, truly home for me. Home can be the building where one lives and for a long time our Tripoli house was my Libyan home until the court case. Thereafter I think I became rootless. When we knew that Bashir was unable to travel and that his last place to live was going to be Chelsea, I made every effort that I possibly could to make it home. People make a home and friends filled that flat with laughter, discussion, good food and wine. We knew it was temporary, but our entire life together had always seemed to be temporary sometimes I wish it could have been otherwise.

As Bashir was unable to travel due to the cancer treatment it was down to me to fly to Jordan to close the flat, sell our car and return with our possessions. I like to imagine I have a guardian angel, as no matter how hard things appear there always seems to be a tiny crack of light enabling me to get through hardships. My brother agreed to fly to Jordan a couple of days after I had arranged most of our affairs to help me with the luggage. This was an absolute blessing; he has always been so solid in his support of his elder but in stature baby sister. It was wonderful also to see Yahya and to have his help, guidance and ever – cheerful face throughout the whole of the visit. It was going to be a demanding and emotional time.

Selling a car is a nightmare at the best of times but doing it with my poor Arabic in the Jordanian car market is not something I would wish to repeat. The sale was further complicated by the required paperwork, as the car had been a diplomatic duty free purchase. This necessitated our driving out to a huge car market complex and negotiating, signing paper after paper, going to the bank and being paid in dollars and having to ensure that all the notes were not fake it was a minefield. The deal was eventually done with Yahya's help, who was patient in the extreme. It was still very hot and dusty and I was in a very male dominated environment and could have been seen as a good target for a rip off. Bodyguard Yaya ensured the mission was accomplished successfully; it was a relief.

For the rest of the trip I used a small rental car and it was fun to nip through the traffic and by this time William had arrived. We went to one of what had been our favourite restaurants, though sadly there was one person missing. As I took off from Amman airport it was yet again a goodbye to another country that had given me an insight into others' way of life and a better appreciation of the hardships people endure compared with mine. I had been feeling hard done by and that life was unfair, but as I went back into Whitelands House that night and saw Bashir, I knew that I had been blessed for the 33 years that we had enjoyed together and hoped that it could be extended somehow, anyhow. Every second had become precious.

Whitelands House could not have been a better location as it meant that friends dropped by for a coffee when shopping in the area and it was easily reached when people came up from outside the capital or from abroad. Consequently the flat was always filled with friends; Bashir could never have felt lonely or bored, as he might have done with just my company. Initially it seemed as if the treatment was progressing well but then Bashir presented a major reaction to the chemotherapy, causing partial kidney failure. Another treatment had to be found and recommenced. The nurses on the chemotherapy out patients were unwearied, kind and encouraging and in his usual way Bashir soon became friendly and on first – name terms with them.

Lamin continued to advise that no buyers had been found; it was depressing. Then, out of the blue, my Tripoli realtor friend instructed me to fly to Libya, as she had been successful in finding a firm, committed buyer. All that was needed was for me to come and close the deal. Before flying it was necessary to have a power of attorney authorised by the Libyan consular section along with all the necessary paperwork regarding the deeds of the house. There was endless bureaucracy with translations, which were time consuming and tiring, coupled with the ever – present worry over Bashir's health. This would be my first visit to Libya without Bashir. There were dark undercurrents that the country was starting to fracture, but on the surface certainly it appeared as if business was booming. If the house was to be sold then I also had to quickly sell some of our beautiful furniture and sent notices of an open house sale to various friends. Bashir never said how distressing all of this must have been for him but was just resolute that it had to be done. I was really unhappy leaving him but selected a window of opportunity when he was not in chemotherapy treatment. He had phone numbers of friends who promised to check up on him, the Marsden was five minutes away, plus a fridge full of his favourite meals. As I left, I had no idea how ghastly the end of the trip would be. We always talked about the illness and what I would do when I was on my own. Bashir was adamant that my future should be safeguarded before his passing. This was Bashir's absolute preoccupation. The last months of his life should have been spent enjoying this cherished time, Bashir's only concern was securing our estate so that he could die peacefully.

I flew into Tripoli and was met by Lamin believing that he was on our side, but chose to stay at the Corinthia Hotel, not wanting to have any connection with the family. We were still under the mistaken belief that they knew nothing of Bashir's illness. What we had not considered at any point was the level of the greed the Shkuka family displayed under the guise and useful conduit of religion.

On the first evening I met the prospective buyer with his huge potbelly, wearing designer Nike gear and holding his crystal sebha beads as if he had just come straight from a nightclub; he was a repugnant looking character who immediately began telling me how he was a well – known judge. Coming from Bani Walid, the former Gaddafi stronghold and strangely not speaking either English or French (the latter forming the basis of Libyan law) I immediately marked him down as a thug. He was obviously a former Gaddafi appointee who had made money in bribes and corruption. I asked how the sale proceeds would be transferred to London and he replied that he had his way, knew all about money laundering and therefore there would be no difficulty. My eyes looked around our home, which we had worked so hard to finance and build. Then my eyes wandered out onto the garden and our beautiful date palm, which had grown so fine and I just could not stand the thought of this man living in our house. If I did the deal, in the future I would be buying a home paid for by the ill – gotten gains of a Gaddafi judge. To the horror and mostly surprise of Lamin, the judge and the Libyan fixer I apologized saying there was no deal. He was obviously furious, and he stomped off. It would have been a great deal for him since we had to sell quickly at a reduced price. When he arrived that night I am sure he thought he had a done deal, having us over a barrel. Today, I have no doubts that it was the right decision but it was to cause much anguish at the time. After so many years of refusing to deal with Gaddafi thugs, people that we both despised, the judge was not an option for either of us and never would be. Although I was nervous calling Bashir that evening I should not have been surprised when he too felt that I had made absolutely the right call. As ever his additional remark was I should believe in God and an alternative was going to turn up and that person would be the rightful new owner of our house, not a thief. Sentimentality had ruled the day rather than perhaps reason. I suggested that perhaps it might be a good idea to visit his elder brother and ask for his advice and help never dreaming what was going to be the result. On agreeing he gave one proviso insisting that Ibrahim came to the hotel and that no one else in the family knew of my visit or the meeting.

Thankfully that morning my brother arrived, as always ever supportive. We arranged to meet that afternoon and visit the house. Even today I shake at that meeting with Ibrahim. When I called despite asking to meet at the hotel he refused and demanded that if I wanted to meet him it had to be at his house where obviously he felt more secure and I would be disadvantaged. Not having seen him in a while and without his Libyan national dress I realized how truly insignificant a man he appeared he had none of the charm or good looks of his younger brother. He was just a diminutive looking man with absolutely no welcome in his eyes.

I had barely had time to sit down when he demanded to know why I had come on my own, blatantly displaying that in fact he knew that Bashir was terminally ill. He continued that he knew I was in Libya trying to sell the house secretly behind the back of the family and this was against sharia law. He added feigned insult in mentioning how I had enlisted the help of a foreigner to make the sale. Additionally he seemed to know I had already been trying to sell our furniture, which he emphasised, was not mine to sell. He completed his tirade in asking if Bashir and I had a joint bank account. Obviously he knew everything, and this information could only have come from one person. It was a diatribe of venomous language and I could not believe what I was hearing. Having come to see this man and ask for help, all I heard was that I was a greedy, bad, Muslim woman. At that point I just should have left but I wanted to try and bring Bashir's brothers and sister on side, have everything out in the open as with their support it would have made Bashir's life so much easier and happier. I tried to explain my circumstances that unless I sold the house I would have nowhere to live and no means of supporting myself. Perhaps he was unaware that I was unentitled to a British state pension and the only future I could see for myself at this point was my being a bag lady under one of the London bridges. I was speaking on deaf ears. Looking over at Lamin and seeking his agreement Ibrahim shouted that as soon as someone was diagnosed as being terminally ill then sharia law was activated and therefore Bashir was no longer in charge of his property. All of Bashir's possessions were now under the jurisdiction of the family as decreed by divine law. Not being able to control myself any longer tears began flowing down my face, with no sympathy whatsoever he lifted his hand and shook it angrily at me saying '*I have to do what my God tells me.*' This gesture and words were repeated several times with the same angry shouting voice and hand gesture. Those were the last words I ever heard him speak and I never want to hear that mean spirited voice ever again. I am unsure whether it was a long seated vengeance for my having married Bashir in the first place, whether he truly believed what he was saying or whether it was just plain *greed*. It was incomprehensible why such a wealthy man would so vindictively go against the wishes of his own, dying brother. I left immediately as there was no purpose for further discussion; the ugly hand gesture and words had said it all. Lamin dropped me at the hotel; I had seen through him and he knew it. In fact it would be almost the last time that I was to see him. On the way to his brother's house that morning he had told me a tale about loyalty, which I will relate later in the story but it epitomises the attitude of this particular Libyan male to females; disposable. Unsurprisingly I decided to make my own way to the airport the next day.

As one might imagine when I met William at lunchtime I was in a dreadful state but he calmed me down. Wisely he advised not letting Bashir know what had transpired with Ibrahim and that a face – to – face retelling of the story would be preferable and less upsetting.

Was it fate? Yes, I am beginning to come round to Bashir's belief. William was free in Tripoli that afternoon and Tariq was coming to collect the furniture that he and his mother had bought the previous day. If it hadn't been for Tariq I would not be where I am today, safe in a London home surrounded by some of the memories of my life with Bashir. Tariq was the North African representative for Cambridge University Press and over the years we had worked together on various English education projects in Libya. In his late twenties with boundless energy, he always showed an amazing generosity towards others, working on projects that he believed would be educationally beneficial to the country. Having spent his early childhood in Edinburgh he also had a love of rugby and founded the Libyan rugby association. The tragedy in his family was that during the revolution his brother had come back from Canada and was killed, dying a true hero. I write all of this about Tariq as he was absolutely pivotal in out – manoeuvring the Shkuka siblings in the sale of our house.

Our home was beginning to look rather denuded after the furniture sale the previous day, but also from the fact that Lamin had been helping himself to things in the house in our absence. He held one set of house keys. The burglar was free to come and go as he wished perhaps thinking that neither of us would return or in the future he would be in charge of the disbursement of our property. I love action men and Tariq is one of these. On seeing my distress and having the situation explained he was immediately on his mobile to a friend who was an estate agent. Half an hour later Arafat appeared, looked around the house and said he knew someone who had money and he believed would want to buy the house. Everything moved very fast from that point. One more phone call and a further half an hour later Ali arrived. I think being with Bashir for so many years I had come to be quite a good judge of character and for some reason or other I wanted Ali to be the new owner. He loved the house, the neighbours across the road were gone and he had always wanted to live in our area. The price was negotiated and all that was left was to tie up the transfer details and work through a lawyer and a deal was done.

I was so grateful that William was with me as he was able to write out a document, while Tariq translated and we had the beginnings of a sale. There was one problem, Lamin had the original house papers I only the copies. I telephoned him and asked him to bring the originals unsurprisingly he told me he was too busy but would arrange an appointment with Ali at a later date. I was beside myself and knew exactly what this meant; he was deliberately stalling. My brother can be extremely forceful when he wants and I handed him my mobile and he in no uncertain terms told Lamin to get in his car and bring the papers immediately. Where Lamin lived was five minutes from our house but about an hour later he slouched up the driveway and thrust the papers into my hand. He tried to interfere in the deal but we had already decided, given the background he was to have no part in the arrangements and Tariq was in charge. I had absolutely no doubt of Tariq's integrity and could hardly believe that he was prepared to help since we were really only acquaintances. Was it fate that he came to pick up the reception table that afternoon or his bad luck? As I was to come to know, it was Tariq with the golden heart. Lamin was forced to hand over the keys to the house and left unsurprisingly, extremely disgruntled. Later that night I was to discover exactly how merciless and ruthless he was to become.

These events were agonizing and were to reach a phenomenally intense climax. I wrote at the beginning that it is a love story between an Arab man and an English woman, about living with a Libyan diplomat during the Gaddafi years and a picture of Libya during those times. Importantly I come to the part of my tale where I will show by the events that happened towards the end of Bashir's life and thereafter, the gender discrimination of sharia inheritance law and how perhaps women can protect and empower themselves with the knowledge from these last chapters. For others perhaps it will give an insight into a culture of which they are unaware.

Thirty - Five

Having been out of the Libyan business loop for a while it was fortuitous when my brother received an invitation to a reception that evening for British business people to network with Libyans and he managed to wangle an invitation for me as well. I had kept my maiden name so we were down as the two Sandovers. It is interesting that Arab women always keep their maiden names while their children take their father's name. Bashir was continually amused when we received an invitation addressed to Mr. and Mrs Sandover I am sure the majority of Libyan men would have found it demeaning. As I have written repeatedly his opinions and outlook on life were very progressive for an Arab. Had they been more traditional it would have been impossible for us to have lasted all those years together so harmoniously. Of course there were ups and downs but we weathered them.

At the reception that night we met a few interesting people one of whom was Dr. Thumi whom I had encountered before at NOC and Wintershall. His firm was probably the premier commercial law firm in the country which had a working agreement with one of the leading London law firms. We chatted and he commented that Ibrahim's assertion that sharia law kicked in at the moment that someone was diagnosed as terminally ill was completely incorrect and he advised us to obtain a doctor's certificate with an assessment of Bashir's state of health and mind. At that time it was just a handshake and a chat but Dr. Thumi was to play a much larger part in the unfolding of our story.

That night I called Bashir but Lamin had already preceded my call giving him the details of the meeting with Ibrahim, probably with a different slant. I could tell from his voice that he was upset but I assured him of the good news with Tarek and that matters would be resolved with his brother. I loathe long distance calls at the best of times and was

289

especially upset that Lamin had interfered. When one is in a weakened state it takes just the tinniest thing to tip the scales and Lamin's call detrimentally altered Bashir's health balance. There were two more long days to go before leaving which I had allocated for clearing our house and packing to bring things to London. The majority of our possessions were still sitting in the warehouse in boxes marked Amman or Gargaresh. Now there was no longer Amman there would only be London. The constant moving, the constant discarding and rebuying by this time was deeply wearing, even more so given Bashir's situation.

I received the unwelcome, unforeseen, shattering phone call the afternoon before we were scheduled to leave. Early in the morning Bashir hardly able to breathe and at the point of collapse had called my friend Lesley. She rushed from Wimbledon dialled 999 and now he was in ICU at Chelsea and Westminster hospital. Quite obviously the strain of my being away, the phone call from Lamin plus the accumulation of the chemotherapy treatment had caused his system to collapse, he had pneumonia. I was absolutely beside myself, I in Libya and he in London, but Lesley assured me that his condition was not life threatening. Naturally I wanted to leave immediately but there was insufficient time to reach the airport. I had to wait an endless night and day. When we finally made phone contact I was able to tell him how much I loved him and he in a very raspy voice told me the same. It was the worst time that distance was ever to separate us.

When taking off from Tripoli the next day William commented that it was good that the pilot took off half way along the runway. I learned there was a warning of surface to air missiles being fired at planes and this necessitated special measures when taking off and landing. In fact, just two days later a Burak aircraft was hit. It was found on that occasion to be from a wedding celebratory missile. Thankfully that plane landed safely and no one was hurt but it was clear that things were extremely volatile.

By the time I arrived at the hospital Bashir was out of ICU and in his own room but with drips giving him antibiotics and in regular need of oxygen. He looked so pale and thin it was just pitiful seeing him in that state. Where was my man? Why had all of this happened to him? His family appeared to have little if no concern for the agony he was going through. I found it hard to believe but it was the reality. For Bashir it was as he had believed they would behave after his death but certainly not before.

It was a further seven days before Bashir was well enough to be discharged from the hospital. During that time Kathy arrived from Canada coming especially to give Bashir her ever – cheerful optimism and wise counselling. She was my friend whom Bashir had known the longest from our Sierra Leone adventure before moving to Canada. Today she is a Judge and her advice on the strategy to be adopted we knew to be invaluable. What I think we failed to fully comprehend at that time was that I was the foreigner, the Shkuka family had their powerful contacts, money and influence. In this respect whatever we did would prove ineffective as in truth they held the aces and were not going to give them up. Their Sharia law interpretation dictated that our valuable house and land was theirs regardless of their brother's wishes. Perhaps most importantly we were up against Libyan sharia law and its plethora of subjective interpretations not British and Canadian law. The two are so diametrically opposed.

Everyone including Bashir felt that the best option would be to make a video begging his family to respect his wishes. Bashir wrote out what he planned to say, working on the words with three members of the embassy. He was pleased with the result. In order for the video to seem authentic and with a verified date it was produced rather like a hostage taking video showing the front page of a newspaper with the date. In Arabic Bashir had a powerful way with words and many Arabic speakers have related being unable to watch the whole of the video, others of its strong impact. It nonetheless had no effect on the Shkukas with the family remaining adamant in their refusal to change their minds. Immans and sharia lawyers in the UK and Jordan were consulted with all confirming that until someone died there was no sharia inheritance law. I copy here the Youtube link to the video for any who would wish to see it. It shows Bashir in ill health, struggling for breath and at his weakest. I dearly wish that we had never had to make this video, as I do not want him to be remembered in this way, but Bashir was determined to see it done. http://youtu.be/316UWg95Rds.

May the blessings of God be upon you and all the members of our family Ibrahim, Ismael, Mahmoud, Lamin and Khadija I appreciate your desire to show compassion to my wife and to fulfil your obligations to her. However, if

you look into your hearts perhaps you will find that God's will is that she should
live in familiar surroundings in London where her brothers and cousins reside.
She sold her properties in London to enable us to live in Libya. Justice would
allow that we sell our properties in Tripoli to allow us and when it is God's will
her to live in London after my death. If you so agree her brothers undertake that
they will release you.

The response from Libyans who viewed this Youtube many of whom we
knew but the majority not was heart – warming and was a good restorative
tonic for Bashir. He was home in Whitelands house surveying life in the
Kings Road from our sitting room window. The pale pink magnolias were
out and Hyde Park was carpeted in golden daffodils spring had arrived.

Thirty - Six

This book could have been called 'Fate, Luck or Chance.' So much of my life has been good luck but at the risk of sounding rather self – pitying there has also been the bad. This book is not about how to survive with a partner who has cancer although the illness is a major part of the end of the tale. I can only say that from personal experience I do not think there is a golden rule and for everyone it has to be different. What I can say is that people want to help and offer support and it is these very people who enabled us both to come out of the tunnel of sadness. Bashir and I are not unusual in that we want to have contact with and be surrounded by people that we like and admire. I have rewritten the word *are* and changed it to *were* and then back again to *are* nothing has really changed and it is still *are* for me. My opinions, thoughts and feelings are unchanged despite the void, the absence. All of Bashir's doctors were one of a kind. Sanjay Bashir's oncologist is very cool. Not in his approach as he is a warm and knowledgeable man, but in his appearance. The two of us would have a guessing game before going into his consulting room, as to what the colour of his socks would be on that particular morning? We lightened the tension this way. Of course there was a bet as to who was going to win and pay for that special bottle of wine. We knew that there was little hope long – term but we clutched at straws for the present; in my mind nonetheless, there was the ever present fear of what was to come. Sanjay was always reassuring and the usual banter that the two had at the end was with Bashir's question 'can I drink my red wine with this medicine?' 'Only if it is a good vintage year?' was Sanjay's response. For me I would have a wide array of Google sourced questions. I am sure that doctors today are totally fed up with lay people questioning and coming up with their own diagnoses and prescriptions. Sanjay showed no such irritations however, and only remarked that it kept him on his toes. The Royal Marsden

Hospital staff members treat those where there is hope but also knowingly work with those who need peace. Annabelle at the Trinity Hospice was further metal in our armour. Initially she made her weekly visits and then towards the end once or twice a week in order to monitor the morphine. I went to the Trinity hospice in Clapham, I think for obvious reasons Bashir chose not to come, that was bringing the end too close when he was still coping reasonably well. It is impossible to write adequately of the admiration I have for the people working in palliative care. A person's face reveals the soul inside and Sanjay and Annabelle have remarkable faces. I think of them often with immense gratitude. All of those years of paying for private medical insurance were to give Bashir peace of mind he believed in the people treating him and in the facilities that were on offer. We had seen so many truly appalling hospitals and medical facilities in our travels around the world and without a doubt people living in the United Kingdom are more than lucky for both the medical facilities and the people working in the hospitals and clinics.

Bashir slowly regained his strength but his voice had become raspy especially when talking on the telephone. It was causing him great distress as he was a man of words and now that was inhibited. An ENT (ear, nose and throat) specialist recommended an operation but that sadly proved unsuccessful. This was followed by a visit to a speech therapist but this likewise proved unsuccessful. The two did not click he needed a quick solution and her exercises were long and laborious with no short – term result the chemistry was completely wrong between them. Thankfully we were to find the right surgeon Mr. Rubin and Bashir had a transplant of fat from his stomach to his larynx. It was an amazing success and telephone calls were no longer a difficulty. His old confidence returned he had a voice.

In the meantime the preparation for the sale of the house progressed. Ali had one proviso that the neighbours would agree to the sale of a few metres of land so that a wall could be constructed separating the two houses thus making them completely separate properties. People can be greedy or opportunists when they can smell a chance and it took a further few weeks for a deal to be negotiated. Finally the papers were signed and sealed between them and it was time for a further Libyan trip to complete the deal. My visit had to be done in secret as if the family had wind that a sale was going to be completed then we knew only too well that they would engineer a reason for the stalling or the aborting of it. Perhaps my greatest fear was of leaving Bashir, given the ICU stay during the last visit. Health wise he seemed to be doing better and the CT scans were showing no further growth of the tumour. It was to be a three – day trip to arrive on the Monday and depart on the 4pm plane on the Wednesday with my believing that I could complete everything in that short time. A meeting was also arranged to meet Dr. Thumi as not only was there the house property to be sold but also the issue of the inherited land and repayment of the loan. Bashir knew by this time that Lamin was not and never had been working on our side leaving the only solution to try for a legal settlement. Besides being very worried and hurt by the complications, we also felt such deep sadness that his family valued property and wealth over the wellbeing and love of a brother. Whatever the truths of Sharia Inheritance law, it was being engineered to prevent the flow of what was just or right.

I opted to stay in the Corinthia hotel as I felt it would be safe from any prying, hustling males. Although in my 60s unfortunately in many cases this does not deter the Libyan wolves. Additionally I felt that by staying here the family would not discover my presence in Tripoli as it was not the sort of place that they frequented. I would be completely on my own with no brother for support. It was reassuring at the airport to be greeted by the ever – friendly face of Yusif as he was to drive me during my stay. On the drive from the airport one passes Bab Al Aziziyah barracks which had been Gaddafi's stronghold and received the endless bombing hits when we were still in Tripoli during the revolution. The strong tremors that we had felt in our house had come from this compound. which the Americans had bombed in 1986, where Gaddafi had his torture chambers, where he had his rooms for his harem of slave girls, where he had met Tony Blair and entertained him in his tent along with many other Heads of State and world leaders. On that late spring afternoon it was just mountain upon mountain of tangled construction metal, broken concrete and cavernous holes in the ground. Yusif happily told me that it was going to become a huge park. If one were superstitious I would think that it is land carrying horrific, bad karma but perhaps nature would revive what had been the most dreaded of places with ghosts laid to rest.

I had two important meetings the following day. The first was to make contact with Dr. Tumi's team who are young, dynamic, friendly and speak

295

excellent English. I felt confident that somehow this land dispute could be resolved in their capable hands. They were in favour of arranging a conference with the whole family. Frankly I did not hold out hope for its success. However, I knew I had to be guided by their knowledge of Libyan culture as to the best way of how things should be done. If it needed a conclave of the family and our lawyers so be it, if that could lead to a successful outcome.

Of much more importance was the evening meeting at the lawyer's office to sign the final house transfer papers; his office happened to be in Gargaresh. There was one final hiccup, the Land Registery offices had been closed since the end of the revolution as the government had wanted to prevent interference with the property documents due to Law No.4. In 2013 the rightful owners were returning to Libya wanting the return and reinstatement of their property. Obviously those occupying the houses wanted the paper trail covered up or destroyed. Ali's lawyer advised that he knew a way into the building and with his contact would be able to verify the papers. A meeting was arranged for the final signing at eleven the following morning. In retrospect it was odd that he had not done this prior to our meeting. Why had he only just decided that this was necessary? Was he incompetent or was there more to it? Perhaps I have seen to many thriller films with conspiracy theories but it did/does seem strange, he was from Gargaresh and perhaps he knew one of the brothers? Perhaps I had been seen in Tripoli the previous evening? Disappointingly that evening the mission was unaccomplished; expectantly I returned the following morning with my suitcase in the taxi ready to head straight to the airport for my London flight.

Tarek, Arafat, Ali and I were seated around the lawyer's desk. Ali and I had put our finger prints on the document (this was truly 18th century although after 33 years in Libya I found it normal. There are still many cases of a thumb print especially for the illiterate elderly in rural areas.) As we were about to sign the lawyer's phone rang. I do not know whether there was actually anyone at the other end of the phone or if it was fabrication. He announced the caller was from the Land Registery advising that the sale could be considered as a sharia inheritance law sale and therefore needed the signatures of the family otherwise the documents might or would be considered invalid at a later date when the Registry reopened. I question to this day how the Land Registry knew that it was to be a sharia sale and in turn knew the lawyer's number? Ali of course had no other option than to say he was unable to sign until he had the family signatures. I think I must have let out a cry of absolute anguish and despair it was the prize being almost in my hands and then snatched away. Arafat left the room, I learned later he was unable to take my reaction and tears, but how could the situation be resolved? I was scheduled to leave in a couple of hours and had absolutely no wish to stay even a second longer as I was deeply concerned how this further bad news would affect Bashir. Once the house sale had failed and now here we were again a second time unable to sell our own property. I called Dr. Thumi who advised that I sign the documents and leave them with Tariq thereafter when the paper from the family was produced Ali could complete. I felt absolute despondency as to what had now turned into a further abortive visit and with no time line as to whether/if we would ever be able to complete. I flew out of Tripoli. Everything was black.

Reflecting on when Ali first came to look at the house I remember immediately warming to him he had an air of respectability and honour. He spoke no English but we muddled through with my Arabic and there was a mutual liking for each other. Houses have a spirit and I have no doubt that our house had virtuous spirits from all over the world. When I had visited China on my antiques hunt from Manila I had bought a pair of beautiful antique carved, renovated doors that were now separating the sitting room from the rest of the house. How many people had gone through those doors or looked through the latticework, on another continent probably 150 years ago? Similarly the house had numerous other touches that had been collected from the various places and countries where we had lived and visited. It was a house with a unique atmosphere. Ali was attracted to the house décor, the garden and especially the palm tree as a good Muslim omen. There is also an edict that there has to be a palm tree among other designated trees in a graveyard. Ali assured me that he would never cut down any of the trees. Here was a man after my own heart. I could see he was speaking the truth.

Later Ali told Tareq that when he saw my absolute distress, despair and tears he made a vow that he was going to own the house and be successful in obtaining the permission from the Shkuka family. Unbeknownst to me Ali called Ibrahim asking for a meeting. Importantly Ali owned gold shops but unlike Ibrahim had inherited these from his father so had been in the business generationally whereas Ibrahim was a new comer to the gold trade. The meeting proved fruitless with Ibrahim being dogmatic that it was sharia law and therefore the property was theirs and accordingly it was the right of the family to refuse to sign. Ali spoke of sharia inheritance law only being enacted after death but this again fell on deaf ears. Ali is slight in stature but has a quiet, forceful presence and when he left Ibrahim's house that night he was even more resolute that justice should be seen to be done.

To bring shame on a family in Libya is disastrous; it can mean that daughters will not have eligible suitors and the family will be shunned at celebrations. Ali was about to use this strategy to obtain the signatures. He started by talking to a couple of owners in the gold market about what had befallen Bashir, of his *Youtube* video and the intransigence of Ibrahim Shkuka, the one who owned the gold mall. Libyans like to gossip especially in the gold market as there is a lot of sitting and drinking coffee together.

In the meantime Bashir had called his nephew Mohamed the eldest son of Ibrahim asking for his help to change his father's mind and those of the other siblings. I have absolutely no doubt whatsoever that the strategy adopted by Ali forced the family to agree to the sale it took less than two weeks. Bashir's sister was the one who held out the longest and eventually her signature was obtained with only that of Mahmud remaining. He was still living alone in the family home a tragic figure having never worked since leaving Prague or had any further relationships. He was by now a complete hermit. Lamin repeatedly reported that he was going to take him to the lawyer's office to sign but it was repeatedly not done. In utter frustration finally Bashir had more than enough of his brother's stalling antics and yelled 'just get it done today'. It had the necessary result but Lamin never telephoned his brother again despite unanswered calls from Bashir begging him to talk.

Whatever you may think of this story on sharia inheritance law and the rights and the wrongs, I think that English law stands firm in that the wishes of the deceased have to be acknowledged and adhered to. Bashir had written a UK will and his requests were clear that everything should be left to me his wife. We had worked together, always pooling our incomes and I had brought my inheritance money from London for the property purchases. We were adamant that we were absolutely within our rights. The family had never made any financial contribution to our estate and in fact on numerous occasions we had given them financial assistance throughout our married years. What distresses me until today is not the financial dispute but rather what it did to Bashir. He was terminally ill, living away from Libya and a family that had shunned him. It caused him enormous sorrow it was in my eyes then and now absolutely and forever unforgiveable.

As soon as Ali had the permission paper from the family the legal documents were signed and he became the rightful owner of what the house will always be called by me our *villa on the avenue of the flowers*. Within hours the money was in our bank in London. Ali had been completely honourable and my fear of having nowhere to live in the future was no longer. That afternoon Ibrahim's eldest son Mohamed telephoned his uncle Bashir asking if he needed help transferring the money to a London bank. He sounded shocked and astounded when Bashir thanked him but advised it was unnecessary. Mohamed also passed on the message at this time that the Shkuka family had let us have the house but the land was for them. Bashir reiterated to Mohamed that it was inherited land and as such belonged rightfully to him, also reminding of the fact that I had paid for the inherited land to be released from the bank loan. This was met with a screaming demand once more that the land was for the rest of the family. Mohamed slammed down the phone. When Bashir tried to call back Mohamed's brother Tarek answered telling Bashir never to call their house again. It was their belief that they had lost their three quarter share in our house but held the cards on the second part of the dispute. We felt certain that if we had asked for help on the transfer Ibrahim certainly would have used his contacts at Central Bank to stall the transaction. Their strategy had probably been to sign the family agreement document and get Ali off their backs. Thereafter they were probably hoping it would be possible to still make a grab for the proceeds of the sale through bank transfer delaying tactics. As I have repeatedly illustrated, in Libya all things are possible nothing is impossible through contacts. Thankfully for once we had been ahead of their game but the family lines had been cut forever.

It was extremely rare for me to see Bashir crying but this time it was endless I held his thin weak body in my arms trying to give him comfort but he knew that he had lost his family and I was now all that he had at the end of his life; how cruel they were merciless.

Thirty - Seven
٣٧

Bashir never in all of those months since his initial diagnosis complained at either the pain from the treatment or his sadness at knowing his time on this earth was to be so limited. He had his Muslim belief that only God can decide the day of your death and he was fatalistic. He wanted everything after his passing to be conducted strictly according to the Islamic last rites and in this respect had briefed me that he wanted his body to be flown back to Libya and buried in the graveyard in Gargaresh near those of his parents. That last telephone call with his nephew Tarek telling him never to call his family again was therefore mind shattering. There had been times together when our tears just flowed and we clung onto each other at what was to come but those terrible words to a man who cared so much for his family was absolutely mortifying. He cried and cried and cried it was unbearable to hear and see. He needed all of his strength and yet he was suffering and deteriorating from the pitiless actions of his family.

A couple of days later Bashir decided he no longer wished to be buried in Libya provided we could locate a Muslim graveyard in London which met his burial criteria. He stated very clearly 'I do not want those hypocrites standing at my grave'. This was an absolutely momentous decision and I was to feel bitter that these were the sort of decisions he was having to make rather than the two of us somehow enjoying our last days together. He warned that when his family discovered that he was to be buried in London they would be vindictive and well understood if I did not agree, realizing how it could affect my future situation. For me whatever he wanted would happen and he would not have to succumb to the wishes of others. We sat together on the computer looking for where he would be buried. I will never know how especially he or I managed it but somehow we each found the inner strength to complete this devastating task. The

300

first and only place we looked was *'The Gardens of Peace'* in Hainault Essex The description, the photos and the phone call confirmed that this was to be Bashir's last resting place. Today as I write this sequence of events I am astounded how we succeeded in finding Hainault together but we did and thus I was able to comply with Bashir's last request.

We no longer had any wish whatsoever to talk, discuss or think about the land dispute and just asked the Libyan lawyers to go ahead with the court case against the family as none of them had come to the conciliation meeting with Dr. Thumi. Bashir's family had disowned him because of property inheritance and left him without family, terminally ill in London. It was all the more important to have my brothers and our friends visiting and everyone rallied around and from those not in the UK he received daily phone calls of encouragement and laughter. Although his eating was becoming laboured there was as ever his wonderful cocktail of fun, love and care with the added ingredients as ever of good food, wine and great social company.

I want to end this chapter on a note of joy and a final picture of the Bashir who had never changed in my eyes since we first met in Sierra Leone. We were to go out for dinner to a Lebanese restaurant. There we were joined by Teresa, who is always wonderful company, and Bashir was in good form, tapping his feet to the background Arabic music that was being played. Later in the evening the music changed and the volume increased and a single Arabic dancer came into the restaurant dancing to the music he so loved. The music was lively and loud and Bashir, as was always his way started clapping and snapping his fingers in time to the music with others in the restaurant joining in. When the dancer arrived at our table there was no stopping the man, despite everything, he was on his feet, once more the elegant dancer of old gyrating his hips and moving to the music with immense pleasure on his face. This is how I want and will remember his last days. It was a joy to see that he could still muster the energy, passion and wish to dance. It took me back to those Sierra Leone nights and the Abba song we had heard so many times when dancing together. Again I wanted to be his *'girl with golden hair'* and to say *'thank you for the music'* for giving Bashir and me that one last, memorable evening.

Thirty - Eight

Extract from my Facebook page 30th June, 2015:

Thursday 2nd July will be the second anniversary of Bashir's passing. Hainault where he was laid to rest is a tranquil place filled with nature and the permanent song of birds and the daily prayers from the mosque. His grave is covered in a carpet of wild flowers. I know that little now remains of Bashir's earthly body save for his bones, those of his delicate kind giving hands. My tears will never cease.

I should have realized better how short our final week together was to be, but one lives with the wish for just a few more weeks or months. Bashir was sleeping much more than he had done throughout his life. His Mediterranean daily routine had always included an afternoon siesta. What was abnormal was his saying that he felt tired this was something new despite the illness. My mother had said the same to my father the night she died. In bed one night he asked me to hold him all night and saying that he felt sorry that perhaps he might be unable to continue much longer with the chemotherapy. I had been begging him since the very start to discontinue the treatment if at any point it was causing him too much pain. He always replied that this would be like committing suicide; he was religious in his beliefs to the end.

That last morning he woke me at 5 am as he was throwing up blood. I made a 999 call and an ambulance arrived promptly and took us to Kensington and Chelsea hospital. This was where he had been earlier in the year in the ICU so I had learnt the ropes by that time. It was a long and tiring day to get the appropriate treatment and try to discover the cause. At one point they were going to send him home but then the bleeding restarted for a few minutes; despite xrays the doctors were

302

unsure of the cause. He was transferred to what I can only call a holding ward waiting to have an exploratory investigation the next morning. On the ward thankfully was a Filipino nurse who had cared for Bashir on his previous stay. John promised to keep an eye on my patient. If I had known today what I didn't know then I would never have left the hospital. By 7pm Bashir said he was feeling really tired and I should leave. Today I can hardly write what happened next without endless tears welling up and streaming down my face blaming myself. His last words to me were 'just leave Susie you are tired and there is nothing you can do here. Go home tomorrow is another day' I never saw him alive again. If only...

I held his hand, kissed and left. I stood in the bus queue never thinking that Bashir was going to be alone in his last moments; it was what I had sworn would never happen. Two minutes later whilst standing on the bus a cold, tingling, shiver came over me that we had not said goodbye properly. I was so exhausted after the day in the hospital and pushed the thought to the back of my mind. I probably hadn't been home more than 45 minutes when Lesley telephoned. She had looked after Bashir when he was admitted to the same hospital some four months earlier. 'You need to come immediately to the hospital I am at the ward.' I was puzzled and worried as to why she was at the hospital, presuming only the worst, that it must be an emergency. Not asking why, I flew out of the door, grabbed a taxi and ran to the hospital. I found a long faced Lesley. I shrieked as I asked her where was Bashir? A young doctor tried to guide me to a side room; that ages – old act that I knew to be a prelude to the worst possible news a death sentence. My husband, my best friend and my lover had died without my being with him. I live daily with the regret that I had not responded to what I felt was his call as he prepared to greet his death. It is my greatest sadness. If only...

Bashir lay stiff, silent and wrapped in white sheets. I knew he had left that lifeless corpse. I just hoped that perhaps his spirit was still somewhere in the room. It had been rehearsed between us and I knew exactly what was required for a Muslim at this time. Bashir always gave me power and despite everything I was able to gather enough strength to ask the hospital to call the Imman so that we could say prayers and wrap his body appropriately. What I demanded of Lesley and what she offered that night was indescribably kind. We talked to Bashir and both held his hands until the arrival of the Imman. He said prayers and covered Bashir's body and head with clean sheets into a shroud. At one point John the Filipino nurse came to the room and gave me condolence and apologised for being unable to stay and give me comfort it was a touching gesture. Later as I was leaving the ward a further nurse came and apologised for the circumstances of his death and I asked what had happened?

It was only then that I discovered that the hospital had incorrectly read the notes and called Lesley rather than me his wife. I was well aware that if I raised the issue over this error I would have been unable to obtain the death certificate immediately and without that we could not as sharia law dictated have Bashir buried. It is imperative that Muslims are buried as rapidly as possible after death. Until a month before his death Bashir had wanted to be buried in Libya which in point of fact would not have conformed to the Prophet's edict. Those last months of his life Bashir tried to do everything to make his passing easier for me and I wonder when he told me to leave that night if he knew what was coming?

As ever I relied on the kindness and support of friends. My lifelong pal Steve strode ahead accompanying me to the hospital the next morning. After endless toing and froing, going from office to office from Westminster Hospital to the Town hall, meeting with the Imman and securing his agreement to come with us to Hainault to say the burial prayers; finally the release form and the death certificate were obtained and the paperwork was complete. Without Steve that day I would have been lost and certainly without the drive and energy to complete the task. It just seemed as if everything was falling into place and by 1 O'clock we had arranged for Bashir's body to be taken to the East London Mosque where it would be washed and rest for the night with special prayers being said in the morning. I had complied with the Islamic rites prior to the burial exactly as Bashir had wished especially with all possible speed.

There had been one moment of relief that morning when an extremely attractive Irish nurse kindly told me she had been with Bashir in his last moments. It had been quick she assured me, he went into a coma and she held him in those last moments. Though not me his wife, at least it seemed in those final minutes he was able to attract a warm hearted, caring person to be at his side.

Rather naturally I had an absolute dread of the reception that I would be given by the Immans at the mosques. After all I was a foreign wife with little if any knowledge of what was to be done at this time and did not wear a scarf or any kind of Muslim attire. My contact with such people in the Middle East and North Africa and even London had been pretty negative and therefore I was prepared for the worst when having to deal with them. I write especially about this as perhaps I too had been caught up in the negative propaganda about Islamic extremism in the media. Without the Chelsea and Westminster Imman I would have been utterly lost. He was open to both my friends and me giving us comfort and directing us over the burial procedures. He took the time to send a detailed letter to Bashir's family telling of the burial and how it had been carried out under strict Sunni Muslim sharia conditions. They never responded to his kindness.

My brother, his wife, the Imman and I drove to the East London Mosque. Parked outside I could see the black hearse the car of death waiting and I clenched my teeth knowing how hard it was going to be to get through the next hours. Thousands of men were leaving the mosque as we arrived and I was advised that 4,000 Muslims come to this mosque for Friday prayers and for daily midday prayer at least 2,500 had raised their voices to give Bashir blessings. Everyone was kind in the most sincere way; I need not have had any fears. There may have been some who would not have shaken my female hand but all of those that I encountered offered me nothing but kindness and sympathy.

I placed my hand gently on the simple pine box containing his body where it remained throughout the journey as my gesture of carrying my husband's coffin. Our friends who through the jungle drum network had made their way to the graveyard were waiting; it was good to be surrounded by friendly faces. I will keep repeating again and again we had chosen a beautiful resting place. Every grave is just an earthen mound with a similar grey marble engraved tomb stone: name, date of birth, date of death, age. After two years a carpet of wild flowers is planted on each and every grave. No one is richer or poorer it is that feeling of equality and uniformity that I think is so special and outstanding. In this Muslim graveyard on that day we were to see and experience what was for all of us a unique funeral sight.

It was a glorious, hot, summer day as it had been on all the momentous days in our married life together. We ladies were asked with utmost respect to remain on the bridge away from the grave; women are not permitted to stand at the graveside during a funeral. Knowing that this would be the situation I was thankful for the thoughtful way in which we were asked. Shortly thereafter the undertaker gestured to come and yet all that I could see was a large group of men none of whom I knew or recognised. On spotting my brothers in the crowd on arrival we found these anonymous men taking it in turns to shovel in the earth to cover Bashir's body. It was explained by the Imman that Muslims believe it is important to pray at a graveside during a funeral and this way one will receive blessings in Paradise. As ever Bashir, even when dead attracted people it was an amazing moment and it boldly displayed a very positive aspect of the Islamic faith. Despite being buried in London, England Bashir's grave had been surrounded; he was not alone. If anyone has an inclination to take a look on the internet at the Garden of Peace, Hainault its name is apt.

2nd July, 2015: On my return from Hainault today I believe that I had done my best in carrying out Bashir's wishes for his burial. I can only imagine what his grave would have been like if it had been in Gargaresh, Libya; unkempt, covered in sand and rubbish, totally neglected. Whilst walking to the grave I talked with two gardeners their faces radiated goodness perhaps there are extra blessings for those who work in graveyards? If I had written this two or even one year ago it probably would have been in anger at the Shkuka family's attitude on finding out that their brother had been buried in England. I was to receive their insulting phone calls, escalating abuse, increasing threats being hurled when I was at my most vulnerable. Evidently they had no respect for their brother's wishes over their own. The final time I was to speak with Lamin he told me a story. It began with a man's brother and wife being kidnapped. The kidnapper told the husband that he would release one of the hostages on the payment of a ransom. 'Which one of them do you think the husband chose?' Lamin asked. His reply said so much 'of course he chose his brother one can never have another brother but one can always have another wife.' The family lost their brother through their own sanctimonious righteousness and cupidity. I question how it can be that the love of a husband for his wife counts for so little in their way of life?

Thirty - Nine

I suppose I should be more comfortable taking the role of heroine in this story, since every yarn should have one. Yet no heroine could claim to be such without a villain, and there were several happy to take that part from my late husband's family. On my next visit to Libya, one more villain would appear to complete the collection of loathsome and soulless people that made our lives so difficult.

We had dealt with Bashir's death sentence and there was much fear, sorrow and heartache to overcome but we had done it together. Now on turning over in our bed at night there was no warmth on the other side just cold, emptiness. Waking in the morning no kiss, no hug to start the day just myself. I was alone for the first time in 33 years, coping with my absolute grief. It was unbearable and relentless but it was the reality of my future.

On the first Monday after Bashir's death I received an abrupt and insensitive call from the Libyan embassy ordering me to come immediately and see the Ambassador. I had just been through the darkest few days of my life and was in no mood to encounter such rude and uncultured men, so refused. We finally agreed that I would go there together with my brother on the Thursday.

What a shame that the ambassador, having lived for some thirty years in London had not assimilated any of the pleasantries and nuances of the English language, culture or indeed any of the genial and warm mannerisms generally attributed to diplomats. He even had the embassy lawyer sitting in on the meeting, which rang alarm bells as it signalled that he needed legal support and counsel. Ibrahim Dabbashi had been passed over for the post of Foreign Minister and I was reminded too of the many brilliant young, career diplomats who had flourished under Bashir's tutelage that should have been occupying that seat.

Being part of the Libyan diaspora who had been living in London in opposition for many years, I suppose this man was an obvious choice. A new set of cronies had taken over, while the local Libyans, who had suffered under the Gaddafi regime for all those years were overlooked, considered incompetent and ignorant. Yet it was these men who had risked their lives to fight and win the war. The newly arrived Libyan diaspora, however, now held the purse strings while their families and chums were awarded lucrative contracts and prestigious jobs. It was to prove a fatal error. Presumably, as the widow of a career diplomat that operated under the old regime I was to receive no help from the embassy.

Unfortunately I had walked into this den thinking that I would be given my rights as a widow of a Libyan diplomat serving abroad simply as a matter of course. I was mistaken. Prior to his death Bashir had discussed with both the Finance and HR Departments at the Foreign Ministry in Tripoli to confirm my rights and the procedures it would be necessary to follow. It was established from these discussions that on his death I would be entitled to three months' salary, funeral costs, a shipment, air ticket and a widow's pension. These rights would give me time to adjust to my new circumstances. Not wasting a moment to claim what they believed were their rights the Shkuka family in the form of Lamin had gone to the Foreign Ministry on the Sunday claiming the last salaries and pension under sharia law. Advising that everything would now have to go through the Libyan court the ambassador tersely and undiplomatically informed us that there would be no salary and no housing allowance, and that if we wanted to challenge this we would have to deal directly with Tripoli. Until today I think the attitude was probably in part racist, gender discriminatory and in part rooted in the fact that the Shkuka family had their contacts and were determined to make my life as uncomfortable and miserable as possible. Another of Bashir's predictions had been fulfilled; by being buried in London he had unleashed a deep lust for vengeance on their part. He had forewarned me.

Prior to my visit and thinking that I was going to be dealing with reasonable people I had made a list of Bashir's FM documents plus an original of the death certificate. I never ever should have handed these over it was an enormous error. Holding no cards in the bargaining stakes we walked away with nothing. After countless letters and stressful visits I eventually managed to have the costs of the funeral and shipment repaid but that was as far as they were prepared to go. On that Thursday I was 65, a widow of a few days, living in a flat I could ill afford, with no income and no job prospects. On one visit to the embassy I was advised that I should find a job. I replied by asking what the embassy would have done if I had been a Libyan widow. The Ambassador replied that I would have been immediately flown back to Libya. This illustrates as much as anything that women are considered little more than an inconvenience for many in the Libyan mindset. More importantly perhaps than any of the financial payments mentioned was their refusal to give me the paper which showed Bashir's final salary payment without which I remain unable to claim my Libyan widow's pension. There is absolutely no action that I can take against them as the embassy has diplomatic immunity. Perhaps in the future, with no intention beyond being a thorn in their side I will stand outside the embassy with a sandwich board and hand out flyers to passers – by, giving details of my book, 9/36.

Hardly able to cope with my situation after that morning, unbelievably there was yet more to come. My lawyer Dr. Thumi telephoned to inform me that he could no longer act on my behalf as my case was now under sharia inheritance and therefore not something his firm dealt with, as commercial law specialists. He recommended an alternative by the name of Mohammed Frogim, and I, unfortunately, accepted his recommendation. Frogim instantly demanded a substantial retainer by Libyan standards of 3,000 Euros and 15% of any funds obtained from the settlement. I sent him the retainer. He turned out to be my final villain.

After two weeks of endless sleepless nights I opened up my laptop and began writing down the circumstances that had led to my current situation due to sharia inheritance law and its gender inequality. What precipitated this nightly writing was my learning that I was to receive one quarter of our property with the family receiving the balance i.e. three quarters, with no mention of the repayment of the loan. This part was ignored it was only later that I was to learn why. In the early hours of that morning as I came to the end of the saga I sat and pondered what was the point of all of this writing? I felt I needed to be more proactive and deliver a reminder or a warning to others; this was how it could become fruitful. Starting from when we had first heard of Bashir's illness I listed the precautionary actions that we had taken and should be taken point by point finally strongly advising foreign wives married to Libyans and Muslim women to protect themselves. I placed the writing ending with a click onto my Facebook page. I never anticipated the number of responses that I would receive from that post from friends and acquaintances worldwide and it prompted the thought that perhaps I had something to say and writing could be the way I could disseminate this message. Shortly afterwards Teri contacted me wanting to put the piece on her blog I was later to learn that this had resulted in over 5,700 hits in less than 24 hours worldwide. There was a message that people wanted to read although my true wish was that women would insist and protect themselves from a situation such as mine. Jarndyce and Jarndyce the legal story of Charles Dicken's Bleak House began to bear similarities to my life with what seemed to be never ending legal procedures. It was from that night that a tiny seed began germinating, but it would take two years before it flowered.

Forty

The final chapters of this book relate specifically to the title 9/36, Sharia Inheritance Law disbursement. I write not to criticize the Islamic legal system or to demand a change, as such an exercise would be futile and it is always important to respect other people's beliefs. A change nonetheless, would be appropriate given the altered role of women in the twenty first century and my opinion too, based on the injustice of my experiences, have to be respected. I wish only to raise awareness and show how this law can be circumvented, by publishing the details of how I was affected by it. The beneficiaries of Sharia Inheritance Law could easily take a moral stance in cases where there is blatant gender marginalization, and make compassionate changes to their claims. This would in no way be an affront to the foundations of the holy law, but merely allow some flexibility where it is needed. Unfortunately, in the case of Bashir's family these paths were never considered. They wanted the money, and found divine justification for greed and theft.

Living in a luxurious, expensive flat in Chelsea, previously paid for by the embassy, was no longer an option given that the embassy from the date of Bashir's death had stopped all rental payments. Prior to the 2nd July, thankfully having sold the Tripoli flat and with the proceeds of the sale now being in London, we had found what I knew would be the perfect home. Bringing Bashir to the flat when it was in a rundown state and knowing that he probably would only be living there briefly was heart breaking for me but for him I cannot imagine. As ever during all of those last months it was he who insisted on the visit, always thinking of my well being over his own. The many touches I see today are as a result of his interior design suggestions; it gives me great pleasure. The end of July was to be the legal flat completion date. It desperately needed renovating, which would take time but I had to leave Whitelands House immediately there was no choice I could ill afford the expensive rent.

311

It is easy to bemoan one's ill fortune and compare one's bad experiences to earlier, happier times. Many spend their entire lives in endless darkness and we must measure our low points not only against other points in our past, but against the backdrop of suffering that occurs all over the world at all points in time. My sadness at this time was alleviated by an offer to stay in Clapham with my absolute saviours Penny and Steve, which could not have come at a better time. I had a huge legal fight with the required completion of reams of paperwork for British probate, copies, letters and translations for the Libyan lawyer, the payment of bills, everywhere were piles and piles of papers needing to be processed. The formalities seemed endless and I struggled through the task. I waded through packing up Whitelands house and donating Bashir's clothes and possessions to a Trinity Hospice charity shop. However, I skipped through the flat renovations after the sale completion. I had known Simon, my builder since he was born and he took on the task industriously, leaving me without any need to worry. With certainty I knew this flat would be the last place I would ever live; I had moved enough. It would be ready by mid September; I had to focus on other matters.

A necessity was to find work and something clicked from way back when I had left school and gone to a tutoring college for my 'A' levels. I felt that I could work as an English tutor; I had the qualifications and just needed some clients. A tutoring agency found me work teaching British, Russian, Saudi, Italian, French and Spanish children wanting to either improve their grades, take exams to pass into a British school or who have learning difficulties. I have taught them all; they are my clients, my meal ticket and also my great pleasure seeing them achieve their goals through my guidance. I had two other strings to my bow; I started working in London and the Home Counties for Cambridge University English exams. Through my Macmillan Publishing contacts I picked up work writing for their new website for exams, and even more thrilling made a half hour film on tips for taking exams. The film was a wonderful learning experience, and great fun to make. http://www.macmillanenglish.com/exams/

In the meantime I still held a belief that perhaps Bashir's family would be honourable and feel they had a moral duty to at least repay the loan plus the one – quarter paltry share from the balance I was to inherit out of the sharia disbursement. In October I moved into my new home living with four deck chairs, two picnic tables and kitchen items borrowed from friends; I owned nothing in London. My possessions were all in boxes packed during the revolution and still stored in Bashir's warehouse on the family land in Gargaresh along with some items of furniture from the house. My hope was that these possessions were going to be shipped to London. Of course I never quite imagined how vindictive and greedy Bashir's family was to be, even after everything else they had done to us.

My October visit to Tripoli saw as ever Yusif waiting at the airport with eyes full of tears having learnt of Bashir's passing. Nothing had changed in the city; there had been no rebuilding since my last visit in May. Bab Al Aziziyah, which Yusif had believed was going to become a picturesque park, was lying in ruins exactly as it was left at the end of the revolution; a hideous reminder, a sore. The mosque, which was reputed to have been one of Gaddafi's nightly hiding places, also prevailed in its bombed ruined state. What was different was the optimism, which had changed to absolute pessimism. If you had a job and your salary was actually paid, you were fortunate. There was mass unemployment given that the expatriate companies had not returned due to the political uncertainty in the country. The Zintan brigades were still in control of the airport and many of the Tripoli checkpoints. The General National Congress, which had been enthusiastically elected in June under the chairmanship of Nuri Abu Shoneen, a member of the Berber party, was proving to be completely ineffective. By awarding themselves rather princely salaries of LD 12,000 a month, a car and a generous Tripoli housing allowance it seemed to many that these people had taken on the job of MP for the money; the muttering had started. Far worse was the GNC's inability to stem the rising violence with the eruption of militias from different factions taking control of towns across the country. The fault lines were widening daily and the idea of national unity was becoming a forgotten utopian fantasy.

Having chosen not to stay at the Corinthia hotel, my three – day stay was at the Thobactus which was not a place for the high – flying government officials and yet was respectable, functional and clean with kind and helpful staff. Being a stickler for time, the appearance of Mohamed Frogim arriving an hour and a half late, chewing gum, over weight, sloppily dressed, carrying a bunch of disorganized papers was a discouraging sight. Here was my final villain. Calling him a lawyer is a misnomer but at that time I believed him to be fully qualified only later discovering through the Libyan law directory that his qualifications restricted him to only appearing in the very lowest Libyan court. Perhaps he had pulled the wool over Dr. Thumi's eyes but before he even opened his mouth I knew that he was going to be a disaster; the worst possible choice. I had with me for support that evening my dear friend Miriem and her sister. I saw their eyes flicker at the sight of the man who was meant to be solving my legal problem. Their doubts were the same as mine although they knew better than me, coming from the society and country. Did he perhaps have a hidden agenda? He was nonetheless mistaken in considering me as a naïve, foreign wife; I had lived and worked in Libya long enough to recognize a crook. As he walked away I commented 'what a buffoon.' He was ridiculous and that is how he came to be known.

The following day at Court saw the predictable passing over of documents and a future court date set for two months hence. Begging the female judge to bring the date forward explaining my financial status, much to the annoyance of the Buffoon Frogim, the timing was reduced to three weeks; a small victory. The non – appearance of the family said much and was not a good indication of the outcome as it showed for them attendance was unnecessary; they had their route to obtaining their goal. My brother had prepared a statement for the Judge detailing a proposal for a settlement but it was refused with the Buffoon barely pushing for its acceptance. We speculated that yes he had a hidden agenda.

That evening over dinner with Tarek there were two more tasks to accomplish on this visit. It was *a Big Ask*. I needed help shipping the packing cases and some of my furniture to London. I wanted our possessions and memories around me in the new flat. I had the shipper lined up but the difficulty was releasing the goods from the clutches of Lamin and the Shkuka family. Tarek agreed to negotiate. I had asked him to distribute those items that I no longer required to deprived families, as my new flat was tiny. It may come as a surprise when I mention poor Libyan families but there are many who are destitute and living barely on the bread line. For those from sub – Saharan Africa and the West who continue to believe Gaddafi's propaganda that Libyans had everything, think again, life was tough and many lived on the hand outs of others and since the revolution their numbers are increasing by the day.

The final task during the visit was to go to the Foreign Ministry. Over the years I had become known to many of Bashir's colleagues who were willing to help having learnt of my treatment from the embassy in London. One such colleague was Dr. Salim Quateen who had been Head of the Legal Department at the Foreign Ministry but had since gone into private practice. Together we went to see the Director of the Department of Administration and Financial Affairs Dr. Khaled Dahan. I knew from experience that to see this man was virtually impossible but with Dr. Quateen we were listened to and notes were taken. He knew nothing of the goings on in London and apologised, saying how surprised he was to learn of my treatment. He confirmed, as I knew to be true, that the pension was for me alone, and the paper I needed on the salary payments should be issued by the Embassy in London. However, the final salaries could only be paid once the family had signed their agreement. By this time I had come to the conclusion that one quarter was better than nothing and on leaving the Ministry advised the Buffoon to obtain the paper from the family saying that it would be paid in London and not in Tripoli and that Dr. Quateen would deliver it to the Ministry for the authorisation. Nothing with the Buffoon was straight forward and he insisted that he should be the one to take the signed paper to the Ministry with the money being paid into his account. Lamin wanted to come to London to collect the money from the embassy. Too many players were angling for their cut and the twists and turns would continue with some of the family agreeing whilst Khadija and Ismael refused. I was back to where I had started. I have no doubt they had commenced fighting amongst themselves as I had seen them do so often over the years. In particular, they quite rightly did not trust Lamin. All of the matters with the Foreign Ministry are until today unresolved.

Leaving Tripoli with so much unfinished business, I was extremely glad to be out of the tension it was not the sunny place of old and was beginning to return to the character of the 80s. The city was rancid with skulduggery, threatening behaviour, austerity and sporadic gunfire that could be heard from my hotel room at night. Shortly after my visit the Prime Minister Ali Zeidan was briefly abducted from the Corinthia hotel. The new phenomena of hostage taking and mob justice was to add to the lawless state of the country. Neither Tripoli nor the wider country seemed to be a good place to stay or live. Perhaps destiny after all had dealt me a good hand. It was 33 years since I had sold the Frognal flat and moved to Tripoli and now my life had come around a full circle with a return to London.

Forty - One

Showing how two people from different cultures and religions can live a happily married life despite all the hardships has been one of the aims of my writing. The result of the sharia inheritance dispute has in no way altered my opinion that 33 years ago I made the right decision in marrying the man I loved, I have absolutely no regrets. From November 2013 through to May 2014 it would be grindingly tough but I still had a belief that justice would be done.

What I had not counted on was the family withholding my shipment. What did they want now? The silver, much of which had been christening gifts, would surely have been rather inappropriate. Why would they want my books? These were deeply treasured which they knew I valued yet ultimately worthless items so this was malice at play, yet again. Each box was marked clearly to show its contents. As of today my books remain in the warehouse in Tripoli unread, covered in desert dust and obviously unwanted by anyone in the family.

After a long drawn out tussle negotiated by Tarek, the Shkuka family agreed for parts of the shipment to come to London. Today I sit in my flat surrounded by memories and keepsakes from all of our travels. A great many of our possessions have been lost along the way but where that has happened I can still remember the times such as collecting shells or stones from certain beaches; those were the sublimely happy times. Bashir had succeeded in his final wish; I had a home. It had been at great cost to him, but I had a home nonetheless.

Balancing my tutoring lessons, I prepared yet again to return to Tripoli for a further court session. Williams's court statement having failed to be filed I felt it essential that somehow or other my voice should be heard by the Judge. With my written statement completed, I sent it to the Buffoon asking for it to be translated. My intuition told me this would not be done. Two days before flying I found my assumption to be correct. Tarek once more came to the rescue; it was translated and waiting for me on my arrival, as was Yusif at Tripoli airport.

What had become a routine drive from the airport into the city showed no changes; everything remaining in ruins by bombing and neglect with Yusif's pessimism even more marked. Many of the young Libyan diaspora who had arrived with such high hopes had left again, unable to cope with power cuts, poor infrastructure, no entertainment, lack of ready – made meals; the comforts of life they had always known. For us it was normal but for them it must have been completely abnormal and unacceptable. Similarly, those who had started off as ministers had either resigned or left the transitional government due to intimidation or a realization that they were unable to deal with the chaos.

Miriem is a tall, distinguished young Libyan woman who came to the court that morning. She is a beacon to other Libyan women, especially engineers, for her persistence in proving that she is as able, if not more so, than her male counterparts. I am immensely proud of her and thankful for her help. As William's statement had been refused by the Judge I was adamant that my now translated statement of my situation should be placed with the court. The Buffoon mumbled to the Judge obviously not wishing for it to be on the record, but Miriem intervened and was successful. This was a great achievement, although there was still no sign of the family. The next appearance was scheduled for February but I had run out of steam and was exhausted so did not request an earlier date. I desperately needed a break from it all and needed to recharge my batteries.

The British Ambassador in Tripoli, knowing of my troubles, had referred me to the only remaining British law firm still operating in Libya and their senior Libyan partner whom I met in London on my return. By this time I had a gut feeling that the Buffoon was not protecting my interests but rather hindering them. My suspicions were confirmed by this lawyer with a future meeting arranged between the two of us and the Head of the Libyan Law Society on my next visit to Tripoli. Many might think that I should have given up at this point, but I wanted and perhaps more importantly *needed* my financial rights. Perhaps I had become rather like my old neighbour; a pit bull.

February arrived and I reluctantly took the flight into Tripoli to be met by the ever – cheerful and kind face of Yusif. A cous cous dinner with

Tarek at my favourite Libyan restaurant *The Ruins,* which is located besides the Roman Marcus Arelius Arch, revived my spirits. February is possibly one of the best months in Tripoli. Spring comes early and the sun is bright in the sky and the sea is a glistening blue. Bashir always used to tell me that the Libyan Mediterranean was unlike any other part of this sea for its unique colour, which was no exaggeration. However, even Tarek, ever the optimist, was depressed at the way things were progressing. Posters with photos of the various candidates standing for the new parliament could be seen on any free space. I noticed many for Dr. Thumi who was hoping to be on the constitutional drafting committee. The rest were just unknown figures and names and as to whether they would be positive or negative for the country, I had little or no idea. What was worse was that it seemed as if there was little enthusiasm to vote. In December the first car bomb had exploded in Benghazi followed by numerous more explosions and now the GN Congress was refusing to disband despite their mandate having expired. It was becoming increasingly clear that the peace was gradually being lost.

That morning in court, the next part of this legal mêlée was to have the land valued in order that there could be a disbursement. When the Buffoon muttered unintelligibly, supposedly requesting the judge to ratify this process, Miriem intervened and once again was successful. Without a doubt he was not on my side; I became increasingly suspicious of his intentions.

That evening the Head of the Libyan Law Society looked at the papers. It was remarked that the fee was quite obviously exorbitant and did not adhere to the guideliness of the Law Society. However, far worse was the feeling that the case was being conducted poorly. Previously unnoticed due to the Arabic language on the Sharia Court Division papers, there was a question asking if there were *any disputes related to the estate,* and it had been marked *no.* A phone call to the Buffoon, who was obviously taken aback and unprepared, admitted that the family had offered him bribes and a cut of whatever they received. Since there was no *cut* available at that time the Buffoon avoided lying by saying he had refused the bribes, but I knew all too well what shady little transaction would occur once any disbursement took place in the future; he would undoubtedly have his share both from the family and myself. This revelation confirmed my total lack of confidence in the man. I had to find another lawyer quickly in this corrupt and troubled land. I had come so far, fought and fought and felt that I still had the energy to continue. However, at that moment I felt totally incapable of making any decisions. I arranged a conference call with William and the two lawyers for five days later between London and Tripoli. These were the days of Skype, unlike those earlier days in Sierra Leone. So much had changed in terms of communications, and ethics. Everyone has to keep up regardless of age, lest they be left behind. Life was no longer pen, quill and decency. It was cut throat and everyone for themselves.

Forty - Two

Libyans had survived forty – two years under Gaddafi's rule relying on their wits and by their strategy of being non – confrontational. After the Thursday conference call from London to Tripoli William and I were unsurprised when this appeared to be the case with the Buffoon and the Libyan lawyers. Not wanting to lose a good deal the Buffoon apparently still wanted to act for me despite my protestations to the contrary. Needless to say he was sacked. I just wanted to be rid of the man. Under British law it would have been compulsory to have advised the judge of the bribe but this was Libya and I was coming to the conclusion that the family had their spider's network and at every turn I was being outwitted. The Buffoon had escaped unblemished.

Had I burnt my boats? There was now the court case with no lawyer plus the two Libyan legal consultants wishing to distance themselves from my case. In truth there was nothing more they could do to help me. I could hardly blame them they had probably pronounced on the legal aspects of the case too strongly and wished to be out of any confrontation, after all I was the foreigner and the Buffoon was the local.

Luck from Egypt was to intervene with an email from Ekatarina advising that Bizante was back in Libya, it seemed as if the lawyer problem could be solved. One phone call and talking to Bizante I knew that I was going to be represented by a true, honest lawyer it was like an enormous weight had been taken off my shoulders for I was truly running out of energy.

Returning to Libya for the fourth court appearance was proving utterly exhausting. I was ground down. No doubt this is what the family had been hoping for. Once more I stayed at Thobactus hotel feeling it to be safe but just days after returning to London it too was bombed a new departure for Tripoli and western Libya; now there were regular bombings, kidnappings and robberies. Tarek and I met with the Buffoon who handed over the papers. In my wish to see the end of him as quickly as possible I neglected to notice that he had returned mostly copies not the original court documents. These were in all probability turned over to the family as he knew where his bread was buttered. In fact at this last meeting he should not have been called the Buffoon but rather Uriah Heap 'ever so humble' but the reality was far from the truth.

The following morning Bizante's son Hussam and I went to the court only to discover that the appearance was the following day. The Buffoon had deliberately given the wrong date in the belief that I would be leaving that afternoon. In fact my departure date was not until the following evening at least that plan had been scuppered. In court the following day we requested, one never demands in a Libyan court that the valuation which had not been carried out needed to be done urgently. It was the usual outdated court procedure of shuffling papers and inserting new ones into the file awaiting a further court appearance. By this time I was well known to the court guard as he had been on duty during the initial hearings with the case of our neighbour and now once more I was back in the family court fighting for my sharia inheritance rights. As I left that day, obviously upset and weeping he followed me outside, warmly shook my hand and gently and kindly assured me that justice would be done. He was a true Libyan. Somehow in all of my troubles I had forgotten the many people of his ilk whom I have met during my Libyan travels; Peace loving, unworldly and religious who are eking out a living but never forgetting and abiding by their God given laws.

So many times I have wished that I could have kept a diary for the past 35 years. But the fear of my writings being found and incriminating the one I loved has always stopped my ever beginning. After court in my hotel room that night for the first time I wrote a diary entry.

May 2014: Tripoli appeared calm but without a doubt there are insidious underlying tensions. There is a terrible sense of a victory lost and as yet an unobtainable peace. People seem to have long forgotten those brave fighters with their thoughts 'for your tomorrow we gave our today.'

Last night from my hotel room I heard gunshots but am told by everyone this is normal. Tonight there have been a few extremely loud bomb blasts and the

windows of my room are shaking. When looking out onto the Tripoli skyline
and hearing those blasts it has resurrected those days and nights of NATO
bombing. Again I feel the nervous tension but I am alone without Bashir's
reassuring touch.

The Libyans remain as always kind and generous in their help and hospitality
to foreigners. When speaking, nearly every sentence shows their obvious
disappointment and frustration at the total lack of progress towards a democratic
Libya. Who is doing what and why is invariably the pessimistic street gossip?
Is it the Gaddafi family fermenting unrest using the stolen billions they have
safely stashed away in offshore accounts? Is it the separatists in the east blocking
oil depots? Or are Islamic State (IS) and Islamic fundamentalists pushing for
their agenda of strict observance of Sharia Law. The current reality is revenge
bombings and killings of Gaddafi's old cronies or for those trying to be voted
onto the drafting committee for the new constitution. Nothing is clear, absolutely
nothing. Meanwhile there is the constant criticism of corruption in all aspects of
the Libyans' daily life.

One can only hope that as the third anniversary nears that Libyans 'will walk
the road together rather than separately' which both short and long term is the
only possible solution for the new Libya. A country of just six million with vast
oil wealth at their disposal to rebuild their country, which is being lost…

I didn't know that this was to be my final visit to Libya in the struggle for
my rights. Back in London shortly thereafter I was stunned to see on TV
rival militias fighting for control of the airport and eventually leaving it
permanently out of action, completely destroyed. I could no longer reach
Tripoli there was no way to fly either in or out.

Today the reality is far worse. Two governments sit at either end of
the country one in the east in Tobruk and the other in Tripoli in the
west and a further UN Unity government recently arrived in Tripoli
but living in the safety of a naval base. IS has taken control of Derna and
Sirte and are carrying out the most heinous, barbaric acts. Just as under
Gaddafi the goal of many Libyans is to leave the country to find a new
decent, peaceful life somewhere, anywhere. There is going to be a brain
drain with nothing stopping the flow. Land values are worthless and
the black market rate is five dinars to the UK pound and there is talk of

devaluation. Life for a European woman would be fraught with danger.

Sharia Inheritance law shows gender discrimination and I am resigned to having lost my nine shares but so too have the family lost their twenty seven shares there are no winners as it will be years before the land returns to its old value. Likewise I know the family will never repay their loans. Perhaps one day they will realise they lost a brother through their greed or perhaps they never cared? For myself I did have a guardian angel I have a home, work and amazing family and friends. Most importantly I live in a country where there is a rule of law and respect. My place of birth was luck, meeting Bashir was my fate.

Bashir you were meant to be the writer of this book I hope I have done our story of thirty – three years justice. There was joy and heartache when we were together but always the strength of having each other. Those last months of your life with neither of us knowing our futures was terrifying but we held onto each other and you made sure that I had a safe place to live despite the best efforts of your family to destroy us.

Your grave is permanently covered in a layer of wild, heather flowers. There is a tree that shades you from the sun and rain. The birds sing and the Imam's daily call over the graveyard says prayers for the dead. You will always be blessed.